# NETWA



# SOLUTIONS

# AND

# SHORTCUTS

# NETWARE SOLUTIONS AND SHORTCUTS

## Batch File Programming for Administrators

**Emmett Dulaney**

M&T BOOKS

**M&T Books**
A Division of M&T Publishing, Inc.
411 Borel Avenue, Suite 100
San Mateo, CA 94402



Printed in the United States of America



**Library of Congress Cataloging-in-Publication Data**

Dulaney, Emmett
NetWare Solutions and Shortcuts / Emmett Dulaney
p. cm.
Includes index. 93-10354
ISBN 1-55851-310-8 CIP

96 95 94 93 4 3 2 1

**Project Editor:** Mike Welch
**Developmental and Copy Editor:** Barbara Hume
**Technical Editor:** Dave Doering
**Production:** Charlene M. Carpentier
**Cover Design:** Lauren Smith Design

*To my parents*
*and all those whose names*
*appear within*

# Contents

# Why This Book Is for You

If you are a network supervisor responsible for maintaining a productive NetWare network, *NetWare Solutions and Shortcuts* is for you.

- Through a valuable collection of batch files, utilities, and routines this book shows you how to automate NetWare and stretch its capabilities beyond the functions you get with the basic operating system.
- Whether you want to automate troubleshooting or simply learn the workings of a quick electronic mail program using just batch files, this book gives you the step-by-step guidelines you need.
- Each chapter is laced with examples of utilities the author has written over the years. Each utility was written to fulfill a specific need, and has proven invaluable over time.
- The floppy disk that comes with this book is ideal for network administrators. It contains 44 ready-to-run batch and executable files.

*NetWare Solutions and Shortcuts* contains a wealth of technical insights that are certain to make managing a network more efficient and productive.

# Introduction

In the 1970s and early 1980s, mainframe computers ruled the business world. They were formidable monoliths whose access was limited, whose costs were high, and whose inner workings were understood by only a privileged few.

These mainframes were giant collection bins of data. Workers entered information into them via terminals, punched cards, magnetic tape, or other means. All employees, providing they had access and security clearance, could reach the same data file and view information identical to that everyone else could see.

Then, in the mid-1980s, the personal computer revolutionized the business world. Middle managers are generally credited with bringing PCs into the business environment. Frustrated by their limited access to and knowledge of the mainframe world, these workers readily accepted what they could own and understand: a stand-alone PC.

With a copy of Lotus 1-2-3 and a thick book, managers could create fairly complex statistical spreadsheets and manipulate the data until it yielded the results they needed—and all without needing to fight for mainframe time. With an inexpensive word processor, they could incorporate the spreadsheet figures into a document and individually address copies of this document to all other managers. Big business took note of the increase in productivity this new technology generated.

With the unlimited potential involved in offering affordable computer access to all suitable employees, the business world bestowed its blessing upon the proliferation of PCs throughout the work area.

A problem soon became apparent, however.

Before, everyone had access to the same information stored in the mainframe. Now, everyone had his or her own information base stored in a personal desktop computer or on floppy disks. If two managers attempted to generate a report using the same formulas, they could come up with different answers if one had data more current than the other. If, for example, the Accounting Department needed a listing of all employee home addresses, accounting personnel would have to assemble it themselves or borrow from the Human Resources Department, completely unaware that the Benefits Committee had only recently finished updating just such a list.

With the mainframe computer, it was possible, up to a point, to run multiple terminals at one time without a noticeable change in processing speed, since the mainframe used a multitasking operating environment. The majority of PCs that went into businesses used MS-DOS, a single-tasking operating system, and running more terminals off a little CPU was not a viable option.

Enter networking.

## The Need for LANs

Local area networks, or LANs, came about as the need to share resources became more and more apparent. If you connect several stand-alone PCs together through cabling and hardware, the individual machines are bound together to handle tasks previously performed on a mainframe. This new ability to share data and resources is relatively inexpensive, yet still enables local computing—the best of both worlds.

In 1983, Novell Inc., based in Provo, Utah, released a system designed to run on MS-DOS machines and enable sharing of files and printers between individual PCs. This local area network operating system evolved, over time, into NetWare.

Workstations on the network essentially run two operating systems: NetWare performs the networking tasks, while the local operating system performs the workstation tasks. A NetWare "shell" program determines which of them will handle the given command by reading each line you type in and attempting to execute it within each directory listed in your PATH statement.

## Why NetWare?

Several vendors offer network operating systems designed to meet the need for microcomputer connectivity. Of all the LANs currently available, Novell's NetWare is considered far and away the operating system of choice. The NetWare network operating system allows individual workstations running other operating systems to access data and applications residing on file servers. Novell has been supplying this product for approximately ten years, in that time frame creating a product second to none in scope and integration. Each release of NetWare has corrected previous difficulties and introduced new, useful features.

NetWare's structure and commands operate virtually independently of each workstation's environment in that the workstation environment (whether OS/2, MS-DOS, DR DOS, or something else) calls on NetWare when given a command that isn't a workstation operating system command. The network operating system then performs the requested function and, once that function is completed, reports the result back to the workstation. The user sees only the result, oblivious to what transpired behind the glow of the monitor.

## Why Go beyond NetWare?

NetWare, while a phenomenal product, is limited in application to the commands and features supplied with the package. To increase productivity, you must look beyond the NetWare application. You must consider generating additional features by incorporating the workstation environment into the realm of available options.

The utilities and tips I describe in this book illustrate methods of enhancing NetWare capabilities by using the two most prevalent workstation operating systems, MS-DOS from Microsoft and Digital Research's DR DOS (now packaged and supplied by Novell). This enhancement uses a combination of batch files and executable (*.EXE and *.COM) programs.

My discussion is based on version 6.0 for both the MS-DOS and DR DOS workstation operating systems. If the commands under discussion don't work with previous versions, I say so.

By intermingling DOS and NetWare, it's possible to generate utilities on a stand-alone workstation that will perform functions across the network. You can create these utilities by using the DOS language already running on the workstation, thus avoiding the need for further investment.

## How This Book Can Help Network Administrators

This book is intended for use by system administrators rather than by ordinary users. One reason I've directed the book to administrators is that you need supervisory rights to NetWare directories and functions in order to create these utilities. Another is that you'll need to use the local hard drive on the administrator's workstation. Many users work on diskless workstations, but I don't know any system administrators who prefer diskless workstations for their own machines.

> **NOTE:** The NetWare version I've used as a starting point for all utilities is NetWare 2.15. This version is the lowest common denominator of the NetWare versions currently in use. All commands I use in this book, unless otherwise noted, are upwardly compatible. I also refer to version-specific commands present in NetWare 2.2 and NetWare 3.11 when appropriate.

Since productivity is a responsibility of supervisors, and since NetWare *requires* supervisor equivalency to access all commands and features of NetWare, the utilities I present are, for the most part, of importance and practicality only to supervisors. Some chapters offer utilities that all users may access and run (electronic mail, for example); even so, the supervisor must first create these utilities.

The suggestions I offer you in this book are the culmination of my years as a system administrator; the utilities are examples of solutions I've found to problems I've run into time and again. I also offer shortcuts I've learned for avoiding those problems in the first place.

In some instances, shareware products have become available that perform similar functions. I strongly suggest, however, that you study the listings and understand how the programs work. Through this understanding you'll gain the knowledge necessary to write applications needed in your discipline, and you'll be able to do so when no other source is readily available.

The first few chapters of this book (Chapters 1 through 4) introduce the concepts and commands available in NetWare and in various workstation operating systems. Once you've gained a clear overview of the commands you can use within each environment, move on to Chapters 5 through 13, which provide in-depth applications using those features and commands. At the end of the book, I've included an extensive glossary and listings of additional utility programs not included elsewhere. All of the programs listed throughout the book are also included, in ready-to-use form, on the enclosed floppy disk.

What this book does is to show you how to use your local operating system (MS-DOS or DR DOS) to enhance your NetWare environment and perform operations that neither system could perform independently.

Using batch and command files, you can increase the number of utilities available to you as a NetWare supervisor as you walk through many examples of marrying the two operating systems. I've explained each program in step-by-step detail. To save you entry time and reduce transcription errors, the floppy disk included with this book contains all the source code you need.

## How This Book Is Organized

Chapters 1 through 4 of this book discuss the language of NetWare and of both the Microsoft and Digital Research disk operating systems. You need to be familiar with the commands these systems use in order to create the utilities presented in this book. Chapters 5 through 13 describe applications you can put together and provide detailed directions for creating utilities. These chapters also give you related pointers on managing network security and on troubleshooting your network. The final section offers a complete glossary and listings of additional utility programs. The book's complete structure is as follows:

| | |
|---|---|
| Introduction | Gives a frame of reference for the purposes of the book. |
| Chapter 1 | Provides an overview of the NetWare language and most commonly used commands. |
| Chapter 2 | Discusses NetWare login scripts and the possibilities for performing operations based upon criteria entered there. |
| Chapter 3 | Covers batch language syntax and operations for MS-DOS and DR DOS, as well as some useful external commands. |
| Chapter 4 | Introduces .BAS, .COM, and .EXE files that externally expand the batch file possibilities. |
| Chapter 5–13 | Show you how to create an electronic mail program, develop a utility toolkit, monitor activity, troubleshoot the network, and so on. |
| Appendix A | Provides a glossary of terms and acronyms. |

| | |
|---|---|
| Appendix B | Offers lists of additional utility programs not covered in the text, but that are included on the floppy disk that accompanies this book. |

## How to Use This Book

This book is intended for you to use as a resource and learning guide. I've presented the utilities in the most generic form possible, unless otherwise specified, in order to let you run them on the greatest number of configurations. Since DR DOS contains all of the MS-DOS commands, I've created the batch files using MS-DOS commands whenever possible. I've also used NetWare 2.15 as a basis for much of the discussion, since it is, in general, upwardly compatible with later releases. You'll also find information on using NetWare 2.2 and NetWare 3.11 for creating administrative utilities. If I use a particular command requiring DR DOS or a specific version of either operating system, I say so prior to the listing.

### Using the code

This book contains a great deal of code. If you type in every entry from scratch, you'll waste a tremendous amount of time. To save you that time, the floppy disk included with this book contains, in executable form, every program presented within. To use the programs, copy them from the enclosed disk to your machine and run them from your hard drive.

The purpose of the listings is to show you how they work and to help me explain why they work. Use the listings as skeletons on which to create your own utilities. Change a few lines and see if the results are more or less than what you expected.

But by all means, don't go out and purchase a BASIC language compiler if you don't intend to alter or experiment with the utilities and merely want to run the ones listed in this book. The disk contains *every listed utility* in executable form.

## Conventions

This book uses the Letter Gothic typeface for text that you type to the screen or that appears on the screen.

Names of keys to press are enclosed inside brackets (for example, <Enter> or <Ctrl>-<F1>).

1 CHAPTER

# NetWare Language

This chapter describes the NetWare command-line utilities. You'll need to use these utilities in implementing the solutions you'll learn about later in the book. The utilities described in this chapter are present in 2.x and 3.x versions of NetWare. I want to make sure you're familiar with these available NetWare command-line utilities before I give you any actual program code listings. What follows is a detailed, but limited, discourse on those commands. Where the possibility of confusion exists, I've supplied clarifying examples.

Novell removed several commands from earlier versions of NetWare and added others as they progressed to the current release. I've identified all version-specific commands for you.

> **NOTE:** This discussion doesn't cover the utilities for NetWare 4.0, a version aimed at the corporate enterprise network environment.

## NetWare Command-Line Utilities

Since you invoke the NetWare command-line utilities by typing a command at the command-line prompt, I use the terms *utilities* and *commands* interchangeably in this chapter. The following discussion represents a compendium of those command-line utilities, or commands, most commonly needed by network administrators.

### ALLOW

You can use this command to examine, set, and change the rights to a directory path or file. Extremely useful in troubleshooting file or directory problems, it replaces the SHOWFILE utility that existed in earlier versions. (GRANT assigns rights, whereas ALLOW lets you view and assign.)

Syntax: ALLOW [path] [rights]

Seven rights are available to users of directories or files. Current versions of NetWare allow for nine ways of specifying these rights, as given in Table 1-1.

**Table 1-1. Specifying file and directory rights in NetWare.**

| ENTRY | MEANING |
|---|---|
| A | Access control (refers to granting of trustee rights) |
| ALL | All rights are granted |
| C | Create and change files |
| E | Erase files and directories |
| F | File scan (dir) |
| M | Modify or change the attributes to a file |
| N | No rights |
| R | Read files |
| W | Write files |

### ATTACH

You can use this command to access another file server without logging out from the original file server. Since the command is issued without parameters, NetWare prompts the user first for a server name and then for a user name on that server.

**BINDFIX**

The NetWare bindery is a database consisting of hidden or system files in the SYS:SYSTEM directory. These system files are encrypted files that contain information about the NetWare server environment, including users, their passwords, printers, or groups. You can use the BINDFIX command to repair a damaged bindery, but it's also extremely useful in removing directories assigned to users removed from the system, deleting trustee rights, and so forth.

The following text shows you what you might see on the screen when you run BINDFIX to perform a bindery fix operation. Notice the two yes/no prompts.

```
F:\SYSTEM>BINDFIX
Rebuilding Bindery. Please Wait.
Checking for invalid nodes
Checking object's property lists.
Checking properties to see if they are in an object
  property list.
Checking objects for back-link property.
Checking set consistency and compacting sets.
Building avail lists and new hash tables.
There are 11 Object nodes and 6 Property Nodes free.
Checking user objects for standard properties.
Warning:  Object TONY property SECURITY_EQUALS has
  incorrect security flags.
Checking group objects for standard properties.
Checking links between users and groups for
  consistency.
Delete mail directories of users that no longer exist?
  (y/n): Y
Checking for mail directories of users that no longer
  exist.
Checking for users that do not have mail directories.
Delete trustee rights for users that no longer exist?
  (y/n): Y
```

```
Checking volume SYS. Please wait.
Bindery check successfully completed.
Please delete the files NET$BIND.OLD and NET$BVAL.OLD
after you have verified the reconstructed bindery.

F:\SYSTEM>
```

### BINDREST

The BINDREST command is the opposite of BINDFIX. It's for restoring to its original state a bindery that BINDFIX has been run on.

### BROADCAST

This command sends a message from the console to all workstations logged on to the network.

### CAPTURE

This command allows NetWare to redirect output aimed at the local workstation printer (or more specifically, to the parallel ports) to the network printer. As long as CAPTURE is in effect, each time you attempt to print, the printed material will be diverted from your local printer to a network printer. When you cancel the CAPTURE command, all material you print will once again print on your local printer. Table 1-2 shows you some examples of the CAPTURE command with different parameters applied.

**Table 1-2. Results of various parameters applied to the CAPTURE command**

| COMMAND | RESULT |
|---|---|
| CAPTURE /Q PRINTQ_0 /nb /nff | Captures the output and sends it to the print queue, without a banner (/nb) or form feeds (/nff.). |
| CAPTURE /SH | Shows the settings currently in effect at the workstation. |
| CAPTURE /C=7 | Uses the default capture settings and prints seven copies of every print job. The number may be anywhere from 1 to 999. |

Table 1-2. *(Continued)*

| COMMAND | RESULT |
| --- | --- |
| CAPTURE/NAME=KAREN BANNER=SCOTT | Uses the default capture settings and prints a banner page preceding each print job. The first half of the banner page in the example will be KAREN. It can be any alphanumeric entry up to twelve characters in length, so long as no spaces are included. The second half of the page, rather than the default of LST, will be SCOTT. Once again, it may be any entry up to twelve characters in length and not containing spaces. |

## CASTOFF and CASTON

You can use the CASTOFF command to prevent other users from sending messages and broadcasts to a workstation. CASTON is the reverse action, once again enabling messaging. Table 1-3 shows you some examples of these commands with parameters applied.

**Table 1-3. Results of parameters applied to the CASTOFF or CASTON commands**

| COMMAND | RESULT |
| --- | --- |
| CASTOFF | Prevents other users from sending messages, but still allows the console to do so. |
| CASTOFF ALL or CASTOFF A | Prevents other users and the console from messaging. |
| CASTON | Re-enables messaging. |

Here's an example of what appears when you type in CASTOFF or CASTON commands:

```
F:\SYSTEM>CASTOFF A
Broadcast messages from stations and the console will
  now be rejected.
Time-clock checking for broadcast has been disabled.
```

```
F:\SYSTEM>CASTON
Broadcast messages from other stations or the console
  will now be accepted.

F:\SYSTEM>
```

### CHKVOL

This command is essentially the same as the DOS command CHKDSK, which does not work on network drives. CHKVOL offers the following information for all volumes on the server:

- Name of the file server
- Total volume spaces
- The amount of space currently used and the number of files
- The number of bytes remaining on the volume
- The number of remaining bytes available to you

NetWare 3.11 also reports on how much space is being occupied by deleted files.

### ENDCAP

This command stops the capturing of data to a remote queue by disabling a previously issued CAPTURE command.

### FLAG

This command allows you to assign or change attributes to a file much as you would with the DOS ATTRIB command, but with more options. Table 1-4 shows you a few examples of using this command with parameters applied, and Table 1-5 lists the parameters available for the FLAG command.

**Table 1-4. Results of parameters applied to the FLAG command**

| COMMAND | RESULT |
|---|---|
| FLAG | Shows the current attributes of all files in the present working directory. |
| FLAG *.EXE | Shows the current attributes of all executable files in the present working directory. |
| FLAG *.EXE SUB | Shows the current attributes of all executable files in the present working directory, and all subdirectories beneath it. |
| FLAG *.TXT S RO | Sets the attributes for all specified files in the directory to shareable and read only. |

**Table 1-5. Available parameters for the FLAG command**

| ENTRY | MEANING |
|---|---|
| S | Shareable |
| RO | Read-Only |
| RW | Read and Write |
| N | Normal (Non-Shareable and Read/Write) |
| T | Transactional (protected by NetWare's Transaction Tracking System, or TTS) |

Listing 1-1 shows you an example of an output listing.

**Listing 1-1. The FLAG utility shows you file attributes.**

```
F:\SYSTEM> FLAG *.*

START.DBD        Shareable       ReadOnly
_FILE_4.DBD      Shareable       ReadOnly
SYS$LOG.ERR      Non-shareable   Read/Write
SUPER.EXE        Non-shareable   Read/Write
TEST.SYS         Shareable       Read/Write
LCONSOLE.EXE     Non-shareable   Read/Write
NET$ACCT.DAT     Shareable       Read/Write
NET$BIND.OLD     Non-shareable   Read/Write
```

```
MSG$V11.DAT      Non-shareable   Read/Write
SNIPEINI.DAT     Shareable       Read/Write
SNIPESYN.DAT     Shareable       Read/Write
$V11.OVL         Non-shareable   Read/Write
NET$DIAL.DAT     Non-shareable   Read/Write

F:\SYSTEM>
```

### FLAGDIR

What FLAG does for files, FLAGDIR does for subdirectories. Table 1-6 shows you the available settings.

**Table 1-6. The FLAGDIR utility's four settings**

| SETTING | MEANING |
|---|---|
| N | *Normal.* Cancels any previously set attributes. |
| H | *Hidden.* This setting prevents the name of the subdirectory from appearing in any listings, but does not prohibit the use of the subdirectory, providing the user knows of its existence. |
| S | *System.* This setting marks the subdirectory as being needed for system functions, thereby hiding the subdirectory from listing operations and preventing it from being copied or deleted. |
| P | *Private.* This setting prevents other users from seeing the contents of a subdirectory unless they have been granted search rights. During a DIR listing, users can see the name of the subdirectory from the parent directory only if they have search rights to that subdirectory. |

### GRANT

This command allows you to grant trustee rights to users or groups for a particular directory. Table 1-7 explains the options you can use with the GRANT command.

Syntax: GRANT [options] FOR [path] TO [name]

**Table 1-7. The GRANT command grants users a variety of trustee rights to a directory.**

| ENTRY | MEANING |
|---|---|
| NO RIGHTS | None of the eight available rights is granted. |
| All | All eight trustee rights are granted. |
| C | The user may Create files and/or subdirectories. |
| D | The user may Delete files or subdirectories. (This NetWare 2.15 option becomes E for Erase in NetWare 2.2 and NetWare 3.11.) |
| M | The user may Modify directory and file attributes, including names. |
| O | The user may Open existing files. (This option is not in NetWare 2.2 or NetWare 3.11; it folds in with other rights.) |
| P | Parental rights enable modifying trustee rights. (This option becomes Access Control in NetWare 2.2.) |
| R | The user may Read files. |
| S | Searching of the subdirectory (DIR) is enabled. This option is referred to as File Scan in NetWare 2.2 and NetWare 3.11. |
| W | The user may Write to files. |

Let's look at a few examples of the GRANT command in use. If you type:

```
F:\SYSTEM\GRANT O R S W  TO HAILEY <Enter>
```

you grant Hailey the rights to open, read, search, and write to the present working directory. If you type:

```
F:\SYSTEM\GRANT ONLY R FOR P: TO JERRY <Enter>
```

you revoke whatever rights Jerry may have had to subdirectory P: and leave him with read access only. If you type:

```
F:\SYSTEM\GRANT ALL FOR SYS:SOFTW TO JENNIFER <Enter>
```

you grant all eight rights to Jennifer for the assigned subdirectory. If you type:

```
F:\SYSTEM\GRANT ALL BUT P TO JENNA <Enter>
```

you grant the remaining seven unspecified rights to the present working directory to Jenna.

### HOLDOFF and HOLDON

These commands are present in most older NetWare versions, but not on the current NetWare 3.11 release. HOLDON lets you prevent users from using a file by electing to hold the file open. HOLDOFF reverses the action and closes the file. While this concept seemed good in theory, it was sometimes flawed in application. These commands have therefore been eliminated.

### LISTDIR

This command lists subdirectories, creation dates, and security information with the following optional parameters:

| | |
|---|---|
| /S | Show subdirectories beneath the requested directory |
| /R | Display the Rights to the subdirectory |
| /D | Reflect the creation Date |
| /A | Show all |
| /E | Show effective rights |

### MAP

You can use this command to show or change the current network drive mappings for the workstation. This command, too, gives you several options. For example:

| | |
|---|---|
| MAP | Shows the current settings |
| MAP X: | Shows the mapping of drive X only |
| MAP Y:=X: | Sets Y equal to X |
| MAP DEL Y: | Removes the mapping to drive Y |

For example, here's what you might see when you use the MAP command:

```
F:\APPL>MAP

Drive  A:   maps to a local disk.
Drive  B:   maps to a local disk.
Drive  C:   maps to a local disk.
Drive  D:   maps to a local disk.
Drive  F:  = BI_ANDERSON/SYS:APPL

SEARCH1:  = Z:. [BI_ANDERSON/SYS:PUBLIC]
SEARCH2:  = Y:. [BI_ANDERSON/SYS:]
SEARCH3:  = C:\PCTOOLS
SEARCH4:  = C:\WP51
SEARCH5:  = C:\PCPLUS
SEARCH6:  = C:\
SEARCH7:  = C:\NOR4.5
SEARCH8:  = C:\DOS

F:\APPL>
```

## NCOPY

Similar to the DOS COPY command, NCOPY is far superior in terms of maintaining file attributes. It's also more appropriate for use with the server. Allowable options are:

- /S Copies Subdirectories and the contents thereof
- /E When used with /S, allows copying Empty subdirectories as well
- /V Verifies the original and the copy to be identical before processing continues

### NDIR

This command lets you list files and subdirectories. It also provides certain specific information about these files and subdirectories. This information includes:

- Filename
- File size in byte
- Date and time the file was last updated
- The attributes assigned to the file
- The owner of the file

After the preceding information, the subdirectory details appear:

- Inherited rights
- Effective rights
- Owner
- Date created or copied

Given without parameters, NDIR brings up a menu screen allowing you to select the options by which a sort will be performed. Given parameters, the search will automatically initiate operation. The available parameters are virtually unlimited, but let's look at the most useful ones.

If you type:

`NDIR FILENAME [NOT]` <Enter>

you can see files matching a particular name, including wildcard characters, or, when using the NOT option, see all files but those specified. If you type:

`NDIR OWNER [NOT]` <Enter>

you can see files owned by a user, or owned by everyone but that user.

If you type:

```
NDIR ACCESS [NOT] BEFORE or AFTER MM-DD-YY
```
<Enter>

you can view files that have been accessed before or after a specified date. The NOT option here is essentially the same as swapping the AFTER and BEFORE. If you type:

```
NDIR SIZE [NOT] GREATER or LESS NNNNN
```
<Enter>

you can view files according to byte size. Again, the NOT option is identical to swapping the GREATER and LESS.

In addition, you can use file attributes in the sort, with [NOT] being an option to precede each. Table 1-8 shows you a few examples of using file attributes in the sorting process.

**Table 1-8. File attributes used to focus NDIR sorts**

| ATTRIBUTE | MEANING |
|---|---|
| EO | View all files that are execute only (X in NetWare 2.2 and 3.11) |
| H | Hidden |
| SY | System files |
| SHA | Shareable |
| RO | Read-only |
| RW | Read and write |
| I | Indexed |
| T | Transactional, or marked TTS |

Table 1-9 shows you a few examples of using the NDIR command with its options.

**Table 1-9. NDIR options used to help find certain files**

| COMMAND | RESULT |
|---|---|
| NDIR F: SUB | Displays all files in F: and its subdirectories. |
| NDIR F: *.EXE SUB | Displays all executable files in F: and its subdirectories. |
| NDIR F: OWNER=MATT SUB | Reveals all of Matt's files in F: and its subdirectories. |
| NDIR F: OWNER NOT=MARLA | Shows all of the files not belonging to Marla in F:. |
| NDIR F: OWNER=BRENDA SIZE GR 500 SUB | Exhibits Brenda's files larger than 500 bytes (thus eliminating viewing a great many batch files and small, unimportant files). |
| NDIR F: OWNER=MARK EO SUB | Indicates all of Mark's executable files on F: and all its subdirectories. |

### NPRINT

Virtually identical to the DOS PRINT command, NPRINT allows you to print existing text files to a network printer from the command line. The options available are equivalent to CAPTURE, including specifying the number of copies, creating banners, and performing other optional functions.

### NVER

This command displays a listing of the NetWare version and information on the workstation, including the DOS level the machine is running, LAN driver details, and IPX and NET information. (You can also obtain IPX and NET information from the workstation by using the commands IPX I and NETX I, but NVER provides the output of both, saving time.) Whenever troubleshooting is involved, always start by using this command-line utility to check the versions of the software you're running.

Another item of interest: For a long time, NetWare required a NETX.COM file corresponding to the MS-DOS release version. For example, MS-DOS 3.3 required NET3.COM, while MS-DOS 4.0

required NET4.COM. DR DOS, on the other hand, regardless of release version, worked with NET3.COM or NETX.COM. Now NETX.COM services all versions of MS-DOS and DR DOS.

Here's what you might see if you invoke the NVER command:

```
F:\SYSTEM>NVER

IPX Version: 3.01
SPX Version: 3.01

LAN Driver:  NetWare Ethernet NE1000  3.00EC (891227)
  V1.00
IRQ = 2, I/O Base = 320h, no DMA or RAM

Shell:       v3.01 Rev. E
DOS:         MSDOS v3.30 on IBM_PC

FileServer: BI_ANDERSON
Novell Advanced NetWare 286 v2.15 Rev. C (08/22/89)
```

### PSC

PSC (Print Server Command) lets you use many of the commands available from the PCONSOLE menu without having to go into PCONSOLE. For example, you can check the status of print jobs and servers by using the following flags (the capitalized characters are all that you need to type to execute the request).

- ABort
- CancelDown
- FormFeed
- MARK
- MOunt form
- PAUse
- PRIvate (to prevent users from using a printer on your workstation)

- SHared (cancels the PRIvate command)
- STARt
- STATus
- STOp

### PURGE

When a user or a network administrator deletes files from the server, the files are actually only *marked* for deletion. They are not erased until the space they occupy is used for another file. This is true whether the files were deleted by means of the DOS commands DEL or ERASE or via the NetWare Filer menu. Using SALVAGE, you can recover a file that's been deleted, but hasn't yet been written over. PURGE, on the other hand, permanently removes files marked for deletion and restores to the server the space those files occupied.

Running PURGE from a main directory will permanently erase all deleted files from that directory and from all subdirectories beneath it. Specifying a filename after PURGE will purge *only* that specific file from the delete list. The PURGE command offers an effective means of permanently disposing of files you don't want anyone else to recover.

### REMOVE

This command lets you remove from a user or group the trustee rights to a file or directory. This command is the antithesis of the GRANT command.

Here are a few examples of using the REMOVE command. If you type:

`REMOVE ALLAN or REMOVE USER ALLAN` <Enter>

you remove Allan from the list of those who have trustee rights to the current directory. If you type:

`REMOVE USER MADONNA FROM F: /SUB or REMOVE MADONNA F: /SUB` <Enter>

you remove Madonna from the list of those who have trustee rights to F: and all subdirectories thereof. If you type:

```
REMOVE GROUP GSC FROM MEMLIST.DAT or REMOVE GSC MEM
  LIST.DAT <Enter>
```

you remove the group GSC from the trustee list to the file MEMLIST.DAT.

**RENDIR**

You can rename an entire subdirectory, providing you have the Modify rights to do so. When you perform this action, only the name is changed. All trustee rights remain the same; users who previously had access continue to have access. One thing to keep in mind, however, is that the MAP commands don't automatically change. You'll have to make manual changes if this subdirectory is included in your MAP statements.

Let's look at a few examples of using the RENDIR command. If you type:

```
RENDIR 140 136 <Enter>
```

you will rename subdirectory 140 to subdirectory 136. If you type:

```
RENDIR . MICHAEL <Enter>
```

you will rename the default subdirectory to MICHAEL. If you type:

```
RENDIR Y: KRISTIN <Enter>
```

you will rename the subdirectory presently mapped to Y: to subdirectory KRISTIN.

### REVOKE

This command revokes *some* of a user or group's trustee rights to a subdirectory or file, whereas REMOVE revokes *all* of the trustee rights. You can do the same thing by means of the SYSCON menu, but REVOKE provides command-line access to the eight rights listed below. To reinstate these rights, use GRANT, the reverse of this command. The capitalized letters of the eight rights are all you need to give. To change more than one right, leave a space between:

- Access control
- ALL
- Create
- Erase
- File scan
- Modify
- Read
- Supervisory
- Write

Here are some examples of the use of the REVOKE command. If you type:

`REVOKE ALL FROM USER WILLIAM` or `REVOKE ALL FROM WILLIAM` <Enter>

it serves the same purpose as the REMOVE command. If you type:

`REVOKE A E FROM TONY` <Enter>

you remove only Tony's rights to Access control and Erase files.

### RIGHTS

Users may issue this command to see which of the effective rights they actually have to a specific subdirectory. The most useful purpose for this command is as a diagnostic tool to help users who are having difficulty accessing files.

Three different permission levels, or levels of access rights, to the same directory may appear as follows:

```
F:\APPL\QA3>RIGHTS
BI_ANDERSON/SYS:APPL/QA3
Your Effective Rights are [RWOCDPSM]:
    You may Read from Files.                (R)
    You may Write to Files                  (W)
    You may Open existing Files.            (O)
    You may Create new Files.               (C)
    You may Make new Subdirectories.        (C)
    You may Delete existing Files.          (D)
    You may Erase existing Subdirectories.  (D)
    You may Change Users' Directory Rights. (P)
    You may Search the Directory.           (S)
    You may Modify File Status Flags.       (M)

    You have ALL RIGHTS to this directory area.

F:\APPL\QA3>RIGHTS
BI_ANDERSON/SYS:APPL/QA3
Your Effective Rights are [RWOC  S ]:
    You may Read from Files.                (R)
    You may Write to Files                  (W)
    You may Open existing Files.            (O)
    You may Create new Files.               (C)
    You may Make new Subdirectories.        (C)
    You may Search the Directory.           (S)

F:\APPL\QA3>RIGHTS
BI_ANDERSON/SYS:APPL/QA3
Your Effective Rights are [        ]:
    You have NO RIGHTS to this directory area.

F:\APPL\QA3>
```

### SALVAGE

You can use the SALVAGE command to recover files that have been erased, so long as they haven't been purged. SALVAGE shows you a list of all deleted files that can still be recovered; you can mark certain files in this list by using the <F5> key. You can then either salvage or purge the marked files.

### SECURITY

An excellent utility for quick scans of the user database, SECURITY shows a listing of security loopholes: accounts with no passwords, users with supervisor equivalency, and other potential security problems.

SECURITY lists the potential security problems on the network in a scrolling format that flies by at the speed of light. It does not, however, correct those problems for you. The best method for viewing the violations is to pipe the output to a file and then print the file out, using NPRINT or any word processing package. To create the file, type:

```
SECURITY > TMPFILE.SEC <Enter>
```

NetWare then creates a file like the following one for further evaluation:

```
File Server Security Evaluation Utility

Checking for network security holes, please wait.

User TONY
   Has no login script
   Is security equivalent to user SUPERVISOR
   Has unlimited grace logins
   Is not required to change passwords periodically
   Can have passwords that are too short (less than 5)
   Does not require a password
```

```
      Does not have a secure password

   User WILLIAM
      Has [RWOCDPSM] rights in SYS:PUBLIC (maximum should
   be [ROS ])
      Can have passwords that are too short (less than 5)

   User ALLAN
      Has no login script
      Has incorrect access security on the SECURITY_EQUALS
   property
      Can have passwords that are too short (less than 5)

   Group EVERYONE
      Has [RWOC  S ] rights in SYS:PUBLIC (maximum should
   be [ROS ])
```

### SEND

If the user to whom you wish to send a message hasn't used the CASTOFF command, SEND allows you to send a short message (45 characters in length or less) to another user presently logged in to the server. In addition to sending to users, you can also specify groups; however, you have no way of knowing which members of the group actually received the message.

The message appears on the bottom line of the receiver's screen, along with a note telling him or her to press <Ctrl>-<Enter> to clear the message. Unfortunately, all processing on the receiver's workstation is suspended until these keys are pressed. Suppose, for example, that user Carol goes to lunch while a complex spreadsheet is recalculating on her workstation. You send her the message "How about lunch?" immediately after she leaves. Carol won't be very happy when she returns an hour later and finds that your message suspended her calculations and she'll have to wait another hour to get the results. You just may be eating sack lunches alone for the next few weeks, so be careful with the SEND command.

### SETPASS

You can use this command-line utility to change your password. Even as a supervisor, you can't use it to change the password of another user, unless you're logged in as that user. To change the password of another user, you must use the SYSCON menu.

Here's an example of what you might see when you use the SETPASS command-line utility:

```
F:\PUBLIC>SETPASS

Enter your old password:
Enter your new password:
Retype your new password:
Would you like to synchronize your passwords on all
attached servers? (Y/N) Y

Synchronizing all passwords...
Password on server BI_ANDERSON not changed.

F:\PUBLIC>
```

The fact that the password didn't change indicates that not all three entries were correct. Since you entered one or more of them incorrectly, the old password is still in effect. A successful attempt will generate a last line of:

```
Password on server BI_ANDERSON synchronized.
```

### SETTTS

This seldom-needed command tells the Transactional Tracking System to ignore logical or physical record locks.

## SLIST

This command lists the servers your workstation now recognizes as accessible. It's particularly useful when you're receiving errors about a server not responding.

## SMODE

For executable files (*.COM and *.EXE), this commands shows how each will use the search mappings in locating data files they need for their operations. The data files usually contain information the executables need to operate. For example, they might contain overlay files or screen parameters describing what type of display is in use.

While there are a few limited uses for this command, it mostly serves as a troubleshooting utility in the event that a data file program needs to read data from more than one type of data file. Table 1-10 shows you the SMODE available modes.

**Table 1-10. SMODE gives you information on executable files.**

| MODE | MEANING |
|---|---|
| 0 | The program will take all instructions from the SHELL.CFG file, and there are no program-specific instructions. |
| 1 | First search the path specified in the execution command, then search the default directory, followed by all search drives. |
| 2 | Search only the default directory. |
| 3 | Look only in the default directory unless the request is a read-only request, in which case, check all search drives. |
| 4 | Reserved by NetWare. |
| 5 | Always search the default directory and all search drives, whether or not a path was specified in the execution command. |
| 6 | Reserved by NetWare. |
| 7 | If data files flagged read-only are opened, then search the default directory and all search drives, whether or not a path was specified in the execution command. |

Table 1-11 shows some examples of the use of the SMODE command.

**Table 1-11. Various results when using the SMODE command**

| MODE | RESULT |
|---|---|
| SMODE | Shows all executable files and their default search modes. |
| SMODE *.* 7 | Changes all executable files in the present subdirectory to the seventh mode. |
| SMODE UPGRADE.* 7 | Changes UPGRADE.EXE and UPGRADE.COM, providing they exist, to the seventh mode. |

### SYSTIME

This command serves a dual purpose. First, it displays the date and time on the server. Second, the workstation issuing the command has its date and time set to that on the server.

### TLIST

This command provides information about the trustee assignment list for the subdirectory. It shows both users and groups. To obtain information on just one file, as opposed to the entire subdirectory, follow the command with the name of the file.

Here's an example of what you might see if you invoke TLIST:

```
F:\PUBLIC>TLIST
SYS:PUBLIC
User trustees:
  WILLIAM   [RWOCDPSM]  (william steen)

Group trustees:
  EVERYONE  [RWOC  S ]

F:\PUBLIC>
```

**USERLIST**

This command displays a list of current file server users, including each user's connection number and the date and time that user last logged in. If you use the /A parameter, the list also includes each user's network and node address. In all cases, the asterisk (*) denotes the user issuing the request.

Here's an example of what you might see if you invoke USERLIST:

```
F:\PUBLIC>USERLIST
User Information for Server BI_ANDERSON
Connection    User Name  Login          Time
----------    ---------  ----------     -------
  1           EMMETT     10-27-1992     7:18 am
  2         * SUPERVISOR 10-27-1992     8:44 pm
  3           BARBARA    10-27-1992     9:54 am
  4           MIKE       10-27-1992     6:41 am
  5           EDNA       10-27-1992    11:42 am
  6           TRACY      10-27-1992     7:32 am
  7           JEFF       10-27-1992     9:14 am
  8           DEBBIE     10-27-1992     8:30 am
  9           JIM        10-27-1992     6:56 pm
  10          LINDA      10-27-1992     8:19 am
```

Here's what you'll see if you use the /A parameter:

```
F:\PUBLIC>USERLIST/A

User Information for Server BI_ANDERSON
Conn User Name  Network   Node Address  Login         Time
---- ---------  --------  ------------  ----------    -------
1    EMMETT     [    600] [   1B2406A8] 10-27-1992   7:18 am
2    SUPERVISOR [    600] [   1B248440] 10-27-1992   8:44 pm
3    BARBARA                            10-27-1992   9:54 am
4    MIKE                               10-27-1992   6:41 am
5    EDNA                               10-27-1992  11:42 am
```

```
6    TRACY                    10-27-1992  7:32 am
7    JEFF                     10-27-1992  9:14 am
8    DEBBIE                   10-27-1992  8:30 am
9    JIM                      10-27-1992  6:56 pm
10   LINDA                    10-27-1992  8:19 am

F:\PUBLIC>
```

### WHOAMI

This command discloses who you are, which file server you're using, what the connection number is, and your login date and time. Table 1-12 shows you the WHOAMI command with its parameters.

**Table 1-12. Information about yourself as a user, generated by the WHOAMI command**

| OPTION | MEANING |
|---|---|
| WHOAMI /G | Shows basic identity information and the groups you have membership in. |
| WHOAMI /R | Shows your effective rights. |
| WHOAMI /S | Adds security equivalencies to the listing. |
| WHOAMI /ALL | Adds your effective rights, security equivalencies, and group membership to the display. |

Here's an example of what you might see if you invoke WHOAMI:

```
F:\PUBLIC>WHOAMI
You are user SUPERVISOR attached to server BI_ANDERSON
  connection 2.
Server BI_ANDERSON is running NetWare 386 3.10 Rev. A.
Login Time:  Tuesday  October 27, 1992  8:44 pm
```

```
F:\PUBLIC>WHOAMI/A
You are user SUPERVISOR attached to server BI_ANDERSON
  connection 2.
Server BI_ANDERSON is running NetWare 386 v3.10 Rev. A.
Login Time:  Tuesday  October 27, 1992  8:44 pm
You are security equivalent to the following:
    EVERYONE (group)
You are a member of the following Groups:
    EVERYONE (group)
You have the following effective rights:
    [ALL]       BI_ANDERSON/SYS:

F:\PUBLIC>
```

## Going On from Here

The commands I've presented in this chapter are the NetWare command-line utilities. While there are a great many of them, they go only so far in the possibilities they offer.

In the next chapter, I'll discuss commands that can execute within the login scripts each time a user logs in to the network. Then we'll cover the DOS commands and start to see how you can use them to enhance those commands listed here.

# CHAPTER 2

# Login Scripts

Are you tired of running from PC to PC to perform cleanup operations and to gather local data? Do you wish there were a way to send messages to users, other than by electronic mail? Would you like to have a way to execute programs immediately on login?

Then I have something to offer that you may find interesting.

But first comes the catch: You have to dig into the NetWare documentation.

Mining through NetWare's documentation requires some serious prospecting. But buried among the basics are some rich references to time-saving functions. One of these time-saving functions is the login script. With login scripts, you can let NetWare perform everyday cleanup operations and gather local data. You can send messages to users without resorting to e-mail. And you can use login scripts to execute programs immediately upon a user's login. Running a LAN without effective login scripts is like digging for gold or jewels without a pick and shovel: You can do it, but it takes a lot of unnecessary work.

Users can have personal login scripts that operate when they log in to a particular server. If no such personal login script exists, then NetWare invokes the system login script on behalf of the user. In the rare case that no system login script exists, NetWare executes the default login script. I'll deal with all of these login scripts in this chapter.

The more workstations you have on your LAN and the more geographically dispersed they are, the more you'll appreciate having login scripts to work for you. By automating network processes through login scripts, you can avoid running around to gather local disk-usage information, to update each user on network-wide changes, or to personalize individual or departmental messages.

You can purchase third-party products that will perform these functions and others for you, but you may need only what NetWare offers for free.

Login scripts have been a part of NetWare almost since the beginning of NetWare itself. NetWare 2.1x, 2.2, and 3.11 all include this login-script capability.

You can enhance any DOS machine by proper use of NetWare's login scripts. But the NetWare documentation glosses over this useful capability, leaving out important details and offering no working examples. Following the sample scripts in this chapter, you can quickly build some useful login scripts.

Novice NetWare administrators will certainly benefit from these examples, but I think veteran network managers will also enjoy looking into an often overlooked feature of the world's most popular network operating system.

## Staking Your Claim

Every user has a login script that automatically activates when he or she signs on to the network. If a user doesn't have his or her own script, then NetWare simply uses the default login script and any existing system script. The two specific rules governing these scripts are that each line can contain only one executable command, and no line can be longer than 150 characters. The network supervisor may change any and all scripts, while individual users may change only their own.

In the following pages, we'll modify the default login script to perform three functions. The first change we make to the login script will allow for the delivery of messages to users, individual and group, upon login. The second modification will cause the system to gather information from each PC on the network, such as number of user files, disk space, available hard disk space, and similar data. The third routine we set up will allow us to specify programs to execute immediately upon login.

## NetWare's Default Login Script

Listing 2-1 shows the NetWare default login script. This login script includes the operations that transpire for a user with no specific script of his or her own (called a personal login script).

**Listing 2-1. A sample NetWare default login script**

```
WRITE "Good %GREETING_TIME, %LOGIN_NAME."
MAP DISPLAY OFF
MAP ERRORS OFF
Remark: Set 1st drive to most appropriate directory.
MAP *1:=SYS:; *1:=SYS:%LOGIN_NAME
IF "%1"="SUPERVISOR" THEN MAP *1:=SYS:SYSTEM
Remark: Set search drives (S2 machine-OS dependent).
MAP S1:=SYS:PUBLIC; S2:=S1:%MACHINE/%OS/%OS_VERSION
Remark: Now display all the current drive settings.
MAP DISPLAY ON
MAP
```

To determine whether a user has a personal login script, you must know his or her User ID. With the rights of supervisor, access SYSCON and select "User Information," and then "Other Information." If you're a user other than the supervisor, and if you don't have supervisor equivalence, then you may follow the same procedures to acquire your own User ID.

Once you know the User ID, you may look in the network MAIL directory and beneath that particular user's subdirectory (for example: F:\MAIL\290067) for a file named LOGIN. If it doesn't exist, then the NetWare uses the default login script.

The default login script writes a greeting to the user, maps a drive to the network drive, and maps a drive to the network drive's PUBLIC subdirectory. In this way, the default login script gives *all* users access to the PUBLIC subdirectory and the network drive before completing the map process. When you begin writing login scripts for individual users, you must include these commands for their network admission to be successful.

## Login Script Commands

Before we begin the actual customization process for a NetWare login script, we need to cover a few of the commands that NetWare allows within the login script environment. This list outlines the login script commands specific to our needs. Most of these commands cannot be executed from the command line; they must exist within the login script in order to function.

### BREAK ON

The BREAK ON command provides a method for terminating the login script process by enabling the <Ctrl>-<C> key combination. This ability to stop the login process is useful in the event that something goes awry and you choose not to complete the login script.

### BREAK OFF

The BREAK OFF command is the exact opposite of BREAK ON in that it disables the ability to break from the routine.

### DOS SET

The DOS SET command appoints local PC variables in the same way as the DOS command SET does. In this manner, it's possible to pass variables such as physical location from the network to an individual PC. One word of caution: The amount of space that you have available for local variables is controlled by the COMMAND.COM file. If you find that you can't load all variables into memory, then you must increase the local PC environment size. (See the MOREENV.BAT listing in Chapter 5.)

### FDISPLAY

The FDISPLAY command works in the same manner as the TYPE command in DOS in that it displays the contents of an ASCII file on-screen. One major difference, however, is that if you specify a file that doesn't exist,

NetWare doesn't generate an error message but continues processing as if it had received no requests.

### EXIT

EXIT "*specifications*" stops the login script process and executes whatever commands are within the quotation marks. Specifications can be for DOS internal commands or for .BAT, .COM, or .EXE files. The only restrictions are that the specifications can't be more than fourteen characters long, and they can't load programs that terminate and stay resident in memory.

### #

The # command allows you to run .COM or .EXE files external to the login process. Again, you can't run programs that terminate and stay resident in memory. Nor may you use this command to run internal DOS commands or batch files.

One method exists for bypassing this restriction, however. Rather than calling the batch file you wish to execute, call the COMMAND.COM file and use the /C switch to accept a command string, with the command string including the batch file. For example,

`#COMMAND /C CODY.BAT` <Enter>

will use COMMAND.COM to execute CODY.BAT and, upon its completion, restore processing to the script.

### INCLUDE

The INCLUDE command allows you to include commands contained in locations other than the login script. One of the major benefits of this command is that it permits you to shorten a group of restrictions in the LOGIN script by placing them in subscripts. You can change the subscripts as frequently as you need to in order to meet current specifications. This concept will be best illustrated when we discuss delivering messages.

### PAUSE

The PAUSE command halts the execution of the login scripts and waits for the user to strike a key before continuing. You would use this command mainly when you're displaying the contents of a file that you want the users to read before proceeding to the next command.

### WRITE

The WRITE command works in the same way the ECHO command works for DOS—by displaying messages on the terminal. You can use NetWare variables so long as they're preceded by a percent sign and typed in capital letters. For example, GREETING_TIME becomes morning, afternoon, or evening, depending upon the actual time. You also may include commands such as *\n* for a new line, or \7 for the computer to emit a beep.

Listing 2-2 shows the default login script with a few of the modifications mentioned previously. This is the script to which we'll make changes from here on out.

**Listing 2-2. A modified default login script designed to pass variables**

```
Remark: Modified Default Login Script
BREAK ON
DOS SET MONTH = "%MONTH_NAME"
DOS SET DAY = "%DAY"
DOS SET YEAR = "%YEAR"
DOS SET HOUR = "%HOUR24"
DOS SET MINUTE = "%MINUTE"
DOS SET WEEK = "%DAY_OF_WEEK"
DOS SET STATION = "%P_STATION"
WRITE "Good %GREETING_TIME, %LOGIN_NAME."
MAP DISPLAY OFF
```

```
MAP ERRORS OFF
Remark: Set 1st drive to most appropriate directory.
MAP *1:=SYS:; *1:=SYS:%LOGIN_NAME
IF "%1"="SUPERVISOR" THEN MAP *1:=SYS:SYSTEM
Remark: Set search drives (S2 machine-OS dependent).
MAP S1:=SYS:PUBLIC; S2:=S1:%MACHINE/%OS/%OS_VERSION
Remark: Now display all the current drive settings.
MAP DISPLAY ON
MAP
```

The primary differences between Listing 2-1 and Listing 2-2 are that we have enabled the <Ctrl>-<C> key combination, and we're now passing variables into the local PC environment with the DOS SET command. Besides passing generic information such as the date and time of the login, we're also gathering the physical station address of the workstation via the P_STATION variable. In local data gathering, utility programs will use this address to differentiate between the two machines.

### Delivering messages

Bear in mind that all users have access to one directory on the network—PUBLIC—regardless of whatever else exists. PUBLIC, therefore, becomes a forum by which a supervisor may leave messages for users or users may leave messages for each other, providing the messages are in ASCII format. These messages will appear in separate files in the PUBLIC directory.

The most straightforward method of viewing such a message file is to use the FDISPLAY command in the login script. Type:

```
FDISPLAY SYS:PUBLIC\REMINDER <Enter>
```

This command looks for a file named REMINDER upon every login. REMINDER is the ASCII file written within the PUBLIC directory. The filename can be any valid DOS name of up to eight characters, with or without an extension. If the file doesn't exist, processing will proceed as normal. If the file does exist, its contents will be displayed on the workstation screen.

One important note is that this command must follow those commands that map the PUBLIC subdirectory in order for the memo ever to be found. It's impossible to display the contents of a file in a directory *before* you've been granted access to that directory. Another item to note: If you wish to give the user enough time to read the reminder before continuing the login, then follow the command with PAUSE.

Suppose the reminder is that time cards are due on Thursday. It's senseless to display the message every day, for the user will simply ignore it after a while. More effective is to display the reminder only on Thursday. To use the login script to cause the message to display on Thursday only, add these lines to your system login script:

```
IF DAY_OF_WEEK = "Thursday" THEN BEGIN
FDISPLAY SYS:PUBLIC\REMINDER
PAUSE
END
```

REMINDER will display only on Thursday, and the PAUSE that requires the user to press a key before the login continues also will appear only on Thursday. If you have a message for more than one day of each week, you can specify a series of commands substituting Thursday for Monday, Tuesday, and so forth.

Imagine, for example, that you need to send a message this coming Friday to the Software Department, reminding them once more of the importance of deadlines. You have several ways of obtaining the desired result, the first of which is to add these lines to the system login script:

```
IF MEMBER OF "SOFTWARE" AND DAY_OF_WEEK = "FRIDAY" THEN
  BEGIN
FDISPLAY SYS:PUBLIC\SOFTWARE.MSG
PAUSE
END
```

This series of commands will work *if* all members of the Software Department are members of the SOFTWARE group. If there is no SOFTWARE group, and all department members belong to the generic EVERYONE group, then the problem becomes more specific.

There are now two possible solutions to the predicament. The first is to modify the login script so that it will show SOFTWARE.MSG on Friday and copy the ASCII file into the MAIL subdirectory of those who should see the message.

The second scenario is to use subcommands in a separate file and key on the LOGIN_NAME. Rather than creating a cluttered login script that searches everyone's name for commands to perform, we can create subcommands that perform the operations elsewhere by exercising the INCLUDE command. (If you have supervisor rights, it would be simpler for you to create a SOFTWARE group and put department members in it. However, I'm trying to show you all possibilities.)

Listing 2-3 shows a login routine that displays the time card reminder for everyone on Thursday and searches for specific messages to deliver to individuals on Friday. In the event that it is not Friday, the subroutine is not used. In the event the user is not one of those listed in the subroutine, processing continues without any indication that the main routine has branched.

**Listing 2-3. Use the login script to display the Thursday REMINDER to everyone, and the Friday "REMINDER" to selected individuals.**

```
Remark: Modified Default Login Script
BREAK ON
DOS SET MONTH = "%MONTH_NAME"
DOS SET DAY = "%DAY"
DOS SET YEAR = "%YEAR"
DOS SET HOUR = "%HOUR24"
DOS SET MINUTE = "%MINUTE"
DOS SET WEEK = "%DAY_OF_WEEK"
DOS SET STATION = "%P_STATION"
WRITE "Good %GREETING_TIME, %LOGIN_NAME."
```

```
MAP DISPLAY OFF
MAP ERRORS OFF
Remark: Set 1st drive to most appropriate directory.
MAP *1:=SYS:; *1:=SYS:%LOGIN_NAME
IF "%1"="SUPERVISOR" THEN MAP *1:=SYS:SYSTEM
Remark: Set search drives (S2 machine-OS dependent).
MAP S1:=SYS:PUBLIC; S2:=S1:%MACHINE/%OS/%OS_VERSION
Remark: Now display all the current drive settings.
MAP DISPLAY ON
MAP
IF DAY_OF_WEEK = "Thursday" THEN BEGIN
FDISPLAY SYS:PUBLIC\REMINDER
PAUSE
END
IF DAY_OF_WEEK = "Friday" THEN INCLUDE
  SYS:\PUBLIC\SOFTWARE

Remark: SYS:\PUBLIC\SOFTWARE
IF %LOGIN_NAME = "KAREN" THEN FDISPLAY
  SYS:PUBLIC\SOFTWARE.MSG
IF %LOGIN_NAME = "JENNA" THEN FDISPLAY
  SYS:PUBLIC\SOF WARE.MSG
IF %LOGIN_NAME = "LANDON" THEN FDISPLAY
  SYS:PUBLIC\SOFTWARE.MSG
IF %LOGIN_NAME = "TONY" THEN FDISPLAY
  SYS:PUBLIC\SOFTWARE.MSG
IF %LOGIN_NAME = "CAROL" THEN FDISPLAY
  SYS:PUBLIC\SOFTWARE.MSG
```

### Information gathering

Depending on the number of PCs on your network and their geographical locations, gathering individual resource details can be time-consuming, if not impossible. Since all users (hence, all workstations) are allowed access to the PUBLIC subdirectory, the PUBLIC subdirectory becomes an area where the PCs may report their status upon login.

At the completion of the defined login execution routine, another process may be started as this login script ends if the processing is diverted through the use of the EXIT command. EXIT allows you to pass control to a DOS batch file that can perform operations on the local workstation. This batch file, if placed in the same PUBLIC subdirectory, is accessible to all workstations and uses none of their memory or disk capacity.

To illustrate, add the following line as the last line to the login script:

```
EXIT "Z:\nWORK.BAT"
```

Now upon completion of login, the Z: drive will be accessed. (Z: will be the PUBLIC directory, since it was the first drive mapped in the NetWare default login script.) The \n serves as a new line character. (The login script has to do it this way, as opposed to F:\PUBLIC\n, because of the fourteen-character size restriction on EXIT commands.)

The diagnostic programs you'll be able to run on your own PC are, of course, dependent on the software that you own; however, Listing 2-4 depicts the batch file WORK.BAT and a representative selection.

**Listing 2-4. WORK.BAT is a batch file designed to perform PC operations based upon the day, leaving the results in PC.LOG.**

```
:WORK.BAT
@ECHO OFF
ECHO ********************************************** >
C:\TEMP.NET
ECHO %STATION% >> C:\TEMP.NET
ECHO %MONTH% %DAY%,%YEAR%          %HOUR%:%MINUTE% >>
  c:\TEMP.NET
C:
DIR C:\NFT | FIND "olume" >> C:\TEMP.NET
IF "%DAY%"=="01" GOTO MONTHY
IF "%WEEK%"=="Monday" GOTO MONDAY
```

```
IF "%WEEK%"=="Wednesday" GOTO WEDS
IF "%WEEK%"=="Friday" GOTO FRIDAY
GOTO END
:MONTHY
CHKDSK /V C: >> C:\TEMP.NET
GOTO END
:MONDAY
CHKDSK C: >> C:\TEMP.NET
GOTO END
:WEDS
C:\NORTON\SD C: /R >> C:\TEMP.NET
GOTO END
:FRIDAY
C:\DOS\MEM /P >> C:\TEMP.NET
:END
TYPE C:\TEMP.NET >> F:\PUBLIC\PC.LOG
```

All workstations that log in maintain one log file, PC.LOG, from which the supervisor can extract information. When each workstation logs on, the login script creates an entry in the log file showing the physical station number, date and time of login, and the C: drive's label to identify which PC generated the information. After that, the batch file performs an examination to see if it is the first of the month; if it is, then a listing of all files on the root drive is piped to the log file. If it's Monday, the DOS command CHKDSK is run to audit the drive for errors. On Tuesday and Thursday, no actions are performed, and the only notation in the log is that the PC logged in at a given date and time. On Wednesday, Norton's Speed Disk is used to render a report on the percentage of disk fragmentation. On Friday, the DOS 5.0 command MEM is employed to gather information on high and low memory in use.

The one item of note is that a temporary file, TEMP.NET, is created on the local PC before the information is transferred to PUBLIC. This is attributable to the fact that access on PUBLIC, while granted to all users, does not include piping operations. If you wish, you can delete the temporary file by adding the line to the end of the batch file to delete all traces from the local drive:

```
DEL C:\TEMP.NET
```

Listing 2-5 shows three days' worth of the PC.LOG file for two representative PCs. On Monday, CHKDSK is run; on Tuesday, no operations are performed, but the login is still reported. Wednesday has a percentage of file fragmentation reported. Notice how helpful having the local drive's volume label as a descriptive definition (ROOM_110 and ACCT_OFFICE) is towards ascertaining which machine is in question. The machines are also differentiated, of course, by the network station numbers (00001B24A2B6 and 00001B24651B, respectively), but I highly recommend setting the local volume name with the DOS LABEL command. If you so desire, you may even relabel the local drive remotely, using login commands similar to those given.

**Listing 2-5. Three days' worth of the PC.LOG file for two PCs**

```
00001B24A2B6
December 23,1991          07:36
Volume in drive C is ROOM_110
Volume ROOM_110    created May 29, 1991 9:01a

 33462272 bytes total disk space
   401408 bytes in 45 hidden files
    73728 bytes in 29 directories
 26683392 bytes in 931 user files
  6303744 bytes available on disk

   655360 bytes total memory
   545024 bytes free
*********************************************
00001B24651B
December 23,1991          07:37
Volume in drive C is ACCT_OFFICE
```

```
 33462272 bytes total disk space
    57344 bytes in 3 hidden files
    61440 bytes in 26 directories
 20387840 bytes in 779 user files
    10240 bytes in bad sectors
 12945408 bytes available on disk

   655360 bytes total memory
   560096 bytes free
*******************************************
00001B24A2B6
December 24,1991          07:39
Volume in drive C is ROOM_110
*******************************************
00001B24651B
December 24,1991          07:40
Volume in drive C is ACCT_OFFICE
*******************************************
00001B24A2B6
December 25,1991          07:43
Volume in drive C is ROOM_110
SD-Speed Disk, Advanced Edition 4.50, (C) Copr 1987-88,
Peter Norton
  Reading disk information...
Total of the entire disk: 79% unfragmented
*******************************************
00001B24651B
December 25,1991          07:44
Volume in drive C is ACCT_OFFICE
SD-Speed Disk, Advanced Edition 4.50, (C) Copr 1987-88,
Peter Norton
  Reading disk information...
Total of the entire disk: 100% unfragmented
```

### Specifying program execution

The pound sign (#), within the login script environment, allows you to run .EXE and .COM files outside of the login, and then return to the login procedure once those files have run. Unlike the EXIT command, the # command allows login execution to continue after fruition. This continuation can be useful for gathering information that you will use after you're logged in.

When you log in to the network drive, NetWare assigns a variable number to each parameter you specify. For example, when Landon signs on, the program he is executing (LOGIN) becomes %0. His login name (LANDON) becomes %1. This holds true whether you issue the command LOGIN LANDON <Enter> or merely LOGIN <Enter>, and then LANDON <Enter>. For any parameter specified after "Landon," NetWare assigns the next higher number: %2, %3, and so forth.

Listing 2-6 shows the login script with a routine added to check for the %2 parameter and act upon it.

**Listing 2-6. If a second parameter of WHO is specified at login, a listing of all users on the system will be given.**

```
BREAK ON
DOS SET MONTH = "%MONTH_NAME"
DOS SET DAY = "%DAY"
DOS SET YEAR = "%YEAR"
DOS SET HOUR = "%HOUR24"
DOS SET MINUTE = "%MINUTE"
DOS SET WEEK = "%DAY_OF_WEEK"
DOS SET STATION = "%P_STATION"
WRITE "Good %GREETING_TIME, %LOGIN_NAME."
MAP DISPLAY OFF
MAP ERRORS OFF
Remark: Set 1st drive to most appropriate directory.
MAP *1:=SYS:; *1:=SYS:%LOGIN_NAME
IF "%1"="SUPERVISOR" THEN MAP *1:=SYS:SYSTEM
Remark: Set search drives (S2 machine-OS dependent).
```

```
MAP S1:=SYS:PUBLIC; S2:=S1:%MACHINE/%OS/%OS_VERSION
Remark: Now display all the current drive settings.
MAP DISPLAY ON
MAP
IF "%2" = "WHO" THEN BEGIN
#USERLIST
END
EXIT "Z:\nWORK.BAT"
```

If the user now logs in by typing:

`LOGIN LANDON WHO` <Enter>

before the EXIT command is actuated, Landon will be shown a listing of who else is on the network at this time. This information can be most beneficial if Landon plans to use SEND or BROADCAST commands.

Any executable file can be specified in similar fashion; some of the best choices include CHKDSK /F if the second parameter is FIX, or any of the multitudes of BACKUP combinations.

## Experiment and Automate

I hope that the three examples of login script modifications I've presented have encouraged you to experiment with automating your own login procedures. If, as a supervisor, you need to send messages, gather PC information, or perform operations upon login, then by all means, start adapting the system default script as soon as you can. If you're a user, many of the same issues hold true except that you'll be able to modify only your own script.

Either way, the possibilities and benefits are endless, and the jewels of automation are only a login away.

3 CHAPTER

# DOS Batch File Language

Batch files are special files containing a list of commands that operate one at a time, whenever the file is called. The batch file language is supported in both MS-DOS and DR DOS, with DR DOS containing all the commands of MS-DOS plus a few more.

Batch files must always be in ASCII format. They must also have the extension .BAT, though you don't have to type in the extension when you call the file into operation. For example, TEMP.BAT can contain a series of operations that will perform whenever you use the command TEMP.BAT or TEMP. The only other restriction is that no line of the batch file can be more than 127 characters long.

You can create these batch files with any word processor that exports to ASCII, or by using either the MS-DOS EDLIN or EDIT (version 5.0) or DR DOS's EDITOR, the latter three of which store output, by default, in ASCII.

The commands contained within the batch file may be DOS commands (internal ones contained within the COMMAND.COM, such as DIR, or external ones contained in the DOS directory, such as COPY). Any command that will run at a prompt may be inserted in a batch file. Or they may be the specific batch file commands listed below.

The processing ceases when all commands within the batch file have been performed or when the <Ctrl>-<Break> keys have been pressed.

### How Batch Files Work

Each time a user enters a command into the computer, COMMAND.COM checks to see if the command is an internal one. If it is, COMMAND.COM executes the command and then reads the next command. If the command is not an internal one, the COMMAND.COM checks the current directory for a file with a .COM extension. If it can't find one, it checks the current directory for a file with an .EXE extension. If it can't find one of those, either, it checks the current directory for a .BAT file. If it can't find a file with a .BAT extention, it repeats the search, in the same order, for every directory listed in the PATH statement.

For this reason, you can't have a .COM or an .EXE file with the same name as a .BAT file, in the same directory, or COMMAND.COM will run the other file and not the batch file. An exception would occur if you were to use the entire filename, including the extension, to summon it. TEMP.BAT, for example, would call TEMP.BAT and not TEMP.COM or TEMP.EXE.

Note that PATH statements contain directory listings where DOS is to look for commands if it can't find the given command in the present working directory.

While it may sound like a wonderful idea to place every directory and subdirectory into the PATH, such a move can slow down processing. For example, suppose you have a PATH that reads as follows:

```
PATH=Z:.;Y:.;C:\PCPLUS;C:\DOS;C:\WP51;C:\;C:\NOR4.5;C:\ D V
```

Now, every time you hit the wrong key and type "DER" instead of "DIR," DOS is going to go through eight directories, one at a time, looking for .COM files, then .EXE files, then .BAT files, only to come back much later and report:

```
Bad command or file name
```

It would be far more advantageous to include in PATH only the subdirectories containing executable files likely to be run. You should never place in your PATH statement directories that contain non-executable files (database files, spreadsheet files, and so forth) or executable files that will be run only when you're in that directory. For example:

```
PATH=Z:..;Y:..;C:\DOS;C:\
```

This approach cuts the processing time on errors in half. (The odds of the other subdirectories containing an executable file that would be called somewhere other than in their own subdirectory are very slim.)

Another waste of time is the replication of entries in the PATH statement. For example, look at this PATH statement from a legitimate system:

```
PATH=Z:..;Y:..;C:\PCPLUS;C:\DOS;C:\PCPLUS;C:\DOS;C:\PCPLUS;
  C:\WP51;C:\;C:\NOR4.5
```

C:\PCPLUS gets searched nine times! It appears within the PATH three times, and DOS performs three searches each time (for .COM, .EXE, and .BAT files). DOS doesn't know that it searched that directory moments ago; if the directory is listed again, DOS searches it again.

Keep PATH statements short and sweet, and your reward will be reduced response time, especially if you're operating in the 286 environment (today's 386 and 486 machines execute the instructions so fast it's hard to perceive any difference).

Once DOS has found a batch file by its command name and loaded it into COMMAND.COM, it reads the file one line at a time. The first line is read, the batch file is closed, and the command read into memory is executed. At the completion of that command, the batch file is reopened, the second line is read, the batch file is closed, and the command read into memory is executed. And so it goes until the batch file has been fully read and executed.

## Batch File Commands

The following are the commands you can use to create batch files, with an explanation of each. I've listed MS-DOS- and DR DOS-compatible commands first, then vendor-specific commands.

### CALL

CALL allows one batch file to summon a second. Upon completion of the second, processing returns to the first. CALL was not a valid command until MS-DOS version 3.3. In earlier versions, you can perform the same function by summoning another version of COMMAND.COM, as shown in Example 3.

*Example 1:*

```
DIR
TEMP
CLS
```

In this example, DOS performs a directory listing, and then processing is diverted to TEMP.BAT. Upon completion of TEMP.BAT, the prompt is restored and the next input is read. CLS never takes place, since processing is diverted from this batch file and never returned.

*Example 2:*

```
DIR
CALL TEMP
CLS
```

DOS performs the directory listing and then runs TEMP.BAT. Once the file is run, processing reverts to this batch file where CLS will be executed.

*Example 3:*

```
DIR
COMMAND /C TEMP
CLS
```

DOS performs the same operations it performed in Example 2. This is the method of choice for MS-DOS versions prior to 3.3.

You can use the CALL command on any line. A batch file may even call itself if operations need to be run more than once, but an ending condition must exist that terminates the processing or the batch file will create an endless processing loop, running over and over without end.

## ECHO

You can use the ECHO command to toggle, off and on, command processing to your terminal and to write messages to the screen. When ECHO is on and you run a batch file, your screen will display the DOS prompt and each line of the file as each line is executed. In order to eliminate this display, the first line of most batch files turns the echo off.

You can use the "@" symbol preceding the command in versions 3.3 and greater. Using this symbol also prevents the prompt and ECHO OFF from appearing as the first command is executed.

*Example 1:*

```
DIR
CLS
```

This example displays the command prompt, then the command DIR, followed by a directory listing. Next, the command prompt appears, followed by the command CLS; then the screen is cleared.

*Example 2:*

```
ECHO OFF
DIR
CLS
```

This example displays the command prompt and the command ECHO OFF. The commands DIR and CLS do not display, but the directory listing is sent to the screen, followed by a clearing of the screen.

*Example 3:*

```
@ECHO OFF
DIR
CLS
```

No command prompts or commands display on the screen, but a directory listing appears, followed by a screen clearing.

The other use for the ECHO command is to display text on the screen as the batch file is processing.

*Example 4:*

```
@ECHO OFF
DIR
CLS
ECHO Change subdirectories to view more
```

No command prompts or commands display on the screen, but a directory listing appears, followed by a screen clearing, and then the text following the ECHO command appears on the screen.

**NOTES:**

- You can use the @ symbol before any command line to prevent it from appearing on the screen and to execute the command without a visual display.
- You can use ECHO OFF at the command line to prevent the prompt from appearing at the beginning of a new line. You can turn it back on with ECHO ON.
- Beginning with MS-DOS 5.0, it's possible to ECHO a blank line to the screen by following the command with a period, like this:

```
ECHO.
```

## FOR

The FOR command allows you to create a list of items (for example, directories or files) and repeat one set command for every item in the list, thereby performing repetitive functions on different items. The list is processed one item at a time. You must assign a variable to the item in the list that is currently being processed. This variable name *must* begin with two percent signs (%%) and then consist of any single letter. The syntax of the command is:

```
FOR %%variable IN (list) DO command
```

FOR, IN, and DO are all required parts of the command. The variable is the single letter and the list may consist of anything, including wildcard characters. The command consists of what will be done to each item in the list.

***Example 1:*** `FOR %%x IN (A B C D E F G) DO ECHO %%x`

This command runs seven times. The first time, it echoes "A" to the screen. The next time, it echoes "B," and so on. To see why, look at the examples that follow.

***Example 2:*** `FOR %%x IN (A B C D E F G) DO ECHO Go Home!!!`

This example runs seven times, once for each variable in the list, and echoes "Go Home!!!" This is a useful method of reiterating a command where the number of times is important, but the actual variables are not.

***Example 3:*** `FOR %%x IN (KAREN DONNA JENNA) DO COPY %%x.TXT A:`

First, KAREN.TXT is copied to the A: drive, followed by DONNA.TXT, and then JENNA.TXT.

***Example 4:*** `FOR %%x IN (*.TXT *.MEM *.DOC) DO DEL %%x`

This command deletes all files ending in the specified three extensions.

NOTES:

- The command called by the DO statement can be only a DOS internal or external command or an .EXE or .COM file. You can't use the FOR and DO combination to execute another batch file. As a workaround for this, you can use the CALL statement as follows:

  ```
  FOR %%x IN (*.TXT *.MEM *.DOC) DO CALL TEMP %%x
  ```

  In this example, TEMP represents TEMP.BAT, or the batch file to be executed.

- If you include a slash character inside the parameter list, NetWare interprets the parameter list as two variables. The first variable is the first character following the slash, while the second parameter consists of all text other than the first character.

  ```
  FOR %%x IN (ABCDEFG) DO ECHO Go Home!!
  ```

  This example prints the "Go Home!!!" command once to your screen, only one variable being present, while

  ```
  FOR %%x IN (/ABCDEFG) DO ECHO Go Home!!
  ```

  prints the line twice, once for variable "A" and once for variable "BCDEFG." Later on in this chapter I'll tell you more about why this method may prove useful to you.

## GOTO

Processing can move from one section of the batch file to another, bypassing portions in between, via the GOTO command. GOTO is followed by a label name. (A *label name* is a line within the file that processing jumps to, bypassing the commands that came between.) The label name must be eight characters or fewer in length, appear in the batch file on a line by itself, and be preceded by a colon symbol (:).

All lines in a batch file that are preceded by a colon are treated as labels and are neither displayed nor executed by NetWare or DOS.

***Example:***

```
DIR
GOTO END
CLS
ECHO Why Haven't You Gone Home Yet?
:END
```

The directory listing is performed and shown on the screen, and then the batch file skips the CLS and ECHO commands and jumps to the END label.

More than one label may be specified for a set of commands to branch the processing to that position. For example, one GOTO statement could send processing to FINISH and one to END, in which case the labels would follow each other as follows:

```
DIR
GOTO END
CLS
ECHO Why Haven't You Gone Home Yet?
:END
:FINISH
```

## IF

You can use the IF command to allow conditional execution of the batch file or portions thereof. There are three conditions, and only three conditions, that the system can check for, as follows:

1. IF EXIST. If a file by a specified filename exists, then the condition is true; otherwise, it is false.

   *Example:*

```
DIR
IF EXIST KAREN.DOC GOTO END
CLS
ECHO Why Haven't You Gone Home Yet?
:END
```

   The directory listing is performed and shown on the screen. If a filename KAREN.DOC exists, then the batch file skips the CLS and ECHO commands and jumps to the END label. If KAREN.DOC doesn't exist, then the screen is cleared and the statement is echoed.

2. IF {variable A} == {variable B}. If two variables are identical, then the condition is true; otherwise, it is false. You would use this conditional setting predominantly with replaceable parameters, described later in this chapter.

3. IF ERRORLEVEL. If an error condition exists that is equal to the number specified, then perform the operation; otherwise, do not perform the operation. An errorlevel of zero always indicates flawless execution of the last command.

   *Example:*

```
BACKUP C:\*.TXT A:
IF ERRORLEVEL 0 GOTO END
ECHO No Files were found to back up
:END
```

   If the backup operation is successful, the errorlevel returned will be zero and no echo will display. If the backup finds no files to back up, however, the errorlevel returned is one and the message is displayed.

Errorlevels may be of any value from 0 to 255. When you're searching for them and more than one is possible, you must always search for the highest number first and the lowest number last. For example, if an operation can return errorlevels of 5 and 6, the statements would need to read:

```
IF ERRORLEVEL 6 GOTO WRONG
IF ERRORLEVEL 5 GOTO RIGHT
```

If all 255 errorlevels are possible and you're interested in only one, a valid shortcut is to use the NOT condition and check for a value, and NOT a value equal to one digit higher:

```
IF ERRORLEVEL 5 IF NOT ERRORLEVEL 6 GOTO
  RIGHT
```

Listing 3-1 shows you a batch file called FINDERR.BAT (also on the disk that comes with this book) that you can use to test for and find an existing errorlevel.

**Listing 3-1. FINDERR.BAT is designed to find existing errorlevels.**

```
:FINDERR.BAT
@ECHO OFF
FOR %%X IN (0 1 2) DO IF ERRORLEVEL %%X00 SET ERR=%%X
FOR %%X IN (0 1 2 3 4 5 6 7 8 9) DO IF ERRORLEVEL
  %ERR%%%X0 SET ERR=%ERR%%%X
FOR %%X IN (0 1 2 3 4 5 6 7 8 9) DO IF ERRORLEVEL
  %ERR%%%X SET ERR=%ERR%%%X
ECHO Existing errorlevel = %ERR%
```

Note that all IF statements can be used in conjunction with NOT in order to reverse their true and false operations. The following file does *not* display the error message upon successful execution:

```
BACKUP C:\*.TXT A:
IF NOT ERRORLEVEL 1 GOTO END
ECHO No Files were found to backup
:END
```

### PAUSE

The PAUSE command causes the execution of a batch file to be suspended until the user presses a key. The message "Press any key to continue . . ." is displayed and processing is suspended until a key is pressed.

This function is useful for preventing text from scrolling past the screen too fast for the user to read. Other common uses for this function include providing reminders to perform such tasks as swapping disks or turning on a printer and similar reminders or instructions.

If you press <Ctrl>-<Break> or <Ctrl>-<C> while DOS is processing a batch file, a yes-or-no prompt appears asking if you wish to terminate the batch file. Any other key combination continues the batch file processing. You can use the ECHO command preceding PAUSE to allow for a more detailed message. For example:

```
ECHO Half of the output has been read,
PAUSE
```

The output to the screen will be:

```
Half of the output has been read,
Press any key to continue . . .
```

If you prefer to have the processing wait for a keystroke but don't want the standard message to print, you can send the output of the command to device NUL (nowhere). For example:

```
ECHO Half of the output has been read, press
ECHO <Ctrl>-<Break> to stop or any other key to
  continue.
PAUSE > NUL
```

This series of commands will echo the two lines as a prompt for a keystroke, but the actual PAUSE string will not be displayed. PAUSE will work as it always has.

### REM

REM allows you to insert REMark statements into the batch file to help explain what is taking place at that position in the processing. The remark statements may be only one line long. If the line is longer than 127 characters, the second line needs to begin with REM as well.

Batch files should always begin with the name of the file in order to facilitate the associatiion of listings with names. One method of doing this is by using REM statement in the following fashion:

```
@ECHO OFF
REM TEMP.BAT
REM 10/12/92 by E.A. Dulaney
REM fragmentation check on frequently used directories
FOR %%x IN (C: C:\DATA C:\DATA\BIN) DO CHKDSK %%x\*.*
```

One word of advice: DOS doesn't know a line is a REM line until it reads the line. This means that it's reading and processing the line before it realizes that the line is meaningless and it must move to the next line. In the interest of shortening processing time, you can use GOTO to jump the REM statements in the following fashion:

```
@ECHO OFF
GOTO START
REM TEMP.BAT
REM 10/12/92 by E.A. Dulaney
REM fragmentation check on frequently used directories
:START
FOR %%x IN (C: C:\DATA C:\DATA\BIN) DO CHKDSK %%x\*.*
```

This entry prevents all REM statements from being read into COMMAND.COM, thereby drastically reducing processing time.

### SHIFT

SHIFT moves replaceable parameters, covered in the following segment, over by one position. If you have three parameters wherein %1=A, %2=B, and %3=C, calling SHIFT will set %1=B, %2=C, and %3 equal to nothing.

Now that I've finished discussing batch file commands, I'll look at ways to pass information to the batch file.

## Replaceable Parameters

Replaceable parameters are variables that have a different value each time the batch file is run. You may specify a maximum of ten parameters, to be numbered %0, %1, %2, %3, %4, %5, %6, %7, %8, and %9.

When a batch file is executed, you can specify parameters by typing the entries on the command line. For example,

```
TEMP ONE TWO THREE <Enter>
```

calls TEMP.BAT and passes the other three entries as parameters to the batch file. %0 is the name of the batch file called, so in this instance, it is TEMP.

```
%1=ONE
%2=TWO
%3=THREE
```

## Environment Variables

You may have established environment variables by means of the SET command. You can read these environmental variables into the batch file by surrounding the variable name within percent signs. For example, to read the PATH statement into the batch file, write the parameter as %PATH%.

## AUTOEXEC.BAT

AUTOEXEC.BAT is a batch file that must be present in the root directory. The workstation BIOS reads it each time a workstation is booted up. COMMAND.COM first reads the CONFIG.SYS file, then reads the AUTOEXEC.BAT as the last operation prior to relinquishing processing to the operator and performs whatever actions are contained there on *every* bootup.

You can use this startup file to establish parameters that you will use for the duration of your boot. Such parameters can include the PATH statement, environmental variables, the commands for starting terminate-and-stay-resident programs (TSRs), and the command-line prompt.

Listing 3-2 shows you an example of a typical AUTOEXEC.BAT listing.

**Listing 3-2. The AUTOEXEC.BAT file establishes your boot parameters.**

```
:AUTOEXEC.BAT
@ECHO OFF
PATH C:\DOS;C:\;C:\UNIX;D:\
SET HOME=C:\DATA
C:\MOUSE1\MOUSE
PROMPT=$P$G
DOSKEY
CD C:\NET
C:\QEMM\LOADHI /R:1 IPX
C:\NET\NET5
F:LOGIN
CLS
CD\DV
DV
```

Lines 1 and 2 perform housekeeping functions—giving the name of the batch file and turning the echo feature off. Line 3 sets the path statement that will be used when not in the network, while line 4 sets a local environment variable. Line 5 loads the mouse driver—a TSR—

and line 6 sets the prompt. Line 7 loads another TSR, and lines 8 through 11 load NetWare. Once loaded, lines 12 through 14 clear the screen and start an interface that will be used on the workstation.

## DR DOS-Specific Commands

All of the batch file commands I've covered so far work identically under MS-DOS and DR DOS. DR DOS, however, offers three commands for which there is no equal in Microsoft DOS, one for which there is an equal only in MS-DOS 6.0, and a new parameter for an existing command. The four new commands are EXIT, GOSUB, RETURN, and SWITCH; IF is the changed command.

Let's look at all of these commands.

### EXIT

This command stops the processing of the batch file and returns processing to the command prompt. EXIT provides a tidy "GOTO END" command that bypasses all the statements that follow it.

### GOSUB and RETURN

GOSUB is much like GOTO in that it redirects processing from one portion of the batch file to another. Unlike GOTO, when GOSUB's statements finish execution, processing is returned to the position in the batch file that originally called it via the RETURN command. Those commands work in the same manner as do their counterparts in the BASIC language. You can't use the GOSUB command alone without a RETURN command following.

*Example:*

```
DIR
GOSUB ROUTINE
CLS
EXIT
:ROUTINE
FOR %%x IN (C: C:\DATA C:\DATA\BIN) DO
  CHKDSK %%x\*.*
RETURN
```

The directory listing appears, followed by CHKDSK on the three subdirectories; then the screen clears and the batch file ends.

### IF

DR DOS adds a fourth IF condition to the available three: DIREXIST, a command that checks whether a directory path exists. If it does exist, the condition is true; otherwise, it is false.

```
IF DIREXIST C:\KAREN THEN GOTO END
```

### RETURN

This command sends processing back to the position in the batch file from which a subroutine was summoned. You must use it in conjunction with either a GOSUB or SWITCH command.

### SWITCH

SWITCH is far and away the most important of the additional commands. It provides interaction between the batch file and the user by prompting the user and then jumping in the file to the label specified by the user.

The maximum number of choices available is nine. Pressing the <Enter> key selects the first choice by default. Listing 3-3 shows you an example of using the SWITCH command.

**Listing 3-3. The SWITCH command provides interaction between the batch file and the user.**

```
:GAMES.BAT
@ECHO OFF
CLS
ECHO Do you want to play
ECHO
ECHO 1. BLACKJACK
ECHO 2. VIDEO POKER
ECHO 3. PINBALL
ECHO
```

```
SWITCH BJ, VP, PB
ECHO Thank you for playing
EXIT
:BJ
CD\CARDGAME
BJACK LEVEL1
RETURN
:VP
CD\CRDGAME2
POKER
RETURN
:PB
C:\PINBALL START
RETURN
```

This entry offers a menu of three choices. Pressing any key other than 1, 2, or 3 loops the input (SWITCH) command, and it awaits a valid entry.

Note that DR DOS doesn't print a blank line when you use "ECHO," but it does print whatever follows the ECHO statement. Therefore, to print blank lines, follow the ECHO command with two or three presses of the space bar.

## MS-DOS-Specific Commands

The CHOICE command became available with the release of MS-DOS 6.0. It serves the same function as the DR DOS SWITCH command. The syntax is as follows:

```
CHOICE [/C:choices] [text]
```

In this command, wherein [choices] are the available options; an errorlevel is returned based upon which one you press. If you select the first choice, an errorlevel of 1 is returned; if you select the second choice, an errorlevel of 2 is returned, and so forth. The text represents the prompt the user sees.

The CHOICE command is case-insensitive, accepting "Y" and "y" as being one and the same. If you use the "/S" parameter, however, you invoke case sensitivity. You can also use the "/T" parameter to time-out the amount of time waiting for a response and force a selection.

## Batch File Examples

In order to illustrate the batch file language, the remainder of this chapter consists of several useful utilities that require only the eight batch commands available in both the Microsoft and Digital Research operating systems. The focus is on counting and various ways that batch files can increment.

### Counting characters

The first illustration of the batch file language is a rather easy one that counts the number of characters in a parameter.

**Listing 3-4. The COUNT.BAT utility uses DOS commands available in both MS-DOS and DR DOS.**

```
:COUNT.BAT
@ECHO OFF
IF "%1"=="" GOTO END
SET A=%1END
:COUNTING
SET COUNTER=%COUNTER%$
FOR %%E IN (/%A%) DO SET A=%%E
IF "%A%"=="END" GOTO FINAL
GOTO COUNTING
:FINAL
IF %COUNTER%==$ SET ANSWER=1
IF %COUNTER%==$$ SET ANSWER=2
IF %COUNTER%==$$$ SET ANSWER=3
IF %COUNTER%==$$$$ SET ANSWER=4
IF %COUNTER%==$$$$$ SET ANSWER=5
IF %COUNTER%==$$$$$$ SET ANSWER=6
```

```
IF %COUNTER%==$$$$$$$ SET ANSWER=7
IF %COUNTER%==$$$$$$$$ SET ANSWER=8
IF %COUNTER%==$$$$$$$$$ SET ANSWER=9
IF %COUNTER%==$$$$$$$$$$ SET ANSWER=10
IF %COUNTER%==$$$$$$$$$$$ SET ANSWER=11
IF %COUNTER%==$$$$$$$$$$$$ SET ANSWER=12
IF "%ANSWER%"=="" SET ANSWER=MORE THAN TWELVE
ECHO %1 HAS %ANSWER% CHARACTERS
FOR %%D IN (A ANSWER COUNTER) DO SET %%D=
:END
```

COUNT.BAT, quite simply, counts the number of characters in an entry by building an environmental variable of the same length, filled with dollar signs ($).

The user begins the routine with the command COUNT PARAMETER. Line 3 checks for the existence of a parameter. If none is found, all other actions are avoided and processing drops to the bottom of the routine.

Line 4 creates the environmental variable A, which is equal to the parameter given and the characters "END." COUNT BILL, for example, sets A equal to BILLEND.

Lines 5 through 9 represent the heart of the program—a loop that continues processing until the variable COUNTER is the same size as the given parameter. Line 6 adds a dollar sign to COUNTER every time it runs, increasing the size one character at a time. Line 7 uses the "FOR /" combination to divide variable A into two sections, the first being the first character of A and the second being everything remaining. The result of running it twice (FOR runs once for every entry between the brackets, once for the first character and again for the remainder) is that A gets set to what it was, minus the first character.

Line 8 checks to see if A is now equal to the phrase "END"—that which was tacked on to the end of the variable back at line 4. If it's equal, processing moves on; if it isn't finished, line 9 loops the process through again. COUNT BILL takes four passes through the loop in the following manner:

| | *Variable* | |
|---|---|---|
| *A* | *COUNTER* | *A (new)* |
| BILLEND | $ | ILLEND |
| ILLEND | $$ | LLEND |
| LLEND | $$$ | LEND |
| LEND | $$$$ | END |

Lines 10 through 23 compare COUNTER, line by line, to determine the length. The counting stops at 12 because that is as long as a filename and extension can be, and it provides a simple check for legitimate entries. Adding additional lines to the routine (IF %COUNTER%=$$$$$$$$$$$$$, and so forth) will enable it to count larger entries.

Line 25 removes the three environmental variables created in the processing, and line 26 wraps it up.

To enable counting of more than one parameter, add the following lines prior to :END:

```
SHIFT
GOTO COUNT
```

### Counting lines in a file

To count the number of lines in a file, the LINES.BAT file will prove useful. This utility is shown in Listing 3-5.

**Listing 3-5. The LINES.BAT utility counts the lines in a file.**

```
:LINES.BAT
@ECHO OFF
IF "%1"=="" GOTO ERROR
FIND /C/V "~~" %1
GOTO END
:ERROR
ECHO Specify a valid filenamc. Example: LINES FILEONE
:END
```

This batch file makes a cursory check to see if a filename has been specified. If no name has been given, action moves to the ERROR routine and the user is given the proper syntax.

Once a filename has been established, a FIND /C is performed on the file. This action counts the number of lines that match a pattern. The pattern given is /V (not) two tildes. In other words, every line that doesn't contain two tildes (~~) in a row is counted and all lines that *do* contain the two tildes are not counted. The FIND /C command, supplied by DOS, will prove useful for many counting operations.

I used the two-tilde sequence because very few lines, if any, are ever going to contain this arrangement within the file. It could easily be replaced by "*@*$&%&" or any other string not likely to appear in the file. By *not* finding the specification, the end result is that every line gets counted and the answer is the total number of lines in the file.

A good idea before using the FIND command is to verify that the file exists and is not a typographical error. The line

```
IF NOT EXIST %1 GOTO ERROR
```

placed after the check for %1's existence, and before the FIND command, will prevent errors from being generated from nonexistent filenames.

### Counting files in a directory or drive

Listing 3-6 shows a batch file that counts the number of files within a directory.

**Listing 3.6. The FILES.BAT utility counts a directory's files.**

```
:FILES.BAT
@ECHO OFF
ATTRIB *.* | FIND /C "\"
:END
```

You can use the ATTRIB (file attribute) command to list every file in a directory. It displays its findings like this:

```
A   C:\COLO.COM
A   C:\FORM.TXT
A   C:\FORM.COM
A   C:\CHECKI
A   C:\HAMMER.BAT
```

Notice that the full path is specified for each file. This means that the "\" character is present at least once in each listing. Using the slash as the item to count and once again using FIND /C, you can determine how many files are in a directory.

What about changing the batch file to count the number of files in any directory, and not just the one the user is presently residing in? Look at Listing 3-7.

**Listing 3-7. The FILES.BAT utility can count files in any directory.**

```
:FILES.BAT
@ECHO OFF
ATTRIB %1\*.* | FIND /C "\"
:END
```

If you give the command "FILES C:\PCPLUS," a count is generated of the files in that directory (ATTRIB C:\PCPLUS*.*). If you now specify only "FILES," a count is given of the files in the root directory (ATTRIB*.*).

What about a count of all files on the drive?

**Listing 3-8. The FILES.BAT utility can count all the files on the drive.**

```
:FILES.BAT
@ECHO OFF
IF "%1"=="ALL" GOTO ALL
ATTRIB %1\*.* | FIND /C "\"
GOTO END
```

```
:ALL
ATTRIB \*.* /S | FIND /C "\"
:END
```

If the user specifies anything other than "FILES ALL," a count is given of the root directory, or the specified directory. If the user requests "FILES ALL," the ATTRIB command begins in the root directory and now runs through all subdirectories (/S). The phrase "GOTO ALL" could be replaced with "GOTO %1" since the parameters are the same.

Finally, to count the number of files on the drive that have been created or modified since you last performed a backup, change the FIND so it no longer looks for "\" and now looks for " A ". Be sure to place one space on each side to prevent finding filenames that begin with the same letter and find only those files which have the Archive bit set.

### Counting characters, lines, and files with one routine

Now that separate batch files have counted the number of characters in a parameter, the number of lines in a file, and the number of files in a directory, it's time to put them all together into one tidy package, as shown in Listing 3-9.

**Listing 3-9. The COUNT.BAT utility handles several counting functions.**

```
:COUNT.BAT
@ECHO OFF
IF "%1"=="LINES" GOTO %1
IF "%1"=="lines" GOTO %1
IF "%1"=="FILES" GOTO %1
IF "%1"=="files" GOTO %1
IF "%1"=="" GOTO ERROR
SET A=%1END
:COUNTING
SET COUNTER=%COUNTER%$
FOR %%E IN (/%A%) DO SET A=%%E
```

```
IF "%A%"=="END" GOTO FINAL
GOTO COUNTING
:FINAL
IF %COUNTER%==$ SET ANSWER=1
IF %COUNTER%==$$ SET ANSWER=2
IF %COUNTER%==$$$ SET ANSWER=3
IF %COUNTER%==$$$$ SET ANSWER=4
IF %COUNTER%==$$$$$ SET ANSWER=5
IF %COUNTER%==$$$$$$ SET ANSWER=6
IF %COUNTER%==$$$$$$$ SET ANSWER=7
IF %COUNTER%==$$$$$$$$ SET ANSWER=8
IF %COUNTER%==$$$$$$$$$ SET ANSWER=9
IF %COUNTER%==$$$$$$$$$$ SET ANSWER=10
IF %COUNTER%==$$$$$$$$$$$ SET ANSWER=11
IF %COUNTER%==$$$$$$$$$$$$ SET ANSWER=12
IF "%ANSWER%"=="" SET ANSWER=MORE THAN TWELVE
ECHO %1 HAS %ANSWER% CHARACTERS
FOR %%D IN (A ANSWER COUNTER) DO SET %%D=
GOTO END
:LINES
@ECHO OFF
IF "%2"=="" GOTO ERROR
FIND /C/V "~~" %2
GOTO END
:ERROR
ECHO Specify a valid filename. Example: COUNT LINES
FILEONE
GOTO END
:FILES
@ECHO OFF
IF "%2"=="ALL" GOTO ALL
ATTRIB %2\*.* | FIND /C "\"
GOTO END
```

```
:ALL
ATTRIB \*.* /S | FIND /C "\"
:END
```

COUNT BILL returns the answer of four characters. COUNT LINES BILL.TXT counts the number of lines in BILL.TXT. COUNT FILES ALL counts the total number of files on the drive, and COUNT FILES C:\LOTUS counts the number of files in that drive. Three functions are served with one batch file that takes up only 1130 bytes of space.

In reality, as previously discussed, if this batch file resides on the C: drive, 2048 bytes, one sector, becomes occupied by the file. If you used three batch files (COUNT.BAT, LINES.BAT, and FILES.BAT), three sectors would be occupied and 6,144 bytes would be required. Designing batch files to serve more than one purpose conserves space and refines efficiency.

### Run a program every fifth boot

Listing 3-10 performs an interesting function, running a specified program at a specified time.

**Listing 3-10. A utility that runs a program every fifth boot.**

```
@ECHO OFF
IF EXIST !BOOT.1 GOTO 1
IF EXIST !BOOT.2 GOTO 2
IF EXIST !BOOT.3 GOTO 3
IF EXIST !BOOT.4 GOTO 4
IF EXIST !BOOT.5 GOTO 5
ECHO BOOT TRACKING > !BOOT.1
GOTO END
:1
REN !BOOT.1 !BOOT.2
GOTO END
:2
REN !BOOT.2 !BOOT.3
```

```
GOTO END
:3
REN !BOOT.3 !BOOT.4
GOTO END
:4
REN !BOOT.4 !BOOT.5
GOTO END
:5
REN !BOOT.5 !BOOT.1
CHKDSK /F
:END
```

The utility shown in Listing 3-10 will run CHKDSK /F every fifth boot of the computer. You can create a separate batch file to perform this operation; BOOT.BAT, for example, is what I've called it on the disk included with this book. But I think it's better for you to add the lines directly to the AUTOEXEC.BAT.

Let me explain what happens here. The user boots the computer on Monday and a small (16-byte) file named !BOOT.5 exists. The file is renamed !BOOT.1 and CHKDSK is run. On the next boot, !BOOT.5 doesn't exist, but !BOOT.1 does, so it's renamed !BOOT.2. On it goes until the fifth boot triggers the action once again. If the computer is booted twice in the same day, there's no danger in the CHKDSK running twice; it will just increment one closer to the time when it will run.

This listing provides an appropriate means of performing an action based upon the boot number. More often than not, however, it's preferable to perform actions based not on the number of boots, but on the day of the week.

### Run a program every Thursday

You might want to run a program automatically on a specific day of the week. Listing 3-11 shows you how.

**Listing 3-11. The CURRENT.BAT utility shows you how to have your computer run a program on a certain day of the week.**

```
:CURRENT.BAT
@ECHO OFF
IF "%1"=="" GOTO GET
DEL $!TEMP.BAT
GOTO %3
:GET
DATE < ENTER.TXT > $!TEMP.BAT
$!TEMP.BAT
:MON
ECHO And how was the weekend?
:TUE
:WED
GOTO END
:THU
CHKDSK /F
GOTO END
:FRI
ECHO Don't forget to initial time cards!!!
GOTO END
:SAT
ECHO !!!!GET OUT OF THIS SYSTEM!!!!
ECHO YOU SHALL BE REPORTED TO THE AUTHORITIES
:SUN
:END
```

Before this routine can run, you need to create another file, called ENTER.TXT. This file contains only one character—a carriage return. Create the file by typing the following commands at a DOS prompt:

```
COPY CON ENTER.TXT <Enter>
<Enter>
<Ctrl>-<Z> <Enter>
```

By having a file that contains *only* a carriage return, you can feed it, via the batch file, into DOS's DATE command, which shows the current date, then prompts the user to enter the new date or press <Enter> to leave it as is.

You can run CURRENT.BAT by merely typing CURRENT. Line 3 checks for parameter %1, which doesn't exist; processing is therefore sent to lines 6 through 8. Line 7 calls DATE and bypasses the prompt by using the carriage return file, ENTER.TXT. The date output is dumped into a file named $!TEMP.BAT in the following format:

```
Current date is Thu  7-23-1993
Enter new date (mm-dd-yy):
```

Line 8 sends processing to the newly created $!TEMP.BAT. Notice that it doesn't *call* the new BAT file; calling would cause it to run $!TEMP, and then return to where it left off in this file. That isn't what you want here; processing completely leaves CURRENT and goes to $!TEMP.BAT.

Since the new file has the .BAT extension, DOS perceives it as an executable file and runs it. $!TEMP runs by sending processing back to CURRENT and feeding in a line of parameters:

```
%0 = Current
%1 = date
%2 = is
%3 = Thu
%4 = 7-23-1992
```

CURRENT.BAT, in operation once more, now has a %1 parameter; thus it slides past the check in line 3. Line 4 deletes $!TEMP.BAT, which is no longer needed, and line 5 sends processing to %3—the day of the week.

On Monday, a message displays on the screen. On Tuesday and Wednesday, no actions take place. On Thursday, CHKDSK runs. Friday and Saturday generate messages that are sent to the screen, while Sunday implements no action.

Now you have a way to execute commands based on the day of the week. What happens if Friday morning an automatic backup occurs on bootup, and Friday afternoon the keyboard slides too close to the CPU and presses the reboot button? When the CPU comes back up, it will still be Friday and another backup will be started. Consequently, it's often necessary to insert a check to verify that the action to take place hasn't already taken place. Between lines 3 and 4 in Listing 3-11, add the following lines:

```
IF EXIST %3 GOTO END
FOR %%E IN (MON TUE WED THU FRI SAT SUN) DO IF EXIST
  %%E DEL %%E
ECHO RAN > %3
```

This insertion will create a file with the name of the day of the week when the process runs the first time, via the new line 6. The next time it attempts to run on the same day, line 4 will see that the file already exists and skip all further processing. When the next day does come, line 5 deletes all old files and line 6 creates a new one.

### Add, subtract, multiply, divide

Look at the lines shown in Listing 3-12.

**Listing 3-12. BASIC lets you do arithmetic in batch language.**

```
:MATH.BAT
ECHO 10 PRINT %1 %2 %3 %4 %5 %6 %7 %8 %9 : SYSTEM >
MATH.BAS
GWBASIC MATH.BAS
:END
```

While no predesignated method exists of doing arithmetic in batch language, one method does exist in the BASIC language, and all versions of DOS come with a BASIC language program. MATH.BAT takes the parameters it has been given and writes them to a .BAS file, adding a line number and command to the beginning and an exit statement to the end. The BASIC language is then brought up (via line 3), running the program, and the answer is generated. For example,

```
MATH 7 * 1.49
```

clears the screen and returns the answer "10.43." This batch file makes it easy to perform immediate calculations from a command prompt, eliminating the need to start an application program such as Lotus or Quattro Pro just to estimate utilization or do a similar calculation promptly.

```
MATH (7^2) - 25
```

raises 7 to the second power and subtracts 25 from the result, giving an answer of "24." Just as in algebra, the brackets require the program to perform the enclosed part of the calculation first.

```
MATH 7*1.49-3
```

gives the answer "7.43." Notice that you don't need to leave spaces between the mathematical elements: "7*1.49" will work as well as "7 * 1.49."

The mathematical symbols that you can use include:

| | |
|---|---|
| + | addition |
| – | subtraction |
| * | multiplication |
| / | division |
| \ | division returning only the whole number—rounding |
| () | perform this operation first |
| ^ | exponential multiplication (^.5 returns the square root) |

MOD uses modulus math and returns the whole number remaining after a division: for example, MATH 22 MOD 7 gives the answer "1"—the whole number left after the division of 22 by 7.

The BASIC program is located in the DOS directory, so if the DOS directory is in your search path everything will work fine. If DOS isn't in your search path, you need to change the line "GWBASIC MATH.BAS" so that it reflects a full path: "C:\DOS\GWBASIC MATH.BAS," for example.

If you're running DOS 5.0, GWBASIC is no longer included; it's been replaced by QBASIC. Change the line to read:

```
QBASIC /RUN MATH.BAS
```

### We're Getting There

The first half of this chapter presented all the commands you can use to create batch files; the second half showed you how to do it. There is but one more chapter of reference before programming begins, and it will discuss creating utilities using BASIC and DEBUG\SID.

4 CHAPTER

# Command Files and Executables

Novell's NetWare offers many commands that perform complex functions. The DOS systems offer a minimum of eight commands that you can use in batch files for enhancing those commands in NetWare. Eight commands however, are not enough.

You need to have many computing functions performed. These functions simply can't be structured merely around CALL, ECHO, and IF statements. For that reason, you must use programming languages to create utilities that fill the void left where the batch language leaves off.

Many languages, such as BASIC, allow you to create programs that work within the confines of their environment. The use of such languages is often sufficient. In order to run the program, however, you must first load the language, and then load the program. Next you run the program, then exit from it, exit the language, and finally return to the prompt where everything began.

It's far better to create stand-alone DOS programs that can run independently of the language used to write them. You can create such stand-alone programs by compiling the program to meet criteria established by the disk operating system.

DOS programs use one of two extensions: .EXE or .COM. Note that .COM programs can't be larger than 64KB, and they exist on the disk in the exact form in which you need to use them. Within these restrictions, .COM files are excellent for very small, compact utilities.

.EXE files, on the other hand, have no such restrictions on their size. They do require DOS to perform processing for them as they run. In brief, .EXE files are always a safe choice since small programs may be .EXE or .COM, but large programs may not be .COM.

## Languages

Any number of programming languages may serve to create utilities, provided you have a method of compiling the finished product into a stand-alone utility. The four most prevalent choices of programming languages today are Assembly, BASIC, C, and Pascal. Each of the four has its own advantages. For your future reference, here is a brief discussion of each of these languages.

### C

C and its offspring C+, C++, and so forth, are the programming languages of choice for the new generation of programmers. More commands are available than most people learn, and the learning curve is minimal compared to that of other languages.

A handful of software companies, particularly Microsoft and Borland, release C software for PCs. The chief disadvantage to users is that it's additional software that doesn't come with any of the operating systems, although it runs equally well with either MS-DOS or DR DOS.

None of the utility programs listed in this book use the C language. However, I strongly suggest that you invest in such if you wish to dabble further. Several language packages are available, ranging in price from $50 to $1,000. Begin small and you can always move up once you have a good understanding of the basics.

### Pascal

Pascal is the programming language of choice for the older generation of programmers. The same software houses offering C also offer Pascal, though C receives more emphasis.

Again, the software is an additional expense since neither operating system includes it; none of the programs listed in this book use Pascal. If you become fascinated by utility programming and you want to involve yourself with it to a greater extent, purchase a Pascal language program if you like a structured environment; otherwise, lean towards C.

### Assembly

The Assembly language is the closest thing to machine language that still exists today. In the Introduction I spoke of the days of mainframe domination. In those days, a lot of programming was done in binary form with a series of switches and values on each of 1 or 0, true or false, in or out—opposing values, no matter what terminology you use. The values generated via those switches formed the instructions on which the computer operated.

Today's Assembly language bears a strong resemblance to the machine language used in those early days, and the only popular software package still on the market aimed at the PC is Microsoft's Macro Assembler, or MASM.

The majority of all Assembly language programming done today is through MS-DOS's DEBUG utility, or its DR DOS counterpart SID (Symbolic Instruction Debugger). Both allow you to alter, display, and execute the contents contained within a file or memory. Due to its cryptic, and sometimes dangerous, nature, however, it's best suited to very small programs, making it ideal for use in creating .COM files.

Because DEBUG or SID is included with the operating system of choice, I'll use it for *all* .COM files in this chapter. I'll give you the program listings in the form of a text file. You may enter the commands one at a time or feed the text file into the debugger of choice. The latter approach allows you to create the entry with a text processor and correct all errors without the risk of being live.

### BASIC

The BASIC programming language has been included with every release of Microsoft DOS since the beginning of computers. GWBASIC was one of the first incarnations, as well as BASICA, BASIC, and a handful of other vendor-specific versions. GWBASIC lasted in latter-day DOS releases until version 5.0, when it was replaced by QBASIC.

QBASIC is simply a stripped-down model of Microsoft's stand-alone program QuickBASIC, which has sold millions of copies. You create and store BASIC programs in QBASIC, using the extension .BAS, not making them immediately executable from the command line.

Leaving the programs in .BAS form, however, makes it possible for you to run them by first calling the BASIC program. With GWBASIC, you perform this function from the command line by typing:

```
GWBASIC TEST.BAS <Enter>
```

With QBASIC, the above command loads the program into memory, thereby making it editable, but it doesn't run it. To run it, you must specify another parameter:

```
QBASIC /RUN TEST.BAS <Enter>
```

One of the advantages of QuickBASIC stripped from QBASIC is the ability to take program listings and turn them into stand-alone .EXE files. In this way, you can turn TEST.BAS into TEST.EXE, and the BASIC language utility need never be loaded into memory to execute the program, which you can now run by simply typing TEST.EXE or TEST at the command-line prompt.

Since some version of the BASIC language is included in MS-DOS with no need to purchase additional software, all of the .EXE files listed in this book will be compiled (stand-alone) versions of MS-DOS QuickBASIC/QBASIC listings.

DR DOS, on the other hand, doesn't include a BASIC language utility. If you're interested in pursuing utility programming and are interested in BASIC, I strongly encourage you to invest in a copy of either QuickBASIC or Visual BASIC. (Visual has an added benefit in that it allows you to generate programs for use with Microsoft Windows.)

**NOTE:** All .COM files will be the result of DEBUG/SID entries. Additionally, all .EXE files will be displayed in BASIC, and all batch files will be given in the format in which they exist: pure ASCII.

## Commands

Space limitations prevent detailed discussion of all DEBUG/SID and BASIC language commands. Many a library shelf has been devoted to books offering those detailed descriptions.

At the same time, it's difficult to view listings and attempt to understand them without some knowledge of the subject matter. For this reason, a *very* brief description of *key* commands follows. I strongly encourage you to research the subject matter further in tomes devoted strictly to the subject.

### DEBUG/SID commands

Table 4-1 shows you the commands you can use with the the MS-DOS DEBUG and the DR DOS SID utilities.

**Table 4-1. DEBUG and SID use the same basic set of commands.**

| COMMAND | RESULT |
|---|---|
| A (Assemble) | Assembles statements into memory. Numeric values must be hexadecimal and entered in segments of four or fewer characters. |
| B (Block compare) | Compares two blocks. (DR DOS only.) |
| C (Compare) | Compares two memory blocks with unequal bytes and their addresses displayed. Thirty-two bytes of memory are examined, unless no ending address is specified. (MS-DOS only.) |
| D (Dump) | Displays the memory contents to the screen. |
| E (Enter) | Allows modification of existing byte values and replaces those values byte by byte. (MS-DOS only.) |
| E (Empty memory) | Used alone, it frees memory. Used with a filename, it loads the file. (DR DOS only.) |

**Table 4-1.** *(Continued)*

| COMMAND | RESULT |
|---|---|
| F (Fill) | Similar to Enter, it changes the byte values, but does so in a broader manner by filling in a specified range with the values provided in a list |
| G (Go) | Runs the program you're editing. |
| H (Hexarithmetic) | Adds and subtracts hexadecimal numbers. |
| I (Input) | Reads values, byte by byte, from a specific port |
| L (Load) | Reads a file into accessible memory. |
| M (Move) | Moves the contents of one range to another location. |
| N (Name) | Allows you to provide a filename to the memory segments you're working on; necessary for saving. (MS-DOS only.) |
| O (Output) | Sends values, byte by byte, to a specified port. (MS-DOS only.) |
| P (Proceed) | Stops the execution of a loop. |
| Q (Quit) | Exits DEBUG and returns you to the system prompt. |
| R (Register) | Displays values of registers and flags. (MS-DOS only.) |
| R (Read file) | Reads a file into memory. (DR DOS only.) |
| S (Search) | Allows a range to be searched for a value. The syntax is S RANGE VALUE. All matches within the range are displayed. (MS-DOS; SR does the same in DR DOS.) |
| S (Store) | Accepts input and stores it, like the MS-DOS E command. (DR DOS only.) |
| T (Trace) | Executes instructions and displays the contents of registers after the execution. |
| U (Unassemble) | The opposite of Assemble, it displays hexadecimal values. |
| V (Values) | Displays the values of the last file read. (DR DOS only.) |
| W (Write) | Saves the named memory to disk. |
| X (eXamine) | Examines CPU states. (DR DOS only.) |
| Z (?) | Displays math coprocessor states. (DR DOS only.) |
| . (period) | Ends data entry and restores a prompt. |

### A limited list of BASIC commands

Table 4-2 shows you a list of the commands you can use in BASIC.

**Table 4-2. BASIC gives its own set of commands to use in creating your own utilities.**

| COMMAND | RESULT |
|---|---|
| ASC (a$) | Returns the ASCII value for the first character of string a$. See Appendix C for a list of ASCII values. |
| BEEP | Cycles the speaker for one-fourth of a second. |
| CALL | As in the batch language, CALL allows you to call another routine. In this instance, however, it must be an Assembly language program. |
| CHR$(a) | The opposite of ASC, CHR$ converts the ASCII number "a" into a character. This command may produce control characters as well as printable characters. For example, LPRINT CHR$(12) forces a carriage return to the printer, and PRINT CHR$(7) sounds a beep. |
| CLOSE | Closes previously opened files. |
| DATA | Provides information to be used by READ statements. The data may be alphabetic, numeric, or any combination thereof. As the entries are read, they are discarded, and the next READ will follow where the last one left off. RESTORE cancels this function and causes READ to jump back to the beginning of the DATA entries once more. |
| DATE$ | A variable you can use to display and set the current date. |
| DIM | Dimension of the maximum sizes a created array can be. |
| END | Quits the execution of the program. |
| ENVIRON | Allows modification of the SET environment inside the confines of BASIC. When the BASIC program is exited, the values which existed before are returned. |
| ENVIRON$ | The counterpart of ENVIRON in that instead of SET variables, it displays the values that presently exist. |
| EOF | Reports whether or not an End Of File condition exists on an opened file. EOF exists when the last segment of information has been read. |

**Table 4-2.** *(Continued)*

| COMMAND | RESULT |
|---|---|
| FOR and NEXT | Cause an execution to continue for a specified number of times, thereby creating a loop. For example, FOR X = 1 TO 25 : CLS : NEXT X will clear the screen 25 times. FOR X = 1 TO 25 : PRINT X : NEXT X will count and print a series of numbers from 1 to 25. The default increment is 1, but you can use a STEP command to change the increment to any desired number. For example, FOR X = 10 TO 250 STEP 10 : PRINT X : NEXT X prints 10, 20, 30, and so on, up to 250. FOR X = 250 TO 10 STEP -10 : PRINT X : NEXT X does the same counting, but in a backward fashion, from highest value to lowest. |
| GOSUB | |
| RETURN | Serve the same function as in DR DOS batch files, branching processing to a subroutine and continuing at the place left off when the subroutine ends. |
| INKEY$ | Returns one key read as input from the keyboard. |
| INPUT | Receives input from the keyboard until the <Enter> key is pressed. INPUT$ reads in string (non-numeric) values. |
| INSTR | Searches one string for an occurrence of another and reports the location of the first such occurrence: INSTR("ONETWOTHREE-TWO","TWO") returns the value 4, the first character location occurrence of the second string within the first. |
| KILL | Deletes files from a disk. |
| LEFT$ | Reads a string from the contents of another string, beginning from the left and going over a specified number of characters. For example, LEFT$("ONETWOTHREETWO",3) returns "1." |
| LEN | Reports the number of characters in a string. For example, LEN("ONETWOTHREETWO") reports "14." |
| LOCK | |
| UNLOCK | Prevent other users from accessing any or all parts of a file, and then restore their ability to do so. It is useful only in a network environment, and true for random-access or sequential-access files. |

**Table 4-2.** *(Continued)*

| COMMAND | RESULT |
|---|---|
| MID$ | Allows one portion of a string to be taken from another by specifying the starting position from the left and the number of characters to take. For example, MID$("ONETWOTHREETWO",4,3) returns the string "TWO" by starting at the fourth character and extracting a total of three characters. |
| NAME | Changes the name of an existing file to a new name. |
| OPEN | Opens a file for reading and/or processing. |
| PRINT | Displays output to the screen or to a file; or the counterpart, LPRINT, sends output to the printer. |
| PRINT USING | Establishes a template in which displayed output is shown. For example, PRINT USING "###.#";.9,.85,7.4 prints the output to fit the template:<br>`0.9`<br>`0.8`<br>`7.4` |
| RIGHT$ | This command is the direct descendant of LEFT$, now returning a specified number of characters, beginning from the right. For example, RIGHT$("ONETWOTHREETWO",11) returns "TWOTHREETWO." |
| SHELL | Allows another executable program or batch file to be run. Upon completion of that program or file, processing continues where it stopped. |
| SYSTEM | Quits BASIC altogether and returns to the operating system prompt. |
| TIME$ | Like its cousin, DATE$, TIME$ allows you to display and change the variable reflecting the current time. |
| WRITE | Identical in operation to PRINT, with one key exception: commas are inserted between values and strings are contained within quotation marks. |
| WRITE# | Writes data to a sequential file, inserting commas and enclosing string values within quotation marks. |

## Programming Samples

To get things started, let's look at two sample programs that serve simple purposes. Notice the syntax of each and compare it with the language descriptions offered previously.

### COM programming

Let's look first at the DR DOS utility in this section. Type:

SID <Enter>

to start the Symbolic Instruction Debugger, and the pound sign becomes your prompt. At the prompt, enter the command S0100.

```
C:\DRDOS>SID
- - - - - - - - - - - - - - - - - - - - - - - - -
*** Symbolic Instruction Debugger *** Release 3.2
    Copyright (c) 1983,1984,1985,1988,1990,1991
    Digital Research, Inc. All Rights Reserved
```

# S0100 <Enter>

Ten digits, separated by a colon and a space, now appear. The first four digits will be different, and they have no significance at this point, but the next four digits will be 0100, as you requested. The last two digits signify the value at this point in time of the byte you're going to change. Type:

B8 <Enter>

Another prompt appears, with the four digits signifying the byte incrementing by one and allowing you to enter another value. Enter the following values and note that in hexadecimal numbers, there are no O's, but zeroes. If the numbers presently in the bytes to be changed are different from those shown here, don't be concerned. You're changing them, and they're likely to presently be set to anything:

```
4655:0101 00 40
4655:0102 00 00
4655:0103 00 8E
4655:0104 00 C0
4655:0105 00 26
4655:0106 00 C7
4655:0107 00 06
4655:0108 00 72
4655:0109 00 00
4655:010A 00 00
4655:010B 00 00
4655:010C 00 EA
4655:010D 00 00
4655:010E 00 00
4655:010F 00 FF
4655:0110 00 FF
4655:0111 87 .
#
```

Notice that the period ended the byte entry and returned you to the pound sign prompt.

Now, you must name and save the entry by entering the filename and the beginning and ending byte addresses. Type:

WCAD.COM,0100,0110 <Enter>

Everything between the specified addresses was written to a file named CAD.COM. Notice that the ending address is 10 when 16 bytes were changed. Notice also how the hexadecimal counting convention works by looking at the four numbers on the right of the colon. Adding 1 to 09 makes it 0A. Adding 1 to 0F becomes 10.

To quit SID, type:

Q <Enter>

and you're back at the system prompt.

Now let's look at the MS-DOS utility DEBUG.

You can do the same thing here that you just saw with DR DOS's SID utility, substituting E for S and N, and W for just plain W, and making a few other changes. Instead of doing that, however, DEBUG will accept a text file as input, allowing you to edit the file and look for errors before creating the COM file.

Using an ASCII editor, create the following file and call it TEST.TXT. Be careful to enter the hexadecimal digits as they appear, and with a space between each set:

```
E 0100 B8 40 00 8E C0 26 C7 06 72 00 00 00 EA 00 00 FF
  FF
N CAD.COM
RCX
0011
W
Q
```

Compile the program by going to the system prompt and typing:

```
DEBUG < TEST.TXT <Enter>
```

Each line of the text file will be read by the compiling utility and the screen will reflect the following:

```
C:\>DEBUG < TEST.TXT
-E 0100 B8 40 00 8E C0 26 C7 06 72 00 00 00 EA 00 00 FF
  FF
-N CAD.COM
-RCX
CX 0000
:0011
-W
```

```
Writing 00011 bytes
-Q

C:\>
```

Do a directory listing and you should see that CAD.COM has been created in your directory. CAD stands for <Control>-<Alt>-<Del>. Calling this utility will reboot your computer.

The program begins entering (E) into memory at byte 0100. All bytes are given values, then the name of the file is specified (N). Next, the registers are called (R and C), the file is written to disk (W), and DEBUG is exited (Q).

Now type CAD and reboot the computer.

### BASIC programming

When discussing batch file commands and the differences between DOS from Microsoft and DOS from Novell, I mentioned that the most striking difference between the two is the SWITCH command that DR DOS has and MS-DOS just recently added by including CHOICE with version 6.0. No other version of MS-DOS includes any capacity for making a selection from a given list of options.

In order to compensate for that lack, Listing 4-1 creates a utility called SWITCH.EXE for earlier MS-DOS versions. This utility performs a similar function to its DR DOS counterpart. (Line numbering, while not necessary in QBASIC and QuickBASIC, is retained in this example to help explain the actions taking place.)

**Listing 4-1. The SWITCH.EXE utility**

```
5  REM SWITCH.EXE / 10/31/92 / EMMETT DULANEY
10 X = 0: ZA = 1
20 BA = INSTR(ZA, COMMAND$, ",")
30 IF BA > 0 THEN X = X + 1: ZA = BA + 1: GOTO 20
40 BC = VAL(INKEY$)
50 IF BC < 1 OR BC > X + 1 THEN GOTO 40
60 MAX = X + 1: X = 0: ZA = 1
```

```
70 BA = INSTR(ZA, COMMAND$, ",")
80 IF BC = 1 THEN CHOIC$ = LEFT$(COMMAND$, BA - 1):
  GOTO 130
90 IF BA > 0 THEN X = X + 1: ZA = BA + 1: IF X < BC - 1
   THEN GOTO 70
100 IF BC=MAX THEN CHOIC$ = RIGHT$(COMMAND$, LEN(COM-
  MAND$) - BA): GOTO 130
110 BA = INSTR(ZA, COMMAND$, ",")
120 CHOIC$ = MID$(COMMAND$, ZA, BA - ZA)
130 OPEN "$TEMP.BAT" FOR OUTPUT AS #1
140 PRINT #1, CHOIC$
150 CLOSE : SYSTEM
```

Lines 5 and 10 perform housekeeping and begin the routine. Lines 20 and 30 count the number of commas contained in COMMAND$, which contains all of the menu choices.

Line 40 accepts keyboard input and line 50 checks to see if the number entered is a valid number or if it's above the number of choices that are available.

Lines 60 and 70 repeat the count, now looking for the entry corresponding to the number entered. Lines 80 through 120 continue the procedure, assigning the choice to CHOIC$.

Line 130 opens a file called $TEMP.BAT, and line 140 writes CHOIC$ into that temporary file. Line 150 performs housekeeping by closing the file and ending.

Now that the given selection has been ascertained and saved into another temporary file, $TEMP.BAT may be called from the first batch file. With the exception of the RETURN command, MS-DOS is now essentially mimicking the SWITCH command in DR DOS.

The MS-DOS batch file in Listing 4-2 uses this new SWITCH command to offer a menu of choices and await an entry.

**Listing 4-2. Using the SWITCH command, you can create the MENU.BAT basic menu utility.**

```
:MENU.BAT
@ECHO OFF
CLS
ECHO.
ECHO DO YOU WISH TO:
ECHO     1. PLAY YAHTZEE
ECHO     2. RUN Q&A
ECHO     3. OPEN PHONE LOG ENTRIES
ECHO     4. START LOTUS
ECHO.
SWITCH YAT,QA,PHONE,123
CALL $TEMP.BAT
MENU.BAT
```

Congratulations! You're now on the fast track to creating utility programs.

5 CHAPTER

# Creating an Electronic Mail Program

Electronic mail has become an important means of communication within the modern office. It enables computer users to leave messages for other users, whether those messages are brief memos or complete documents. It's hard to imagine anyone investing heavily in productivity and not investing in such a time- and paper-saving device.

Numerous vendors package and market electronic mail programs, complete with a variety of related features. An unfortunate drawback is that many of these programs take more time to learn than to operate. In addition, the cost of the package seems directly proportional to the urgency of your need.

After investing in a beginning NetWare LAN system, however, a small- to medium-sized organization may not have the funds to purchase an electronic network mail package (although the cost of such applications is reasonable compared to the price of most networks). Or you may be a network administrator who prefers creating your own programs for your workplace.

You can create your own electronic mail program, using a few inexpensive, readily accessible software components: some DOS code, the AUTOEXEC.BAT file, and some leftover hooks in NetWare.

At the very least, this project can give you a good example of what you can do with batch files. Consequently, this chapter serves as a teaching tool, helping you to understand how you can combine these available commands to create programs to meet the needs of your own work environment.

The following low-frills mail system may lack elegance, but it does provide an inexpensive way to effectively relay messages between users. Best of all, it uses the existing NetWare structure and illustrates an affinity between DOS and NetWare. This cohesiveness manifests the principles I covered in the preceding four chapters.

Although this electronic mail program is fully functional, I present it as a learning aid. It illustrates the manner in which batch files work with NetWare and with NetWare's underlying structure. Step by step, I've presented and discussed each portion of the utility in order to examine the intermingling of the two environments. Subsequent chapters will bring executable files into the equation, but for now we'll start with a simple example.

## Background Information

Earlier versions of NetWare included a crude mail program to free smaller offices from the need to invest in yet another program after their recent considerable outlay of cash. In the interest of developing a third-party aftermarket, however, Novell removed the program in later versions of the software. While this crude e-mail program is now missing, the very structure upon which it was built still exists. Programmers who know what they're looking for can still use this structure.

For example, each time you add another user to your user list, NetWare creates another MAIL directory for that user and assigns a unique subdirectory. That user, once logged in, can examine the files in his or her directory. All other users, however, except for those with supervisory rights, will get the message "file not found" if they attempt to look at the contents of the same subdirectory.

For small networks, with one server and a limited number of employees, an off-the-shelf e-mail program can seem a luxury. Given Novell's introduction of a 10-user version of NetWare a couple of years ago, the number of smaller LANs will continue to increase significantly. Also, this user-created program lets you send whole files across the LAN, serving not only for delivery of mail but also for file copying.

Of course, the e-mail approach I offer you has its limitations. For one thing, today's e-mail packages are often loaded with software extras, not the least of which is a refined word-processing package dedicated to e-mail activity. With the batch program I'm giving you here, you're largely restricted to using your own word processor and the DOS COPY CON command. In addition, I don't recommend this approach for large networks with multiple servers, where cost would be of less concern.

In short, what I'll give you in this chapter is a series of batch files that show you how to create your own e-mail program in NetWare. There are some compelling reasons to consider doing this. Saving money on a third-party e-mail package ranks as the most obvious reason, while learning the workings of such a system serves as another.

**Step 1**

To keep the process as simple as possible, we'll use as an example a small LAN with a C: drive available to every user. (Users without C: drives—in other words, users who are running diskless workstations—may use the F: drive for the same effect.)

First, you need a list of all users on the system. Next, log in as Supervisor or as a user with supervisor equivalence and access SYSCON. From the main menu, select "User Information," and then "Other Information." This process will give you a User ID of eight characters for each user.

Now, if F: is your server drive, look at F:\MAIL. You'll see subdirectory names of five to six characters in length generated from the User ID. The list you come up with will be similar to the following:

| | |
|---|---|
| ALLAN | B0025 |
| DONNA | 11004D |
| ERNESTINE | E003B |
| JENNIFER | A001D |

| | |
|---|---|
| JERRY | D0033 |
| KAREN | 290067 |
| LORRAINE | 20007 |

The DOS SET command lets you make each user's name equal to the path where his or her electronic mail will reside. One potential problem with SET, however, is that the environment size is determined on startup by COMMAND.COM. The default assignment is 160 bytes, a space that must also include your PROMPT, PATH, and COMSPEC. If you don't change the environment allotment, you'll encounter the dreaded "Out of environment space" error message.

### Step 2

Listing 5-1 shows you MOREENV.BAT, the first batch file we're going to create. It will be summoned by the AUTOEXEC.BAT file on startup and establish more system environment room by running COMMAND.COM again with more space allotted.

**Listing 5-1. The MOREENV.BAT batch file begins your e-mail program.**

```
:MOREENV.BAT
IF NOT EXIST ALREADY.RUN GOTO MOREROOM
GOTO END
:MOREROOM
ECHO ONETWOTHREE > ALREADY.RUN
COMMAND /E:480 /P
:END
```

This batch file sets the environment space to 480 bytes—sufficient for the seven-person operation in our example—but the number can be anything from 160 to 32,768.

MOREENV creates the file ALREADY.RUN during its operation to prevent a loop from occurring wherein the new COMMAND.COM accesses the same batch file the old one did and starts yet another COMMAND.COM, ad infinitum.

AUTOEXEC.BAT summons this batch file upon startup in the following manner:

```
:AUTOEXEC.BAT
CALL MOREENV.BAT
DEL ALREADY.RUN
prompt $p$g
F:LOGIN
```

**Step 3**

You've now created more local system environment space and you've logged in to the server. Now you can find out who you are with the NetWare command WHOAMI. (The batch file I'm going to show you will use WHOAMI to determine who is sending mail.) The next step is to create a batch file named YOU.BAT that you can use in a variety of ways. This file is shown in Listing 5-2.

**Listing 5-2. YOU.BAT is the second batch file you need for your e-mail program.**

```
:YOU.BAT
@ECHO OFF
CLS
IF NOT "%1"=="" GOTO ASCERTAIN
C:
WHOAMI | FIND "You are" > TEMP.BAT
TEMP.BAT
:ASCERTAIN
IF NOT "%1"=="are" GOTO NEXT
SET ME=%3
DEL TEMP.BAT
SET ABC=%ME%
:NEXT
IF %ABC%==ALLAN SET ME2=\MAIL\B0025
IF %ABC%==DONNA SET ME2=\MAIL\11004D
IF %ABC%==ERNESTINE SET ME2=\MAIL\E003B
IF %ABC%==JENNIFER SET ME2=\MAIL\A001D
```

```
IF %ABC%==JERRY SET ME2=\MAIL\D0033
IF %ABC%==KAREN SET ME2=\MAIL\290067
IF %ABC%==LORRAINE SET ME2=\MAIL\20007
```

The same batch file is called twice. The first time this program is called, there is no additional parameter, %1, so WHOAMI is run and the line containing that information is parsed out into a file named TEMP.BAT, which will look something like this:

```
You are user KAREN attached to server SERVER_ONE con-
  nection 2.
```

Next, TEMP.BAT is run.

Notice that this file is summoned from the middle of YOU.BAT. You never use a CALL command; therefore, YOU.BAT is completely closed and exited, and TEMP.BAT is run.

TEMP.BAT in turn accesses YOU.BAT once again, by virtue of the first word of the sentence. Once again, there is no CALL command contained in TEMP.BAT, so all processing reverts to YOU.BAT with a given set of parameters:

%0 = You
%1 = are
%2 = user
%3 = KAREN
%4 = attached

Since parameters exist on the command line this second time YOU.BAT is executed, processing jumps over lines 5 through 7.

The third parameter tells who the user is and sets the variable ME equal to that value (KAREN). The NEXT subroutine in YOU.BAT sets the user's mail directory equal to the variable ME2 by looking at the first variable. In other words, once the batch file knows who the user is, the batch file also knows what that user's mail directory is.

**Step 4**

Knowing who the user is and what that user's MAIL subdirectory is, you'll be able to look in that directory and determine if the user has mail waiting. All new mail will have the extension .DAT to differentiate it from previously read messages. The following text shows how the program indicates that mail is waiting.

```
F:
CD %ME2%
IF EXIST *.DAT ECHO You have new mail.
PAUSE
```

**Step 5**

The users must be able to know that they have mail, and should also be able to read it, remove it, or save it and send mail to other users. Before the discussion continues, let's look at all four batch files that we've discussed so far.

I've already given you YOU.BAT and MOREENV.BAT in their entirety. At this point, you need to add the line CALL MAIL.BAT to follow login processing in the AUTOEXEC.BAT file, as illustrated in the following code:

```
:AUTOEXEC.BAT
CALL MOREENV.BAT
DEL ALREADY.RUN
prompt=$p$g
cd c:\net
c:\qemm\loadhi /r:1 ipx
c:\net\net3
f:login
c:
CALL MAIL.BAT
```

With this addition, the AUTOEXEC.BAT file can now call the principal portion of the program, MAIL.BAT. Had you entered the

CALL command earlier, it would have caused the AUTOEXEC to hang, since MAIL.BAT did not exist.

Next, add the meat of the electronic mail program, as shown in Listing 5-4:

**Listing 5-4. The MAIL.BAT electronic mail utility**

```
:MAIL.BAT
@ECHO OFF
IF NOT "%1"=="" GOTO %1
SET ALLAN=\MAIL\B0025
SET DONNA=\MAIL\11004D
SET ERNESTINE=\MAIL\E003B
SET JENNIFER=\MAIL\A001D
SET JERRY=\MAIL\D0033
SET KAREN=\MAIL\290067
SET LORRAINE=\MAIL\20007
CALL YOU.BAT
F:
CD %ME2%
IF EXIST *.DAT ECHO You have new mail - use %0 READ to
  view
PAUSE
GOTO END
:READ
IF NOT "%2"=="" GOTO VIEW
CLS
ECHO New messages are:
C:
DIR F:%ME2%\*.DAT | FIND /V "Volume" | FIND /V
  "Directory" | FIND /V "(s"
ECHO Saved messages are:
DIR F:%ME2%\*.-AT | FIND /V "Volume" | FIND /V
  "Directory" | FIND /V "File not" | FIND /V "(s"
ECHO Use %0 %1 FILENAME.EXT TO VIEW
GOTO END
```

```
:VIEW
F:
CD %ME2%
IF NOT EXIST %2 ECHO Invalid File Name and/or Extension
IF NOT EXIST %2 GOTO END
MORE < %2
REN %2 *.-AT
ECHO Message has been saved. Use MAIL PURGE FILENAME to
  permanently remove.
:PURGE
IF "%2"=="" ECHO You must specify a File Name
IF "%2"=="" GOTO END
IF NOT EXIST %2.-AT ECHO Invalid File Name. Leave off
  the Extension.
IF NOT EXIST %2.-AT GOTO END
F:
CD %ME2%
DEL %2.-AT
GOTO END
:SEND
IF "%3"=="" ECHO Correct syntax is MAIL SEND Path Per-
  son
IF "%3"=="" ECHO Such as MAIL SEND C:\WP\LETTER %ME%
IF "%3"=="" GOTO END
SET ABC=%3
CALL YOU B40
F:
CD %ME2%
COPY %2
SEND "You have received mail" %3
ECHO MAIL HAS BEEN SENT
SET ABC=%ME%
CALL YOU TOO
GOTO END
:COMPOSE
```

```
IF "%2"=="" ECHO Correct syntax is MAIL COMPOSE Person
  Document.DAT
IF "%2"=="" ECHO Such as MAIL COMPOSE %ME% LETTER.DAT
IF "%2"=="" GOTO END
SET ABC=%2
CALL YOU B40
F:
CD %ME2%
CLS
ECHO Begin writing. . . use {CTRL-Z} on a blank line
  when finished
COPY CON %3
SEND "You have received mail" %2
ECHO MAIL HAS BEEN SENT
SET ABC=%ME%
CALL YOU TOO
:END
C:
CD\
```

## How The Electronic Mail Utility Works

1. The following steps are executed when the MAIL program is called. If you specify MAIL with no parameters, the batch file assumes that this is the first time it has been summoned, and assumes it was summoned by the AUTOEXEC.BAT (the CALL command that was added). Therefore, it sets the workstation's initial parameters equal to every user's mail subdirectory, and then calls YOU.BAT to determine which user is using it at the workstation. Now, having the USER and USER's Subdirectory, it checks for files with the extension .DAT and echoes that there is new mail waiting (if indeed there is) before going to the END of processing and returning control to any lines that follow in the remainder of the AUTOEXEC.BAT.

2. If you specify MAIL READ from the command line, the batch file will look in your subdirectory and list all files with the extension .DAT as new messages and all files with the extension .-AT as saved messages. This method of differentiating new files as .DAT and old files as .-AT lets you know in the middle of the day that new mail messages exist without having to reboot and run AUTOEXEC.BAT again.

   Note that the operations performed, while accessing the F: drive, actually take place on the C: drive. The reason for using the C: drive involves non-supervisory users who don't have the necessary permissions to establish temporary files on the F: drive. If they try to perform the e-mail operation on F:, they'll get the error message "Intermediate file error during pipe." This error message means, in plain English, that the user can't create the temporary files necessary for the piping operation on the F: drive. Since there are no permissions, trustee rights, or other such restrictions on the C: drive, you can do error-free piping.

3. If you use the command MAIL READ {FILE-NAME-.EXT}, it will display the specified letter, one screen at a time, through the batch file's use of the MORE command. Note that the batch file uses MORE to read the input, rather than reading the input and then piping to MORE. In this manner, the batch file can use the command on the F: drive. If this explanation seems confusing, bear with me for a moment, and read the next paragraph.

   The command DIR | MORE creates a temporary file that contains the output of the DIR command. The pipe symbol (|) causes this temporary file to be created. That temporary file is then opened and read into the MORE command, which displays its contents one screen at a time.

   Because a temporary file is created and then removed, you must have the necessary permissions within a directory to create and remove files if you use this command. On the other hand, the command MORE < JERRY.DAT does *not* create or remove files. The MORE command is called and it is fed the file JERRY.DAT, which it displays one screen at a time. In short, the pipe (|) creates temporary files, and the redirection symbols (< and >) do not. MORE has nothing to do with it. The same is true with DIR | SORT or any other command using a pipe.

Back to business. No matter what filename you specified, the file, after you've looked at it, is renamed with the extension .-AT, thereby saving messages and differentiating them from new messages. If you wish to view the message again, enter the same command as mentioned previously, using the new extension. If, on the other hand, you no longer desire to save this message, you can also purge mail files (discussed next).

4. MAIL PURGE FILENAME will remove mail files permanently. Note that you don't specify an extension here. This operation deletes only files with the extension .-AT. Those files still unread and still using the .DAT extension can't be removed until someone has opened and viewed them. Any other files stored within this mail subdirectory are also left alone, as long as they don't have the .-AT extension.

5. If you've created a document that you want to send to another user, you may do so with the command MAIL SEND {PATHNAME} {PERSON} wherein PATHNAME is the full path of the file, and PERSON is the USER's name on the network. For example,

```
MAIL SEND C:\QA\QADOC\LETTER.DAT KAREN
```
<Enter>

sends a copy of LETTER.DAT to Karen. Bear in mind that the extension must always be .DAT in order to appear as a new file when someone checks to see if he or she has mail. Bear in mind as well, if you explain the functions of this program to the users on your network, that most users hate typing in full directory paths.

The e-mail utility ascertains Karen's subdirectory by accessing YOU.BAT once more. This time another parameter is given by the statement that calls it B40. (This is, in fact, a throwaway parameter that merely causes the action to jump to ASCERTAIN, and then to NEXT without resetting the ME parameter and slowing down processing.) The file goes to the other user's subdirectory; then a message is sent to that user (providing he or she isn't using the CASTOFF feature) informing the user that he or she has mail. If the user isn't logged in, no such message is sent.

Finally, YOU.BAT is summoned again with another dummy parameter to set ME2 back to the original user's subdirectory.

Operating the MAIL command in this manner allows you to create documents with your favorite word processor and use its features to create spell-checked, word-wrapped documents before mailing.

6. If you want to send a quickie memo, instead of going to the trouble of accessing a word processor, writing, and exiting to the command line, you can use a shortcut. MAIL COMPOSE {PERSON} {FILENAME} uses the DOS COPY CON command and accepts input directly from the CONsole (keyboard). A blank line will appear and you can type whatever message you wish, pressing <Enter> for each new line. You can correct mistakes on the line you're currently working on by using the <Backspace> key and typing over the error, but you can't change a line once you've entered a carriage return at the end of it.

After you've written your memo, press <CTRL>-<Z> at a blank line, and then <Enter>. Like SEND, COMPOSE places the document in the other user's subdirectory, sends that user a message if he or she is logged in and not using CASTOFF, and returns variable ME2 to your subdirectory.

Unlike SEND, COMPOSE doesn't leave a copy of the memo in any other directory for you to refer to later on. This quick messaging method is intended for one-time memos, not for keeper messages. Think of it this way: COMPOSE moves the file and SEND copies the file.

7. When you read the previous sentence, a little light bulb should have turned on over your head. You can use MAIL SEND to copy a file from anywhere and place it inside a user's mail subdirectory. If the file doesn't have the .DAT extension, then it won't show up as being mail, but it will be there for the user to access as needed. Consider the following chain of events:

```
MAIL SEND C:\F15\F15.ZIP ALLAN <Enter>
```

copies the archived file F15.ZIP into Allan's mail subdirectory. Now, suppose you want to send a new message. You can type:

```
MAIL COMPOSE ALLAN F15.DAT
Hey, I just dropped you a copy of F15.
Unpack it and hide it in with your
  spreadsheet program like the Boulder office
  does.

At lunch, I'll copy the instruction manual
and leave it in your box.
Jerry.
^Z
```

to send him a memo telling him that the file has been left for him.

Note that the file to be copied is referred to in the batch file as %2. Nowhere is a restriction or extension given. Therefore, not only may you copy a single file, but you can use wildcards as acceptable entries as well. For example, if you type:

```
MAIL SEND C:\F15\F15.* ALLAN <Enter>
```

you copy all F15 files over to the mail subdirectory.

### Enhancements

There's one key difference between generating utility files to speed up an application on your part and designing utilities that will be used by seven people to send mail back and forth. When you create a utility for your own use, you needn't be as concerned with documentation as you must when other people use your utility. When you write it, you know how it works. When you use a utility someone else wrote, it's harder to ascertain how processing takes place.

To make the MAIL program easier for users to understand, you can add a help function to it. Starting with the fourth line from the end, change MAIL.BAT to look like this:

```
CALL YOU TOO
GOTO END
:HELP
:INFO
:INFORMATION
:?
CLS
TYPE MAIL.HP
ECHO.
PAUSE
```

```
CLS
:END
C:
CD\
```

Next, create a file in the same directory as MAIL.BAT, name it MAIL.HP, and type the following:

```
ACCEPTABLE MAIL COMMANDS ARE:
  MAIL READ - to check for new messages
  MAIL READ {FILENAME.EXT} - to read a message file
  MAIL PURGE FILENAME - to delete messages
  MAIL SEND {PATHNAME} {PERSON} - to send a mail file
  MAIL COMPOSE {PERSON} {FILENAME} - to write a file
```

If a user types MAIL, followed by any of the four required variables (MAIL HELP, MAIL ?, and so forth), the user will see this help file displayed until he or she presses a key.

Here's a question for you to think about. Why is MAIL.HP a text file, and why do you type it to the screen when you could display the same information by using ECHO statements?

The answer is implied in our early discussion of batch files. Batch file lines are read one line at a time, the batch file closed, the command carried out, the batch file opened, and the next line read, and on and on and on. Processing six ECHO statements as opposed to one TYPE command would significantly increase the amount of time required to carry out the action.

Always look for ways to perform the action quickly and allow the computer to start processing something else.

## Wrap-Up

MAIL.BAT is a multipurpose batch file program that creates an electronic mail program for NetWare. Lacking the complex features of a more expensive program (such as a full-fledged text editor), it allows you to enable electronic mail on a NetWare LAN without investing additional money. The process also teaches you quite a bit about creating your own programs by using DOS and NetWare commands and a little simple programming.

For this electronic mail system to function properly, MOREENV.BAT and AUTOEXEC.BAT *must* reside on the hard drive of each networked workstation. YOU.BAT and MAIL.BAT can reside in the network's PUBLIC directory, where all logged-in network users can access it.

For practice, consider other enhancements you could make to the program to amplify its effectiveness. For example, if a user types

```
mail send c:\qa\qadoc\letter.dat karen <Enter>
```

instead of

```
MAIL SEND C:\QA\QADOC\LETTER.DAT KAREN <Enter>
```

the program won't work. Why not? And what can you do to rectify the situation?

What happens if the user issues this command but specifies a file, or a user, that doesn't exist? What if the user mistypes the receiver's name?

What if the user gives the command MAIL LOOK?

Think; try to answer these questions to the best of your ability. Think of ways to circumvent the problems they pose. If you want to compare thoughts, Appendix A at the end of this book contains some solutions to these problems. But many, many ways of foiling such problems are possible; there isn't only one right answer.

# 6 CHAPTER

# Optimal Server Maintenance

Local area networks, since their inception, have evolved from conveniences that allowed peripheral sharing to necessities important for aggregate operations. In this evolutionary process, increasing demands have been placed on the server to be consistently dependable. Workstations must also be in a state of constant readiness; the moment they are powered up, they are expected to establish unfailing connection with the server.

If an ounce of prevention is worth a pound of cure, then an hour of file system maintenance is worth a month of server reconstruction and restoration. Running a LAN without a minimum level of upkeep is like flying a private plane without performing mandatory system checks. The plane may fly flawlessly for several months—until one day the fuel line breaks just as you're cresting the Appalachians.

"Optimization" is a relative word, contingent on the type of LAN being operated: the network operating system itself, the number and quantity of workstations, the number of hours LAN users access its services, and so forth. As more and more users and applications come to depend on the server, more possibilities exist for crises to occur. Routine maintenance becomes even more important—and it must be regular.

The next three chapters of this book cover computer optimization. This chapter is aimed at the server—the heart that pumps blood to the appendages. The chapter focuses on the kind of maintenance that *must* be performed by someone possessing supervisory rights.

The second chapter in this section, Chapter 7, involves basic knowledge of DOS-based workstations. This kind of maintenance may be performed by a user or a supervisor, depending on the user's level of competence and experience. The chapter is designed to stand alone, and can be shared directly with users. If these users knows what they are doing, there shouldn't be unanswered questions.

The third chapter in this section, or Chapter 8, contains information and utilities relevant to both the server and the workstations. Once again, at this level, either a user or a supervisor can perform the maintenance, but I *highly* recommend that the supervisor perform the operations described in Chapter 8.

## The Server

While "maintenance" is a term that can describe everything from performing backups to reinstalling the operating system, I assume that as a supervisor responsible for the upkeep of a server, you know how to handle these tasks. The next few pages discuss maintenance features that supervisors often overlook; yet these features can accelerate the response time of databases, reclaim disk space, attenuate backup time, and increase server response performance.

## Optimizing Databases

A quick look at the software shelf tells you that there are as many database vendors as there are addresses in Silicon Valley. While each database looks and performs differently, according to its manufacturer's specifications, most share a common set of problems that result in inefficient disk usage. These problems fall into two key categories: the way information is stored in a record, and the way records are stored in a file.

When database file forms are designed, each of the fields in a record is assigned a certain amount of character space. Every new record gets this amount of space. If an entry doesn't use all of this space, blank space is allocated in the index and data files. For example, if your form contains an address field and the length of the field is sixty characters, when you add an address of thirty characters, another thirty characters of blank space is assigned. This padding allows you to make longer entries later if you need to.

The inefficiencies inherent in this methodology are two-fold. First, bytes of disk space that could be used elsewhere are inappropriately assigned to the index *and* data files. Second, when you search the field for information (..Main Street..), the database must search sixty characters of each index rather than thirty; the search takes twice as long as it should.

You can easily correct this problem by finding the record with the longest data length for each field and setting the length of each field on the form to its current maximum value. For example, if the longest address entry consists of forty characters, then change the maximum field length to forty. This change reduces the size of the index and data files, effectively decreasing search time.

The second problem inherent in databases involves the method by which records are stored within the file. Try this test of storage caliber: if you have 1,000 employee records and delete all 1,000, will your file sizes revert to only the size of the form design? With almost every database, the answer is no. Even though most software packages don't allow you to restore a deleted record, they fail to release the space previously occupied by the record.

Q&A, by Symantec, serves as an excellent example of what I'm talking about. Q&A restores *none* of the space previously occupied by deleted records. To recover the data space, you must copy the file design to another file, using the File/Copy/Copy Design process. If you didn't delete all the records—a more plausible scenario—then you must copy into the new database any records that were not deleted via File/Copy/Copy Selected Forms. You must then delete the original database and rename the new one to the original name. The new .DTF and .IDX files now reflect the records remaining and the file sizes are the least possible, allowing for prompt searches.

While all of this may seem like a great deal of work, it's certainly worth the effort, considering that people so seldom get around to this kind of cleanup and the disk space returned is considerable.

Let's look at an example of this operation on a database that, at one time, contained 34 employee records. I deleted 29, leaving only five. I haven't shown all the steps specific to Q&A. The following steps demonstrate the most important aspects, however, including those applicable to other databases as well.

As you follow this discussion, note what commands you type in and what your results are.

### Step 1: Look at the file sizes

```
C:\QA\DATA>DIR ONE.*

Volume in drive C is EXAMPLE
Directory of C:\QA\DATA

ONE DTF     67584 10-05-92   9:57p
ONE IDX     34304 10-05-92   9:57p
2 file(s)   101888 bytes

C:\QA\DATA\QA
```

## Step 2: Copy the files to another

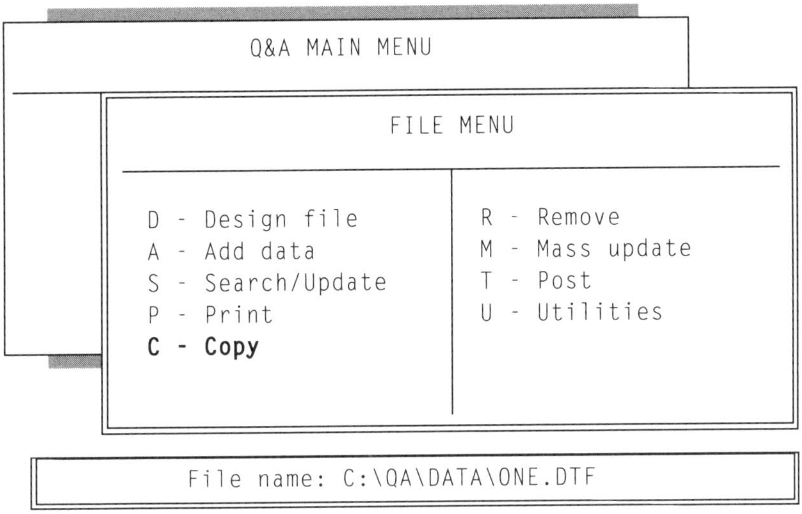


**Figure 6-1. Select copy**

## Step 3: Copy the form design

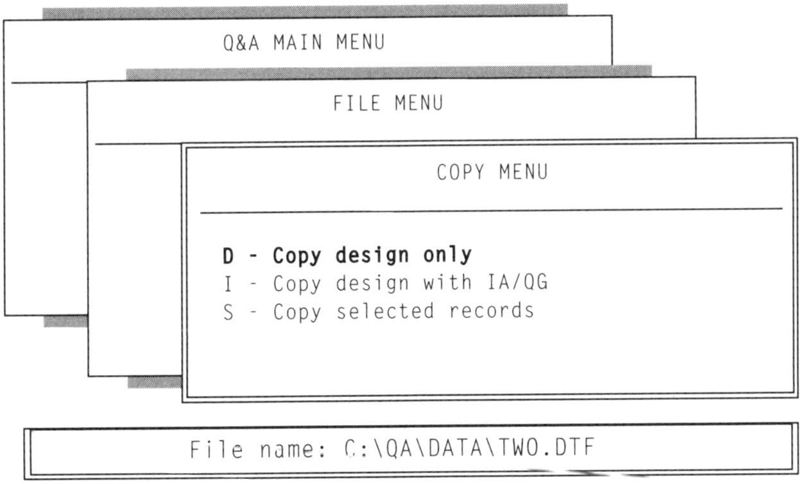


**Figure 6-2. Copy the form design first**

### Step 4: Copy all forms

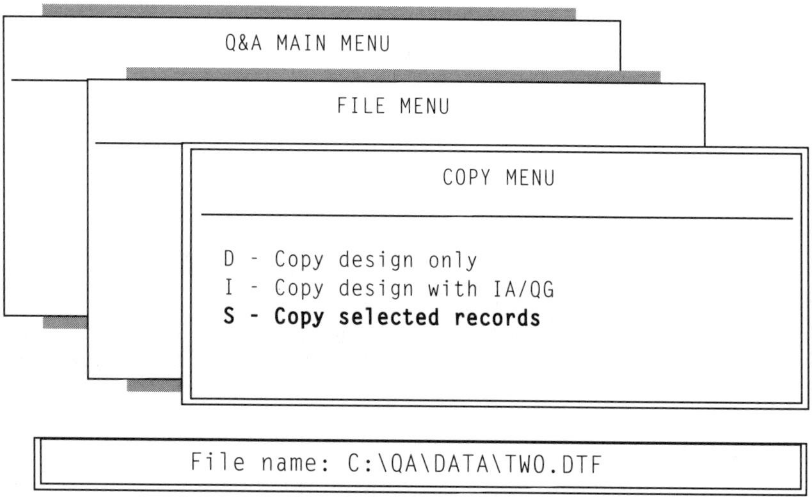


**Figure 6-3. Copy all forms to the new/empty database**

### Step 5: Look at the size of new database files

```
C:\QA\DATA>DIR TWO.*

Volume in drive C is EXAMPLE
Directory of C:\QA\DATA

TWO DTF      43520 11-21-92   3:27p
TWO IDX       9728 11-21-92   3:27p
2 file(s)    53248 bytes
```

### Step 6: Delete the first database, and rename the second

```
C:\QA\DATA>DEL ONE.*

C:\QA\DATA>REN TWO.* ONE.*
```

```
C:\QA\DATA>DIR ONE.*

Volume in drive C is EXAMPLE
Directory of C:\QA\DATA

ONE DTF     43520 11-21-92   3:27p
ONE IDX      9728 11-21-92   3:27p
2 file(s)   53248 bytes

C:\QA\DATA>
```

**NOTE:** What I've just shown you is a classic example of the way many databases work. It would not be possible to go into such great detail about all database programs, so I chose one that I consider representative.

Table 6-1 is a table of other selected databases and the steps they require to restore indexes and data files to their true size in the event some, or all, records have been removed.

**Table 6-1. Different databases use different processes for rebuilding index and data files after deleting forms.**

| SOFTWARE | METHOD |
|---|---|
| dBASE | The PACK command removes all files marked for deletion, but you must use ZAP to recover the disk space if all files have been deleted. The space is not restored, however, until the file has been closed. |
| FoxPro | Same procedure as dBASE. |
| Paradox | Space previously used by removed files is written over by new records as they are added. EMPTY will rebuild the database and set file sizes to their minimums with no records. |
| Reflex | Rewrites the data and indexes as the data changes. No additional steps are required. |
| ThinkTank | Similar to Q&A. Writes the records to a file, and then creates a new database and reads the records back in. |

## Recovering Disk Space

A network manager is obligated to safeguard users' files. One primary way to do that is by performing centralized LAN backups on a nightly basis. When disk space is wasted on the server, then media space also becomes wasted on the backup.

Users can waste server disk space in two unrelated ways. The first way is by keeping outdated files on the network. The second way is by storing duplicate versions of the same file in different locations. Both waste disk and media space and increase backup time.

### Eliminating unneeded files

When DOS performs operations involving the pipe (|) command, it creates temporary files while the output of the first command is written to a file. (In virtually every instance, the temporary file will be in ASCII format.) That output is then read back in and used as input by the next DOS command. If the series of commands completes their execution flawlessly, the temporary files are removed upon termination of the program that called them. If the command series can't complete, the temporary files remain on the disk for eternity. They're never used again, nor are they ever eradicated by internal software.

These files can appear in any subdirectory. They usually appear in pairs and begin with $T, followed by a six-digit sequential number. For example, requesting from the server root directory the command

```
dir /s | more
```

and then crashing out of the routine before completion (using key combinations such as <Ctrl>-<C>, <Ctrl>-<Alt>-<Del>, or <Ctrl>-<Break>) causes the following two files to be written in the root directory:

```
$T100012 20903   4-30-92  1:13p
$T100013     0   4-30-92  1:13p
```

You can locate all DOS temporary files by using "DIR $T* /S" with DOS 5.0, "FF $T*" from Symantec's Norton Utilities, or the

NetWare "NDIR $T* SUBDIRECTORY" command. Each of these commands will give you a complete list of temporary files, although each will be in a slightly different format. Listing 6-1 shows you the results you might get from these different utilities.

**Listing 6-1. You can choose from among several ways to locate DOS temporary files.**

**Norton Utilities:**

```
F:\> FF $T*
FF-File Find, Advanced Edition 4.50, (C) Copr 1987-88,
Peter Norton

F:\PUBLIC
        $t300001   0 bytes   2:18 pm  Thu Sep 10 92
        $t300002   0 bytes   2:18 pm  Thu Sep 10 92
        $t300003   0 bytes   1:14 pm  Wed Sep 16 92
        $t300004   0 bytes   1:14 pm  Wed Sep 16 92

4 files found
```

**NetWare:**

```
F:\>NDIR $T* SUBDIRECTORY
SYS:PUBLIC
File Name   Size   Last Modified   Accessed   Created   Flags    Owner
---------   ----   -------------   --------   -------   -------  -------
$T300001    0      9-10-92 2:18p   11-02-92   9-10-92   [W----]  WILLIAM
$T300002    0      9-10-92 2:18p   11-02-92   9-10-92   [W----]  WILLIAM
$T300003    0      9-16-92 1:14p   11-02-92   9-16-92   [W----]  WILLIAM
$T300004    0      9-16-92 1:14p   11-02-92   9-16-92   [W----]  WILLIAM
       4 files using 0 bytes

Total: 4 files using 0 bytes
Total disk space in use: 16384 bytes (4 blocks)
Sub-directories not found
```

**MS-DOS:**

```
F:\>DIR $T* /S

Volume in drive F is SYS
Directory of  F:\PUBLIC

$T300001    0    9-10-92    2:18p
$T300002    0    9-10-92    2:18p
$T300003    0    9-16-92    1:14p
$T300004    0    9-16-92    1:14p
        4 File(s)  47251456 bytes free

F:\PUBLIC>
```

Many applications allow you to specify where you want their temporary files to go so you'll know where to find them in the event of a failure. Setting all such applications to one "junk" subdirectory can facilitate the process of finding temporary files.

Let's use Q&A from Symantec for our example once again. In Listing 6-2 I've reproduced a setup page from Q&A, an application I use once again to represent the way many application programs allow you to establish these variables.

**Listing 6-2. The Q&A setup page, showing how applications let you direct their temporary files to a selected directory**

```
                    SET GLOBAL OPTIONS
-------------------------------------------------------------
Type the Drive and, optionally, the Path where the fol-
lowing kinds of files will be stored. This will save
you extra typing because Q&A will always know where to
look first for these files:

Q&A Document files:  C:\QA\TEXT\
Q&A Database files:  C:\QA\DATA\
Q&A Temporary files: C:\JUNK\
```

```
You can make the program execute menu items as soon as
you type the first letter of the selection. (If you
select this option, you may have to re-record macros
that expect ENTER after the letter.)

Automatic Execution:  Yes  No
```

Other files you may not need any longer include those ending with extensions .BAK (backups of edited files), .CHK (unrecoverable file fragments), and .ME (readable document files included with software packages). Don't discard application READ.ME files, however, unless you're quite sure you don't need them any longer.

NetWare creates several files that supervisors should check—and delete—regularly. If auditing has been enabled on the server, keep an eye on SYSTEM\NET$ACCT.DAT. This file contains a three-line entry for every user login activity. While condensed in a binary form (extractable with PAUDIT.EXE) to make it as small as possible, it does, nevertheless, grow to sizable proportions over time. Delete this file to regain the space, and a new one will be created with the next user logging action.

Old mail directories are another disk-space waster. No one can read the information still in mail directories for former users or write to those users, so delete the directories. The easiest way to perform this task is to use NetWare's two hidden, system files—NET$BIND.SYS and NET$BVAL.SYS—that store information about users, including their passwords, rights, directories, and so on. These two files constitute what is known as the system *bindery*. Running BINDFIX.EXE will rename these two files and create them again from scratch, in the process giving you the option of deleting mail directories for users no longer on the system.

One word of caution, however. After running this utility, delete the files NET$BIND.OLD and NET$BVAL.OLD. This is what the bindery files get copied to, and since they're no longer hidden or system files, it's far easier now for snooping users to import and read them.

### Removing duplicate files

Duplicate files comprise the single largest unnecessary consumption of resources. Duplication doesn't mean having two files by the same name in different directories with different contents—for example, DESQVIEW\READ.ME and QA\READ.ME. Duplication means having two *exactly* identical files in more than one directory.

Listing 6-2 consists of three short programs which, when run together, will find all duplicate files in existence across the server. You must create these three programs in the root directory of the server. Only the Supervisor can run them. You can generate these programs by means of any text editor; they consist of one batch routine and two short BASIC programs summoned by the batch file.

**Listing 6-3. A routine for finding duplicate files, consisting of three programs**

```
:DOUBLE.BAT
ECHO OFF
ECHO SEARCHING THE SERVER
NDIR F: SUBDIRECTORY BRIEF > FIRST.DAT
C:\DOS\GWBASIC ONE.BAS
ECHO SORTING . . .
SORT < SECOND.DAT > FOURTH.DAT
SORT < THIRD.DAT >> FOURTH.DAT
C:\DOS\GWBASIC TWO.BAS
CLS
DEL FIRST.DAT
DEL SECOND.DAT
DEL THIRD.DAT
DEL FOURTH.DAT
TYPE FIFTH.DAT
ECHO (results stored in FIFTH.DAT)
```

```
10 REM ONE.BAS
20 DIR$="": PRINT "COMPILING . . ."
30 OPEN "F:\FIRST.DAT" FOR INPUT AS #1
40 OPEN "SECOND.DAT" FOR OUTPUT AS #2
50 OPEN "THIRD.DAT" FOR OUTPUT AS #3
60 LINE INPUT #1, TEST$
70 IF INSTR(TEST$, "tal disk") > 1 THEN CLOSE: SYSTEM
80 IF INSTR(TEST$, "YS:") > 1 THEN DIR$=TEST$: GOTO 60
90 IF RIGHT$(TEST$, 1) <> "a" AND RIGHT$(TEST$, 1) <>
  "p" THEN GOTO 60
100 IF ASC(TEST$) < 76 THEN PRINT #2, TEST$;"_";DIR$:
  GOTO 60
110 PRINT #3, TEST$;"_";DIR$: GOTO 60

10 REM TWO.BAS
20 CHECK$="": PRINT "COMPARING . . ."
30 OPEN "F:\FOURTH.DAT" FOR INPUT AS #1
40 OPEN "FIFTH.DAT" FOR OUTPUT AS #2
50 LINE INPUT #1, TEST$
60 IF LEFT$(TEST$, 23)=LEFT$(CHECK$ ,23) THEN PRINT #2,
  CHECK$: PRINT #2, TEST$
70 CHECK$=TEST$
80 IF EOF(1) THEN CLOSE: SYSTEM
90 GOTO 50
```

The first portion of the program shown in Listing 6-3, DOUBLE.BAT, is the batch file. It uses the NDIR command to organize a listing of all files on the server before summoning ONE.BAS into execution. (I've given you the two basic programs in GWBASIC form as a lowest common denominator, but you can just as easily create and execute them using MS-DOS 5.0's QBASIC.)

ONE.BAS reads the output of NDIR, appends the directory name to the end of each file listing, and divides the listing into two separate files: one containing filenames with the first character from A through K, and the second, L through Z. (The two files are necessary because the DOS SORT command doesn't work exceptionally well with large files.) By operating with two separate files, you minimize the possibilities for SORT problems.

DOUBLE.BAT comes back into action, sorts the two files, and combines them into one before summoning TWO.BAS, which now compares the first 23 characters of each entry. These 23 characters comprise the filename, extension, and size; if all are identical, and if the date and time are also the same, the files are most likely duplicates.

If duplicates exist, the results are printed to FIFTH.DAT, which is then printed to the screen, and all temporary files are deleted. Listing 6-4 is an example of a complete duplicate file listing. With this information, you can remove those files not critical to operations.

**Listing 6-4. The output from DOUBLE.BAT gives you information that enables you to eliminate duplicate file listings.**

```
$V11      OVL   2915  6-19-89 12:00a  _SYS:PUBLIC
$V11      OVL   2915  6-19-89 12:00a  _SYS:SYSTEM
2         BAT     20 10-28-88  9:11a  _SYS:APPL/CHA/MENU
2         BAT     20 10-28-88  9:11a  _SYS:CH20200/MENU
5         BAT     12  5-18-89 11:32a  _SYS:CH20200/MENU
5         BAT     12  5-18-89 11:33a  _SYS:APPL/CHA/MENU
AUTOEXEC  BAT     57  5-13-91  9:43a  _SYS:CH20200/STARTUP/NCR
AUTOEXEC  BAT     57  5-13-91  9:44a  _SYS:CH20200/STARTUP/AST
CONFIG    SYS     86 11-10-90 11:03a  _SYS:CH20200/STARTUP/AST
CONFIG    SYS     86 11-10-90 11:03a  _SYS:CH20200/STARTUP/NCR
CONSOLE   COM    103  1-27-91 12:38a  _SYS:LOGIN
CONSOLE   COM    103  1-27-91 12:38a  _SYS:PUBLIC
DESQVIEW  DVS   1024  9-20-90 12:35a  _SYS:APPL/DVMAC
DESQVIEW  DVS   1024  9-20-90 12:35a  _SYS:APPL/QA3
ERR$V11   DAT   3118  6-19-89 12:00a  _SYS:PUBLIC
ERR$V11   DAT   3118  6-19-89 12:00a  _SYS:SYSTEM
EVENTLOG  EXE  16656  8-03-90  6:46a  _SYS:APPL/WSROOT
EVENTLOG  EXE  16656  8-03-90  6:46a  _SYS:CH20200/STARTUP
HELP$V11  DAT   3722  6-19-89 12:00a  _SYS:PUBLIC
HELP$V11  DAT   3722  6-19-89 12:00a  _SYS:SYSTEM
```

```
IBM$V11    OVL    2915  6-19-89  12:00a  _SYS:PUBLIC
IBM$V11    OVL    2915  6-19-89  12:00a  _SYS:SYSTEM
LCONSOLE   EXE  118855  4-16-90  10:27a  _SYS:PUBLIC
LCONSOLE   EXE  118855  4-16-90  10:27a  _SYS:SYSTEM
MENU       BAT      17  5-18-89  10:51a  _SYS:APPL/CHA/MENU
MENU       BAT      17  5-18-89  10:51a  _SYS:CH20200/MENU
MSG$V11    DAT   12468  6-19-89  12:00a  _SYS:PUBLIC
MSG$V11    DAT   12468  6-19-89  12:00a  _SYS:SYSTEM
QA-SCRIP   DVS    1066  1-10-91  12:03a  _SYS:APPL/DVMAC
QA-SCRIP   DVS    1066 10-24-90  10:50a  _SYS:APPL/QA3
QAPRINT3   ZIP   28416  8-29-90   7:36a  _SYS:APPL/QA3
QAPRINT3   ZIP   28416  8-29-90   7:36a  _SYS:APPL/SURVEY/QA3
RDEMO      EXE   59430  1-27-91  12:46a  _SYS:SYSTEM
RDEMO      EXE   59430  1-27-91   2:47a  _SYS:PUBLIC
READ       ME     5289  5-03-90   3:11a  _SYS:CH20102
READ       ME     5289  5-03-90   3:11a  _SYS:CH20200/ANYWHERE
REP        COM     384  1-01-80   0:16a  _SYS:CH20102
REP        COM     384  1-01-80   0:16a  _SYS:CH20200
RUNCHA     BAT      40  8-07-91   8:33a  _SYS:CH20200/STARTUP/NCR
RUNCHA     BAT      40  8-07-91   8:34a  _SYS:CH20200/STARTUP/AST
START      DBD   20894  1-27-91  12:46a  _SYS:SYSTEM
START      DBD   20894  1-27-91  12:47a  _SYS:PUBLIC
```

## Wrap-Up

Optimizing a server incorporates trimming databases to their most efficient levels and disposing of unneeded files. By doing so, you enable the server to access files more quickly, find the needed information, and be prepared for the next transaction. An additional benefit to server optimization is the saving of your media and your time during backups. I recommend that you follow the outlined steps on a regular basis for the highest rate of return.

The next two chapters of this book contain additional information about workstation optimization and about optimization for servers. The questions at the end of Chapter 8 relate to Chapters 6, 7, and 8.

7 CHAPTER

# Optimal Workstation Maintenance

A personal computer is much like a car, a home, or any other tangible investment in that keeping it trouble-free requires routine maintenance. Workstations can last for years without causing problems if you perform preventive maintenance at regular intervals.

Defining the interval is the tricky part. Not only must you take into account the type and age of the workstation you own, but also the quality of the environment and the quantity of the workload. In this chapter, I've drawn up for you a service schedule of standard preventive maintenance that you may modify to satisfy your own needs.

In the previous chapter, I discussed routine maintenance of the network server. Workstations, of course, outnumber servers on the typical network. Diskless workstations require relatively little effort to maintain, since they contain fewer components that may fail. Consequently, this chapter concentrates on workstations containing hard drives.

At the very least, you should consider the outline given here as a minimum guideline to preparing your own preventive maintenance schedule. Based on the type, age, and usage of individual workstations, your actual maintenance schedule may vary somewhat from the guidelines in this chapter.

Let's look at the maintenance chores you should perform on a weekly, monthly, and yearly basis.

## Weekly Maintenance Tasks

Several maintenance tasks, although tedious, are important enough to the safety of your data to perform every week, without fail. These tasks include backing up your data, scanning for viruses, running CHKDSK, and looking for TSR programs.

### Backups

I can't stress enough the importance of backups. Backups offer you your *only* form of recovery in the event of a hard drive failure (short of disk mirroring, used in some network environments). Many people who understand this fact still fail to perform backups on a routine basis. If the data on the hard drive has any value whatsoever, then back it up. If it has no worth, then delete it so you can put the hard drive to better use.

From the day your hard drive was manufactured, it was a given that it would fail; *when* it will fail is the only uncertainty. If you don't perform regular backups of your valuable data, then you're playing with odds worse than you could get at the racetrack.

You must always back up your data to removable memory devices—floppy disks or data cartridges. Backups performed from one hard drive partition to another are subject to the same failure of the drive or controller card; don't expect to save your data this way. For example, if you install two hard drives in your machine and use one to back up the other, what do you do when a fire destroys your machine?

One possible solution involves three sets of transportable media backups. Rotate these three sets on a weekly basis, keeping the two most recent in the office and the third at your home. In this manner, if something goes wrong with your most recent backup, you can refer to the next most recent, without losing everything. Likewise, if something happens to the office, you have a complete backup set at home.

Several methods of performing backups are available. The DOS BACKUP and RESTORE commands have one thing in their favor: they came with DOS when you purchased your machine and therefore require no additional investment. They are sometimes unreliable, however.

You can purchase one of several programs designed to simplify the backup procedure. Two that I recommend are FASTBACK PLUS by 5th Generation Systems, Inc., and Mountain Tape Systems Software. Mountain Tape is an excellent choice if you back up to a data cartridge, while FASTBACK is designed for floppies. FASTBACK PLUS 3.0 allows for incremental appending backups, a feature not offered in previous versions of the software. Both products feature data compression to minimize the number of media required and prove to be quite reliable on recovery attempts.

If you're doing backups and storing the media in safe places, you're far ahead of most people.

### Virus scanning

Run a scan for viruses. The need for this step depends on how accessible your system is to other users and to the outside world via modem or other means of remote communication.

In particular, you need to check your COMMAND.COM file. COMMAND.COM is, quite simply, the DOS command processor. It provides the user interface, contains resident commands, summons the ambulatory commands, and generally enables your computer to understand what you typed in on the command line. Altering this file is the easiest method of disabling or injuring your hard drive.

When DOS was installed in your workstation, a copy of COMMAND.COM was placed in the root directory. When you copied the files from your floppies onto the hard drive, COMMAND.COM was copied again into your DOS directory.

The simplest way to examine for degradation is to compare these two versions of the file and look for discrepancies. You can make this comparison by typing at the command line:

`COMP C:\COMMAND.COM C:\DOS` <Enter>

If you don't have COMMAND.COM in your DOS directory, dig out your original DOS disks and copy it in. If the COMPARE command comes back with anything but a match, a discrepancy exists that you need to look into.

Beginning with version 6.0, MS-DOS added an anti-virus utility (licensed from Central Point Software) that searches for over 1,000 strains of three types of viruses. The three types that this utility searches for include boot sector viruses that affect the DOS operating system by loading themselves into memory; infections in all executable files; and Trojan horses—application programs that contain contaminated code.

You can initiate the virus scan with the MSAV command. Specifying the "/L" parameter following the MSAV command limits the search to local (non-networked) drives only. You should use this parameter on user workstations, but the supervisor's workstation should also scan the networked drives.

MS-DOS also includes a TSR program that you can start up from the AUTOEXEC.BAT on every bootup with the VSAFE command. This program will constantly check all new files for viruses.

### Running CHKDSK

You should run CHKDSK to verify that no corruption has taken place on the hard drive and that the integrity of the file structure is intact. For example, Listing 7-1 shows you what you might see if you run CHKDSK and corruption has occurred.

**Listing 7-1. Running CHKDSK on a hard drive where corruption has occurred**

```
C:\>CHKDSK

Volume EMMETT_D created 11-15-1992 3:58a
Errors found, F parameter not specified
Corrections will not be written to disk

2 lost allocation units found in 1 chains.
16384 bytes disk space would be freed

 142024704 bytes total disk space
     90112 bytes in 3 hidden files
```

```
     540672 bytes in 66 directories
   56836096 bytes in 1781 user files
   98287616 bytes available on disk

       8192 bytes in each allocation unit
      19015 total allocation units on disk
      11998 available allocation units on disk

654336 total bytes memory
516896 bytes free

C:\>
```

To remedy this problem, run CHKDSK again, using the "/F" parameter. The "/F" parameter will fix the corruption and restore the space, as shown in Listing 7-2.

**Listing 7-2. Running CHKDSK again with the "/F" parameter added**

```
C:\>CHKDSK /F

Volume EMMETT_D created 11-15-1992 3:58a

2 lost allocation units found in 1 chains.
Convert lost chains to files (Y/N)?Y

  142024704 bytes total disk space
      90112 bytes in 3 hidden files
     540672 bytes in 66 directories
   56836096 bytes in 1781 user files
      16384 bytes in 1 recovered files
   98287616 bytes available on disk

       8192 bytes in each allocation unit
      19015 total allocation units on disk
      11998 available allocation units on disk
```

```
    654336 total bytes memory
    516896 bytes free

C:\>
```

What becomes of the lost allocation units? DOS converts them into a file in the root directory in the form of FILExxxx.CHK, wherein xxxx represents an incrementing number. In this example, the following file was created and added to two existing ones:

```
C:\>DIR *.CHK

Volume in drive C is EMMETT_D
Directory of C:\

FILE0000.CHK     16384 12-10-92    1:51a
FILE0001.CHK     40960 12-10-92    1:51a
FILE0002.CHK     16384 01-20-93   12:31a
        3 file(s)        73728 bytes
                      84541440 bytes free

C:\>
```

**NOTE:** If you answer "No" to the "Convert lost chains to files?" prompt, the lost blocks are freed up so that they may be reallocated; none of the data in these blocks is recoverable.

*.CHK files are always indicative of DOS cleaning out data that it can't interpret. It's safe to delete these files.

### Looking for TSRs

Run MEM /C to see what kinds of programs are running on the workstation when no real activity is taking place. TSRs load from the CONFIG.SYS file and batch files and stay in memory until needed.

Classic examples of these programs are spell checkers activated with the press of a function key, or the mouse cursor, which awaits movement from a mouse to emulate its actions on the screen.

Run MEM /C and look for TSRs that get loaded but are not needed on the workstation. Because they're resident in memory, they steal processing time from other applications that may need the memory space.

Listing 7-3 shows you what you might see if you run MEM /C to look for TSRs.

**Listing 7-3. Run MEM /C to search for TSR program.**

```
C:\>MEM /C
Modules using memory below 1MB:

Name          Total      =   Conventional   + Upper Memory
--------  ------------   --------------   ------------
MSDOS      14477  (14K)   14477     (14K)    0      (0K)
SETVER       624   (1K)     624      (1K)    0      (0K)
QEMM386     2432   (2K)    2432      (2K)    0      (0K)
ANSI        4208   (4K)    4208      (4K)    0      (0K)
DBLSPACE   47248  (46K)   47248     (46K)    0      (0K)
COMMAND     2912   (3K)    2912      (3K)    0      (0K)
DV           224   (0K)     224      (0K)    0      (0K)
MOUSE      14992  (15K)   14992     (15K)    0      (0K)
DV         43824  (43K)   43824     (43K)    0      (0K)
DOSKEY      4144   (4K)    4144      (4K)    0      (0K)
COMMAND     3216   (3K)    3216      (3K)    0
Free      517088 (505K)  517088    (505K)    0      (0K)
```

```
Memory Summary:

Type of Memory       Size       =   Used          +    Free
--------------   -------------   -------------  ------------

Conventional      654336  (639K)  137248  (134K) 517088 (505K)
Upper                  0    (0K)       0    (0K)      0   (0K)
AdapterRAM/ROM    394240  (385K)  394240  (385K)      0   (0K)
Extended (XMS)   1048576 (1024K)  983040  (960K)  65536  (64K)
--------------   -------------   -------------  ------------
Total memory     2097152 (2048K) 1514528 (1479K) 582624 (569K)

Total under 1MB   654336  (639K)  137248  (134K) 517088 (505K)
EMS is active.
Largest executable program size                  517072 (505K)
Largest free upper memory block                       0   (0K)
MS-DOS is resident in the high memory area.

C:\>
```

## Monthly Maintenance Tasks

Some maintenance chores need only monthly performance. These chores include deleting temporary files, defragmenting hard drives, and directory sorting.

### Deleting temporary files

Delete all temporary files that no longer serve a purpose. Edited batch files change the extension of the original from .BAT to .BAK. With the .BAK extension, the file is not executable and serves no real purpose on the system.

To locate these files, run the following from the command line:

```
C:\>DIR *.BAK /S <Enter>
```

If the command finds too many files for you to see them all before they scroll off the screen, you can send the output to MORE and view the findings one screen at a time:

```
C:\>DIR *.BAK /S | MORE <Enter>
```

The files you find with this command can be safely deleted. You can also delete those files containing the extensions .CHK (see the CHKDSK discussion earlier) and .$$$ (temporary files created during piping operations and not properly removed after execution).

### Defragmenting

Use a commercial defragmenting utility to defragment the hard drive. MS-DOS 6.0 comes equipped with DEFRAG, a utility for defragmenting the drive and placing all files into contiguous blocks.

If you're not using MS-DOS 6.0, the best solution is the SPEED-DISK program packaged with Norton's Utilities. This program will read all the programs on your hard drive and rewrite them in one continuous file. It also updates the file allocation table (FAT). Newer copies of Norton's Utilities save a copy of your FAT into a file that you can use to restore your hard drive in the event of an accidental formatting.

When a file is originally placed on the hard drive, it occupies a certain amount of space. You then create another file that fills in space beneath the first, and so on and so on in the fashion shown in Figure 7-1:

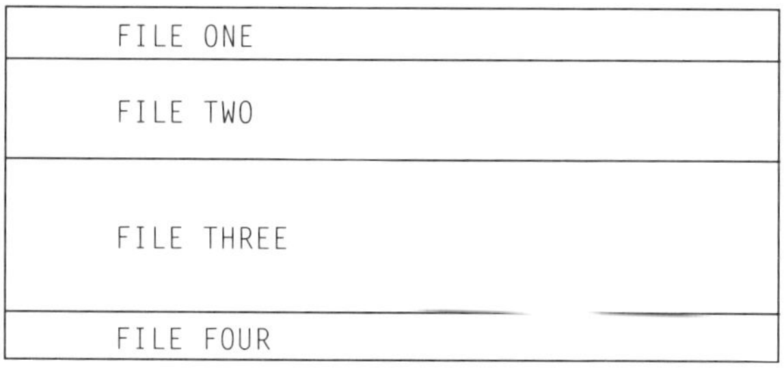


**Figure 7-1. A simple diagram of initial (continuous) file allocation**

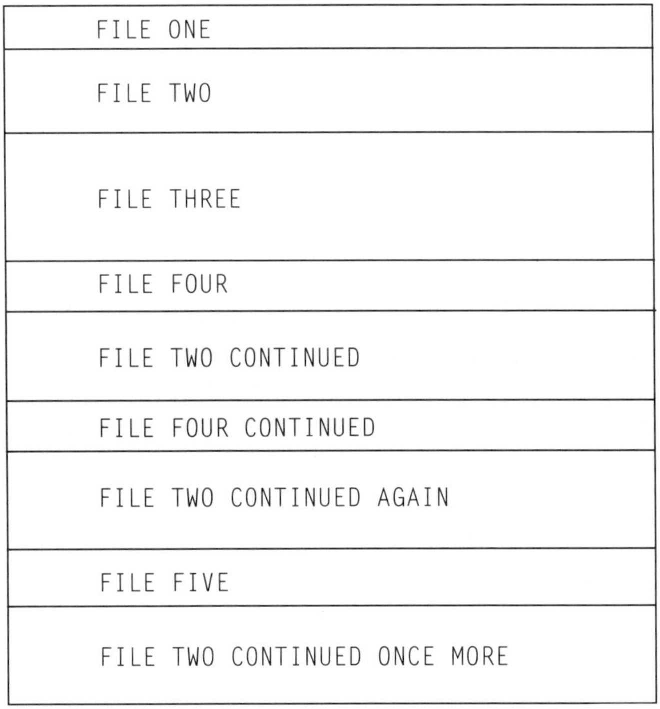


**Figure 7-2. A simple diagram of noncontinuous file allocation**

Suddenly, it turns out that File Two is a word processing document that contains your autobiography. Consequently, as time goes on and you have more fascinating experiences, you need to add a few more pages to this file. You bring it up in your word processor, add to it, and then save it.

But there's no room for the addition, since the file is blocked in by other files. Therefore the additions are written at other positions on the hard drive in the next available slot, and a pointer is added to the first portion to indicate where the rest lies. This process repeats each time you make an addition to the file.

The file is now discontinuous, or fragmented, as shown in Figure 7-2.

This splitting of file portions is known as *fragmenting*. While you can view your file and change, add to, and delete from it, the fragmentation slows your system response time by causing hard drive heads to search several places to bring up one file.

Fortunately, you can use the following batch file to generate a list of the fragmented files on your computer. Since program files don't change in size, the only directories you need to address are those containing data files, where you read, write, and rewrite.

To change the directories inside the parentheses to depict your directory names, use the batch file shown in Listing 7-4.

**Listing 7-4. FRAGMENT.BAT helps you find your fragmented files.**

```
:FRAGMENT.BAT
@ECHO OFF
CLS
ECHO Working . . .
FOR %%F IN (C:\ C:\DATA C:\QA\QADATA C:\OTDATA) DO
  CHKDSK %%F *.* >> HOLD.TMP
CLS
FIND /V "bytes" HOLD.TMP | FIND /V "All" | FIND /V
  "Volume"
DEL HOLD.TMP
```

Running the FRAGMENT.BAT batch file results in a display on your screen similar to this one:

```
C:\BLANK.EXE Contains 2 non-contiguous blocks
C:\FILE0001.CHK Contains 2 non-contiguous blocks
```

In this example, the subdirectories DATA, QADATA, and OTDATA contain no fragmented files; therefore, nothing is listed.

Note that another word for "contiguous" is "adjoining." These noncontiguous blocks are all files that are not connected as one, or files that are fragmented.

Now that you have a listing of all fragmented files, you need to do something about it.

MS-DOS 6.0 comes equipped with DEFRAG, a utility for defragmenting the drive and placing all files into contiguous blocks. Other defragmenters are available as well.

If you're not using MS-DOS 6.0 and don't own any of the Norton or other utility software packages, you can minimize some of the fragmentation with the XCOPY command, being certain to turn on the verify feature. With the foregoing examples, you can use the XCOPY command in this way:

```
XCOPY FILE.TWO D:\CLEAN /V
DEL FILE.TWO
XCOPY D:\CLEAN\FILE.TWO C:\ /V
```

This process will correct *some* of the fragmentation, but purchasing a good utility program like Norton's is money well spent.

#### Directory sorting

Do a directory sort to put all directory entries into alphabetic order. This arrangement makes it easier for you to find files when issuing DOS commands. The best method of performing the sort function is with a Norton Utilities program known as DS or Directory Sort. To use it, go to the root directory and, at the command line, type the following:

```
DS N C: /S <Enter>
```

This utility sorts all files on the C: drive in alphabetic order by name. It does so for all subdirectories as well. This optional step can prove quite useful whenever you have to locate a file in a large directory.

## Yearly Maintenance Tasks

Some maintenance tasks need only yearly performance. These tasks include the removal of duplicate files, compressing the entire drive, optimizing setup, and deleting unnecessary operating system files.

### Removing duplicate files

Ridding the workstation of duplicate files is as important on the workstation as on the server. Nothing is as complete a waste of disk space as storing duplicate files.

DOS files and other executables are often copied into directories other than their own by someone needing them in a different location. COMMAND.COM is a good example; it's needed in the root directory, but not in the DOS directory.

Utility programs are another example. You copy a file into your root directory because you need it right now. Later, you decide to install the entire utility package on your hard drive. You now have a file existing in two places: the utilities directory and the root directory. Another cause of the file-duplication problem is packaged software that contains commands that you already have on your system.

DUPES.BAT is a batch file that I've included on your disk as an ASCII batch file. Working in conjunction with a QBASIC utility called STRIP.BAS, DUPES.BAT can help you locate duplicate programs on your hard drive. Listing 7-5 shows you this batch file.

**Listing 7-5. The DUPES batch file helps you find duplicate programs.**

```
:DUPES.BAT
@ECHO OFF
CLS
IF NOT "%1"=="" GOTO CHECK
:COMPILE
@ECHO OFF
ECHO Generating list of files . . .
CHKDSK /V > C:\FULL.LST
ECHO Compiling . . .
QBASIC /RUN C:\STRIP.BAS
```

```
ECHO Sorting . . .
SORT < C:\TEMP.$$$ > PRN
ECHO Process complete.
ECHO Print FULL.LST for a complete listing of the hard
  drive.
GOTO END
:CHECK
ECHO Searching and Comparing . . .
CHKDSK /V | FIND "%1" | SORT > C:TMPFILE
ECHO N >> C:TMPFILE
COMP < C:TMPFILE
:END
```

The DUPES batch file performs in two different ways. Running it with no parameters generates a printout of all files on the drive, sorted into alphabetic order. Listing 7-6 shows you what such a printout might look like.

**Listing 7-6. DUPES.BAT lists all your files alphabetically.**

```
GAMES
GAVEL.WPG
GENIUS.VRS
GO.BAT
GOCHA.BAT
GOODEXIT.BAT
GORILLA.BAS
GRAB.COM
GRAB.COM
GRABBER.DOC
GRAFTABL.COM
GRAFTABL.COM
HEAD.EXE
HEAD.EXE
HELP.BAT
HELP.EXE
```

```
JOB.LBL
JOBLBL.DTA
JOBLBL.HDR
JOBLBL.IDX
JOBLBL.SRT
JOHNS
JOIN.EXE
JOIN.EXE
KEYBGR.COM
KEYBIT.COM
KEYBOARD.DTA
KEYBOARD.HDR
KEYBOARD.IDX
LABEL.COM
LABEL.EXE
LABELS.BAS
LABELS.WPM
LB-UPGRA.DTA
```

This printed list, because it's alphabetical, makes it easy to scan through the compendium and look for duplicates. In this small portion of an example printout, you can see numerous files with the same name and extension, including GRAB.COM, GRAFTABL.COM, HEAD.EXE, and JOIN.EXE.

An added benefit of the program is that it creates a file called C:\FULL.LST, which is a complete listing of all files on your hard drives, including their respective directories and subdirectories. You can print out this file and store it in a safe place in case of a hard drive crash or corruption.

Now that you've found the suspected duplicates, you can go on to the second part of the process. DUPES checks the suspected duplicate files and ascertains whether or not they are true duplicates of each other. The following text shows what you might see if you run the DUPES command:

```
C:\>DUPES GRAB.COM

C:\GRAB.COM and C:\EAD\GRAB.COM
Eof mark not found
Files compare ok

C:\>
```

If the files are exact duplicates, you'll hear no noise from the CPU and the last line of the message will be "Files compare ok." This message tells you that they are truly identical files and one may be deleted. Notice that running DUPES.BAT in this fashion displays the full path of both files, making their removal relatively simple.

If the files are different, the CPU will emit a beep and the last line of the message will change. For example:

```
C:\>DUPES HEAD.EXE

C:\HEAD.EXE and C:\QA\HEAD.EXE
Files are different sizes

C:\>
```

Since these files are different sizes, they can't be exact duplicates. Only when you see the message "Files compare ok" can you be sure the files are duplicates and you can delete one.

Note here that DUPES.BAT, when run to generate a printout, takes the complete file listing C:\FULL.LST and removes from it references to directories and subdirectories. Only by stripping down to the actual filename is it able to locate possible duplicates. The batch file language won't permit such filename isolation; therefore, it's necessary to use a QBASIC program called STRIP.BAS, which strips the aforementioned information away. Listing 7-7 shows you this program.

**Listing 7-7. STRIP.BAS helps you isolate filenames.**

```
OPEN "C:\FULL.LST" FOR INPUT AS #1
OPEN "C:\TEMP.$$$" FOR OUTPUT AS #2
DO WHILE NOT EOF(1)
  INPUT #1, ln$
  DO WHILE INSTR(ln$, "\") > 1
    ln$ = RIGHT$(ln$, LEN(ln$) - (INSTR(ln$, "\")))
  LOOP
  IF INSTR(ln$, "t") < 1 THEN PRINT #2, ln$
LOOP
CLOSE
SYSTEM
```

This utility is very straightforward in operation. It reads each line of C:\FULL.LST, and checks to see if the line contains a "\" character. If so, it takes only what is to the right of the character. In this way, "C:\BOOKS\NETWARE\ONE.BAT" becomes "BOOKS\NETWARE\ONE.BAT," then "NETWARE\ONE.BAT," and finally "ONE.BAT."

All filenames that CHKDSK generates are automatically given in uppercase format. As a result, if a lowercase "t" is contained in the line, the line is not a filename, but rather a part of the message generated anytime CHKDSK is run. These lines, all of which contain a lowercase "t," are tossed away and only the filenames are kept to a temporary file.

Once the temporary file is created, DUPES.BAT then sorts the file and prints the output. One word of caution is in order here: The sorting process time will vary, depending on the number of filenames. The more files on the system, of course, the longer the sorting process takes. During the sorting operation, processing is done on memory and not on the drive. No lights flash. The computer may appear to be hung when in fact it's using memory to sort the file. Be patient during the sorting operation and take into account the number of files on the drive.

### Entire drive compression

DR DOS comes packaged with a utility known as SuperStor, a data compression utility that works not on individual files, but on the entire hard drive partition. The partition becomes compressed in such a manner that it's now able to hold more data, thereby simulating a larger drive.

In essence, *all* the data on the drive is compressed. Another drive location becomes necessary as a temporary holding facility where these files may be decompressed for usage. It takes only moments to create a SuperStor drive and transform all existing data to conform to the new dimensions.

The problem comes, however, if you ever need to change the drive back to a non-SuperStor drive. In doing so, you must remove *all* files, as the drive is virtually reformatted to its old self.

Listing 7-8 shows the CHKDSK listing for the C: drive of a 40MB hard drive configured according to the old MS-DOS standard of 32MB on drive C: and 8MB on drive D:. The system was converted to DR DOS and C was prepared as a SuperStor drive.

**Listing 7-8. SuperStor provides data compression on a complete hard disk partition.**

```
Checking internal SuperStor drive tables.
Volume in drive C: does not have a label


 65,658,880 bytes total disk space.
    139,264 bytes in 6 hidden files.
    147,456 bytes in 18 directories.
 11,804,672 bytes in 552 user files.
     32,768 bytes in 4 pending delete files.
 53,534,720 bytes available on disk.

    655,360 total bytes of memory.
    504,112 total bytes of free memory.
    503,392 bytes in largest free memory block.
```

The 32MB partition practically doubles, allowing for more bytes than was previously available with no programs loaded. The device list and compression statistic screens show yet more interesting information, as shown in Figure 7-3:

```
    Main Menu                System Device List

 Prepare                  A: DOS Floppy drive
 Remove                   B: DOS Floppy drive
 Statistics               C: Fixed SuperStor partition
 Help          F1         D: DOS Fixed disk
 Exit          Esc        E: SuperStor host device (was drive C:)
```

```
            Drive C Compression Statistics
```

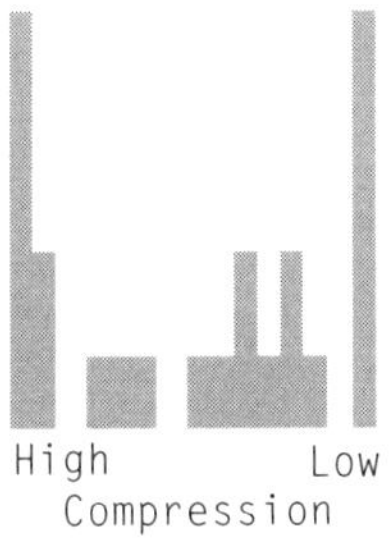


```
SSTOR Bytes used:        12115968
SSTOR Free (est):        52658176
SSTOR Total (est):       64774144
Actual Bytes Used:        6313472
Actual Free:             26329088
Actual Total:            32642560

     Compression ratio = 1.9:1
        Space Savings = 48%
```

**Figure 7-3. Data Compression Utilities Copyright © 1991, AddStor Inc.**

Note first that a virtual drive E: has been created as the SuperStor host, or temporary workspace for decompressing drive C:'s files as they're needed. Also note that the compression ratio is actually 1.9 to 1; a 48% space savings has been generated.

Depending on the kinds of files on your drive, however, the compression ratio can fluctuate severely. Table 7-1 shows the average compression ratio for the most common file types.

Table 7-1. Compression ratios for various file types

| FILE TYPE | COMPRESSION RATIO |
|---|---|
| Executable files | 2:1 |
| Spreadsheets | 3:1 |
| Documents | 3:1 |
| Databases | 5:1 |

In addition to the compression, SuperStor allows you to designate a portion of the disk to remain decompressed in the event you have files you don't want compressed. If you select this option, another drive letter is created to indicate the location of the decompressed portion of the drive. The original drive letter indicates the compressed portion.

After the compression has taken place, you need to modify the CONFIG.SYS file to include two new device drivers. SSTORDRV.SYS must come first, followed by DEVSWAP.COM. DEVSWAP performs a reassignment of drive letters between the compressed drive and the decompressed drive. If this device isn't loaded, the computer will still function perfectly, but the root drive won't be the default. (For example, E: could contain the DOS directory as opposed to C:.)

You can create a maximum of eight SuperStor partitions for any one drive, and the maximum partition size is 512MB (256MB prior to SuperStor). Listing 7-9 shows a before-and-after CHKDSK listing once SUPERSTOR is added to the workstation.

**Listing 7-9. CHKDSK can show you how much space you save by compressing your files with SuperStor.**

```
CHKDSK listing before SuperStor:

BEFORE:
Volume William's created Sep 16, 1992 1:21p

 33462272 bytes total disk space
```

```
    57344 bytes in 4 hidden files
    75776 bytes in 33 directories
 26134528 bytes in 747 user files
  7194624 bytes available on disk

   655360 bytes total memory
   533120 bytes free

CHKDSK listing after SuperStor:

AFTER:
Volume William's created Sep 16, 1992 1:21p

 65658880 bytes total disk space
    65536 bytes in 4 hidden files
   262144 bytes in 32 directories
 27942912 bytes in 746 user files
 37388288 bytes available on disk

   655360 bytes total memory
   466128 bytes free
```

If you're using MS-DOS 6.0, you'll find a similar utility by typing DBLSPACE <Enter> at the command-line prompt. The utility name stands for "DoubleSpace"; the hard drive space is virtually doubled.

If you're using a previous version of MS-DOS, no such utility is included free of charge, but several are available in the $100 to $200 price range. SuperStor is available as a stand-alone utility, and Stac Electronics markets STACKER that serves the same function. One additional note about the stand-alone STACKER is that you can also use it with a dedicated compression card to further enhance compression and decompression time.

### Optimizing setup

When a workstation boots up, DOS reads the CONFIG.SYS file from the root directory immediately after the DOS operating system to determine what drivers to load, how to allocate memory, and generally establish the environment. How that environment is defined can, and does, determine the performance of the workstation in terms of speed, random-access time, and processing execution.

You can establish five key factors in the CONFIG.SYS to enable quicker data retrieval speed and decrease processing time. All five serve that same purpose, but in slightly different ways. Let's look at the five key speed factors in the CONFIG.SYS file.

1. BUFFERS. This entry in the CONFIG.SYS file refers to the number of storage buffers DOS creates upon workstation startup. Buffers hold information that has been retrieved from the hard drive, with each buffer roughly equal to one sector. You can retrieve and access information held within a buffer much more quickly than information still resting on the hard drive. Without a buffer statement, DOS creates a bare minimum allocation of memory based on the amount of conventional memory available on the workstation.

   The more buffers there are, the more information you can readily access. The bad part is that the more buffers there are, the more memory is being used up and the less main memory space is available for use by programs and applications. I highly recommend setting your buffers to at least BUFFERS=40.

   DR DOS allows you to specify BUFFERS *or* HIBUFFERS, in which case the memory is allocated out of high memory instead of conventional memory. This approach provides the best of both worlds, allowing a high number of buffers to be established without subtracting from the conventional memory available for use by applications.

2. FASTOPEN maps the location to files and directories as you open them. As a result, if you summon a file a second time, the system can find it more quickly because you've already accessed it once. Ideally suited for databases that are constantly opened and closed throughout the day, FASTOPEN can also be loaded in expanded memory to leave as much conventional memory free as possible.

   FASTOPEN is useful *only* with files retrieved more than once. For files not retrieved more than once, BUFFERS serve the purpose of decreasing access time.

3. The number of files that can be opened simultaneously defaults to eight if there is no FILES= statement in CONFIG.SYS. Eight is considered the minimum; 255 is considered the maximum.

   Much like the BUFFERS= statement, the FILES= statement allocates conventional memory that is set aside and will be used when multiple files are opened at the same moment. It also takes away from the amount of memory available for programs and applications. However, networks often require that many files be opened at the same time; I guarantee that eight will never be enough.

   FILES=30 allots space for 30 files and limits the number of open files to no more than 30. This setting leaves enough room for most NetWare applications and creates the most efficient use of the FILES= option.

4. The HIDOS option in DR DOS and the DOSHIGH option in MS-DOS allow you to load as much of the operating system as possible into high memory. Again, this frees the lower, conventional memory for use by applications and programs.

5. SUPERPCK is a disk-caching utility included with DR DOS. A disk cache is a section of memory that stores information on frequently accessed disk sections. By storing the information here, the system can more readily retrieve it than by physically reading the drive. Disk caching is a refinement of the buffers idea.

   SUPERPCK not only greatly decreases the amount of time required to retrieve data, but also the time required to write, modify, and save it. You can also load it into extended memory, in which case it uses only a portion of conventional memory as an address. The same purpose and function is accomplished in MS-DOS via SMARTDRV.SYS.

   Because both utilities are memory hogs, they're useful only on workstations with extended or expanded memory. Like FASTOPEN, memory cachers greatly improve their performance on files that are accessed more than once during the course of the computing session; instead of just mapping the location, they actually copy the accessed file into the cache.

   Listing 7-10 is a sample of a CONFIG.SYS file. The order in which you set up the variables doesn't matter, but the order in which drivers are loaded often does.

**Listing 7-10. This sample CONFIG.SYS file showing FILES= and BUFFERS= entries**

```
DEVICE=C:\DOS\SETVER.EXE
FILES=40
BUFFERS=40
DEVICE=QEMM386.SYS
DEVICE=ANSI.SYS
DOS=HIGH
```

Additional methods of optimizing the setup include common-sense approaches to establishing environmental variables. For example, the PATH statement should contain paths to the most commonly used utility directories first to decrease search time. Additionally, the PATH must never contain addresses to directories that contain no executable utilities (database directories, for example), since the only files that PATH searches for are .COM, .EXE, and .BAT files, in that order.

**NOTE:** Beginning with MS-DOS 6.0, you may specify NUMLOCK in the CONFIG.SYS to override the workstation's default as to whether or not the numeric keypad number lock is on at startup. This utility has been needed for a long time, and will replace many public domain utilities which have been serving the purpose for a number of years.

### Deleting unnecessary operating system files

You may delete certain system files from each workstation without harm, providing you don't intend to use the workstation for international code pages. Table 7-2 shows you a list of these files.

**Table 7-2. System files that are frequently expendable**

| |
|---|
| 4201.CPI |
| 4208.CPI |
| 5202.CPI |
| COUNTRY.SYS |
| DISPLAY.SYS |
| GRAFTABL.COM |
| KEYB.COM |
| KEYBOARD.SYS |
| PRINTER.SYS |
| NLSFUNC.EXE |

Additionally, if the workstation is not a 386 or higher, you may delete the following files:

```
EMM386.EXE
MEMMAKER.*
```

## Wrap-Up

Optimizing the workstation ensures that it's running at its peak performance level in terms of processing. As a chain can only be as strong as its weakest link, a network can only be as good as its components. A lightning-fast server can send information to a workstation, but from that point on, it's up to the workstation to present the information, modify it, and send it back to the server. All components must work together, and all must be at their best if processing is expected to be at its ultimate.

In this chapter I discussed optimization on the server. In the next chapter I will discuss optimization that's relevant to the server and the workstation alike. The questions following the end of Chapter 8 pertain to Chapters 6, 7, and 8.

# CHAPTER 8

# Optimal Server and Workstation Maintenance

The previous two chapters discussed optimization of servers and workstations, respectively. This chapter discusses optimization techniques that you can use on both platforms.

## Allocation Units, Sectors, and Space

Answer the following question in one word or less: If you have a disk with 1,000 bytes free remaining, and you'd like to copy the following files from your hard drive to that floppy, would they fit?

```
Q        BAT        43 11-03-92  11:59a
AUTOEXEC BAT       199 11-03-92  12:00p
DIRECTOR BAT       219 08-17-91  11:36p
FINDER   BAT        29 08-17-91   7:24p
RUNCHA   BAT        73 04-19-89  11:55a
PATHRS   BAT        79 10-17-92  11:54p
FINDUR   BAT        18 09-27-92   8:20p
FINDERR  BAT       257 10-24-92   9:00p
        8 file(s)          917 bytes
```

And the answer is . . . a resounding no.

To explain why, let me give you an analogy. When you build a house on a plot of ground, the ground the house is built on usually occupies more space than the actual house. If not, no one would ever buy lawn mowers and cordless weed-eaters.

The developer lays out plans for building sites and maps out lots. A buyer purchases an individual lot, and then builds whatever type of house suits his or her needs. While all of the houses built in the development are different, the lot size remains the same.

When you save a file on a hard drive or a floppy drive, the same thing takes place. The amount of space the file uses isn't equal to the number of bytes in the file, but rather to the nearest DOS lot size, referred to as an "allocation unit." While lot sizes depend on land developers, allocation unit sizes depend on which drive and media you're operating from. Consequently, it's rare for the file size and the allocation unit size to be equal.

If you create a batch file of 10 bytes on your C: drive, the amount of available disk space doesn't decrease by 10 bytes. In most cases, it will decrease by 2048 bytes—the standard C: drive allocation assignment. (This number changes with disk compression utilities, often to an even higher number!)

Now let's look at a basic language utility called WASTED, shown in Listing 8-1. This utility, which runs only on local drives with MS-DOS 5.0 and higher, reports the true number of bytes in use by a file.

**Listing 8-1. The WASTED utility tells you how many bytes a file is using.**

```
REM WASTED ALLOCATION SPACE ROUTINE
REM by Emmett Dulaney
CLS:SHELL"DEL $DOLITLE.*":PRINT "Preliminary work in
  progress..."
REM CALCULATE HOW MANY BYTES ARE IN EACH ALLOCATION
  UNIT
SHELL "CHKDSK > $DOLITLE.DOC"
OPEN "I", #1, "$DOLITLE.DOC"
DO
```

```
  LINE INPUT #1, UNIT$
         IF RIGHT$(UNIT$, 5) = "space" THEN S =
           VAL(UNIT$)
         IF RIGHT$(UNIT$, 4) = "UNIT" THEN EXIT DO
LOOP
CLOSE #1:B = VAL(UNIT$):SB = 0
REM OBTAIN DIRECTORY LISTING
INPUT "Specify files: example *.BAT, PS.*, *.*, etc. ";
  D$
INPUT "Search subdirectories [n/y]: "; S$
IF S$ = "y" OR S$ = "Y" THEN D$ = D$ + " /S" : SB = 1
SHELL "DIR " + D$ + " /A-D > $DOLITLE.DOC"
OPEN "I", #1, "$DOLITLE.DOC"
A = 0 : U = 0
DO
    LINE INPUT #1, FL$ : X = 0
    IF RIGHT$(FL$, 5) = "bytes" AND SB < 1 THEN EXIT DO
    IF LEFT$(FL$, 6) = "Total " THEN EXIT DO
    IF RIGHT$(FL$, 1) = "a" OR RIGHT$(FL$, 1) = "p"
      THEN
         D = VAL(MID$(FL$, 13, 10))
         IF D < B THEN
              A = A + (B - D) : U = U + B
         ELSEIF D >= B THEN
              X=D MOD B:A=A+X:Z=((D\B)*B): U = U + Z
         IF X > 0 THEN U = U + B
         END IF
    END IF
LOOP
REM PRINT TOTALS
IF SB > 0 THEN LINE INPUT #1, FL$
T = VAL(FL$) : CLOSE #1
PRINT : PRINT "There are "; T; " files which occupy ";
PRINT USING "##,###,###"; U;
PRINT " bytes": PRINT "of ";
```

```
PRINT USING "##,###,###"; S;
PRINT " total available in sectors of ";
PRINT USING "#,###"; B
PRINT "The total occupied yet unavailable bytes = ";
PRINT USING "##,###,###"; A
PRINT USING "##.##"; ((A/U) * 100);
PRINT "% of allocated space is vacant."
```

Using this utility, you can ascertain the true size of files such as Q.BAT, which we were earlier led to believe was occupying only 43 bytes. Here's what you might see if you use WASTED to check the byte size of Q.BAT.

```
C:\>WASTED

Preliminary work in progress. . .
Specify files: example *.BAT  PS.*, *.* , etc. ? Q.BAT
Search subdirectories [n/y]: N

There are  1  files which occupy 2,048 bytes
of 33,462,272 total available in sectors of 2,048
The total occupied yet unavailable bytes =      2,005
97.90% of allocated space is vacant.

C:\>
```

As you can see, 2048 bytes is more than the DIR listing showed to be in use by all the .BAT files combined. This file alone wouldn't fit on the floppy disk, given its size and the remaining space. Almost 98 percent of the lot/allocation unit set aside for it is lost, unavailable for use by anything else.

If you use the WASTED utility to look at all eight files, you'll find similar statistics.

```
C:\>WASTED

Preliminary work in progress. . .
Specify files: example *.BAT  PS.*, *.* , etc. ? *.BAT
Search subdirectories [n/y]: N

There are  8  files which occupy     16,384 bytes
of 33,462,272 total available in sectors of 2,048
The total occupied yet unavailable bytes =     15,467
94.40% of allocated space is vacant.

C:\>
```

Suppose you use the WASTED utility to examine all .BAT files on a drive. Here's what you might see:

```
C:\>WASTED

Preliminary work in progress. . .
Specify files: example *.BAT  PS.*, *.* , etc. ? *.BAT
Search subdirectories [n/y]: Y

There are  35  files which occupy     88,064 bytes
of 33,462,272 total available in sectors of 2,048
The total occupied yet unavailable bytes =     62,311
70.76% of allocated space is vacant.

C:\>
```

But as molecules can be broken into atoms, allocation units can be broken into sectors, each sector constituting 512 bytes. The variable in the equation is the number of sectors in each allocation unit. For the most part, it depends on the drive you're on. Not taking into account the results of using compression utilities, the most common assignments are one cluster (512 bytes) to the A: drive, two (1024 bytes) to B:, four (2048 bytes) to drive C:, eight (4096 bytes) to drive D:, and so on, in exponential order.

If the same 35 .BAT files, then, were located on the D: drive rather than on the C: drive, the results would be different. Let's run the WASTED utility again.

```
C:\>WASTED

Preliminary work in progress. . .
Specify files: example *.BAT  PS.*, *.* , etc. ? *.BAT
Search subdirectories [n/y]: Y

There are  35  files which occupy    176,128 bytes
of  8,888,320 total available in sectors of 4,096
The total occupied yet unavailable bytes =    150,395
85.00% of allocated space is vacant.

C:\>
```

Because the batch files are on D: instead of C:, they occupy twice as much space as before, and *over* twice the amount of unused space is left to waste. Think of how much more efficient it would be if the 35 .BAT files were on the A: drive!

Rule number one, then, becomes to keep the smaller files on the lowest letter drive.

The second rule is to make the files as large as possible and avoid as many small files as possible. How can you accomplish this goal?

Consider the eight batch files that were listed earlier and found to occupy 16,384 bytes. Let's take a quick look at three of them in Listing 8-2.

**Listing 8-2. Three separate batch files**

```
Q.BAT
ECHO OFF
CLS
```

```
CD\QA3
WF
QA
CD\
EXIT

FINDER.BAT
CLS
CHKDSK /V | FIND "%1"

FINDERR.BAT
@ECHO OFF
FOR %%X IN (0 1 2 ) DO IF ERRORLEVEL %%X00 SET ERR=%%X
FOR %%X IN (0 1 2 3 4 5 6 7 8 9) DO IF ERRORLEVEL
  %ERR%%%X0 SET ERR=%ERR%%%X
FOR %%X IN (0 1 2 3 4 5 6 7 8 9) DO IF ERRORLEVEL
  %ERR%%%X SET ERR=%ERR%%%X
ECHO Existing errorlevel = %ERR%
```

All of these files are very straightforward, serving but one purpose each. Q.BAT starts a Q&A application program, FINDER.BAT locates a file in a "whereis" manner, and FINDERR.BAT finds and reports the existing errorlevel.

Suppose these three files were joined together in a single, unified file. Look at Listing 8-3.

**Listing 8-3. Three conjoined batch files**

```
:BATCH.BAT
@ECHO OFF
CLS
IF "%1"=="" GOTO NOPARM
GOTO %1
:Q
CD\QA3
WF
```

```
QA
CD\
GOTO EXIT
:FINDER
SHIFT
CHKDSK /V | FIND "%1"
GOTO EXIT
:FINDERR
FOR %%X IN (0 1 2 ) DO IF ERRORLEVEL %%X00 SET ERR=%%X
FOR %%X IN (0 1 2 3 4 5 6 7 8 9) DO IF ERRORLEVEL
  %ERR%%%X0 SET ERR=%ERR%%%X
FOR %%X IN (0 1 2 3 4 5 6 7 8 9) DO IF ERRORLEVEL
  %ERR%%%X SET ERR=%ERR%%%X
ECHO Existing errorlevel = %ERR%
GOTO EXIT
:NOPARM
ECHO Usage BATCH {Q FINDER FINDERR}
:EXIT
```

Now, instead of typing "Q," you must type "BATCH Q," for a total of six additional keystrokes. But look at what you gain with those few added keystrokes:

```
AUTOEXEC BAT       199 11-03-92  12:00p
FINDUR   BAT        18 11-12-92  10:33p
DIRECTOR BAT       219 08-17-91  11:36p
RUNCHA   BAT        73 04-19-89  11:55a
PATHRS   BAT        79 10-17-92  11:54p
BATCH    BAT       468 11-12-92  10:46p
        6 file(s)       1056 bytes

C:\>WASTED

Preliminary work in progress. . .
Specify files: example *.BAT  PS.*, *.* , etc. ? *.BAT
Search subdirectories [n/y]: N
```

```
There are   6   files which occupy    12,288 bytes
of 33,462,272 total available in sectors of 2,048
The total occupied yet unavailable bytes =    11,233
91.41% of allocated space is vacant.

C:\>
```

There are now two fewer files than before, and the DIR listing shows that 139 more bytes are being used than before. But more importantly, the WASTED utility shows that the number of occupied bytes has dropped 25 percent from 16,384 to 12,288—a savings of 4,096 bytes, or eight clusters. You could obtain even greater space savings if you were to combine all eight tiny batch files into one large file.

## File Compression

Reducing the byte size of files follows the earlier discussion of saving disk and backup media space. If you can reduce the size of the file without hindering functionality and performance, then you can optimize space more advantageously. In the preceding chapter, we discussed total drive compression; now we're interested in individual files.

Four exceptional utility programs are available that allow you to reduce the size of your files without danger to your data. Three of these are available from the same vendor; the fourth is from another. There are four, as opposed to one, because each serves a different purpose. These utilities are PKLITE, SQZ!, PKZIP, and PK Data Compression Library.

### PKLITE

Following are two identical listings of the NetWare PUBLIC subdirectory containing NetWare system files. Listing 8-4 shows executable files in their standard format, while Listing 8-5 lists the same files after I've used PKLITE to reduce their size. In this case, I obtained an average savings of 38 percent within the directory by compacting the files without losing any of their operability. Those files that retained their original size contain graphical overlays and cannot be safely reduced.

**Listing 8-4. A display of file sizes before using PKLITE**

```
Volume in drive F is SYS
Directory of  F:\PUBLIC

LCONSOLE EXE   118855   4-16-90  10:27a
RDEMO    EXE    59430   1-27-91  12:47p
CASTON   EXE    11079   1-27-91  12:47p
SYSCON   EXE   265683   1-27-91  12:48p
FCONSOLE EXE   214380   1-27-91  12:48p
REVOKE   EXE    18183   1-27-91  12:48p
MAKEUSER EXE   114464   1-27-91  12:48p
NDIR     EXE    42581   1-27-91  12:52p
LRESTORE EXE    24576   1-27-91  12:53p
PCONSOLE EXE   135697   1-27-91  12:53p
CAPTURE  EXE    39655   1-27-91  12:53p
PRINTDEF EXE   147955   1-27-91  12:53p
MENUPARZ EXE    51632   1-27-91  12:53p
PRINTCON EXE   109056   1-27-91  12:53p
ATTACH   EXE    30118   1-27-91  12:53p
SESSION  EXE    92415   1-27-91  12:53p
CHKVOL   EXE    19255   1-27-91  12:53p
FLAG     EXE    26615   1-27-91  12:53p
```

**Listing 8-5. A display of file sizes reduced 38 percent after using PKLITE**

```
Volume in drive F is SYS
Directory of  F:\PUBLIC

LCONSOLE EXE    56705   5-04-92  10:16p
RDEMO    EXE    20761   5-04-92  10:16p
CASTON   EXE     7092   5-04-92  10:16p
SYSCON   EXE   142739   5-04-92  10:16p
FCONSOLE EXE   101273   5-04-92  10:17p
```

```
REVOKE   EXE    12362   5-04-92  10:17p
MAKEUSER EXE   114464   1-27-91  12:48p
NDIR     EXE    26450   5-04-92  10:17p
LRESTORE EXE    24576   1-27-91  12:53p
PCONSOLE EXE    72628   5-04-92  10:17p
CAPTURE  EXE    24656   5-04-92  10:18p
PRINTDEF EXE    75362   5-04-92  10:18p
MENUPARZ EXE    51632   1-27-91  12:53p
PRINTCON EXE   109056   1-27-91  12:53p
ATTACH   EXE    30118   1-27-91  12:53p
SESSION  EXE    49229   5-04-92  10:18p
CHKVOL   EXE    13290   5-04-92  10:18p
FLAG     EXE    17337   5-04-92  10:18p
```

PKLITE works on all executable files (.EXE and .COM) that do not contain overlays. Average file compression is 45 percent, and the difference in file operation is transparent in terms of operating time and actions. The following text gives you an example of PKLITE in action.

```
C:\>PKLITE *.EXE
Copyright 1990 PKWARE Inc. All Rights Reserved.

File: BABY.EXE may contain overlays. Compress (y/n)? N

Compressing: CHOP31.EXE
Original Size: 36960 Compressed Size: 18647 Ratio: 49.6

File: CMP.EXE is already compressed

Compressing: EVENTLOG.EXE
Original Size: 16656 Compressed Size: 14185 Ratio: 14.9

Compressing: FALL.EXE
```

```
Original Size: 23116 Compressed Size: 18683 Ratio: 19.2

Compressing: LASTBOOT.EXE
Original Size: 5120 Compressed Size: 4309 Ratio: 15.9

Compressing: MLX.EXE

Unoptimal relocation data detected, rearrange for
  better compression (y/n)? Y

Original size: 35312 Compressed size: 19513 Ratio: 44.8

FILE: EXEHDR.EXE is a Windows or OS/2 program and
  cannot be compressed

File: UNIQ.EXE is already compressed

C:\>
```

### SQZ!

What PKLITE does for executable files, SQZ! from Symantec does for spreadsheets. This add-in program automatically compresses worksheets when you save them and decompresses them when you read them. With an average space savings of approximately 50 percent, once again there is no noticeable increase in the amount of time required to retrieve or save the spreadsheet.

### PKZIP

PKZIP comes into play by allowing you to save all files that you rarely use, but don't want to get rid of, in one archived file. Using imploding and compressing, you may take last year's notes and memos and shrink them into one file a fraction the size of the previous files. For example, the five following documents:

```
032991 DOC23160  3-29-91       9:53a
041391 DOC23470  4-13-91       7:21a
041591 DOC17070  4-15-91       1:05p
042291 DOC33670  4-22-91       8:33a
042391 DOC24300  4-23-91       2:01p
```

when compressed become:

```
DOCS      ZIP    57400  5-01-92       3:19p
```

The new single file is 47 percent the size of the original five files. Think of 47 percent in terms of tapes or floppies, and the figure becomes even more significant.

#### PK Data Compression Library

The last of the utility packages is PK Data Compression Library. This package is an all-purpose ASCII or binary data compressor, allowing reduction in the size of data files used by C, C++, Pascal, Assembly, Basic, and Clipper applications.

One other useful tool, not a utility per se, is SHEZ. Since PKZIP and PK Data Compression work from command-line prompts, you can sometimes find it confusing to decide how to phrase the command for the operation you wish to carry out. SHEZ is a menu-and-mouse interface between the user and the PK utilities that enable you always (within reason) to get the results you expect. Modestly priced, it's a worthwhile investment for those less than comfortable with command lines.

Table 8-1 lists the vendors and current prices of the utility packages I've mentioned in this chapter.

**Table 8-1. Vendors of size-reducing software**

| UTILITY | PRICE | PURPOSE | VENDOR |
|---|---|---|---|
| PKLITE | $46.00 | Compress executable files | PKWARE, Inc.<br>9025 N. Deerwood Drive<br>Brown Deer, WI 53223<br>(414) 354-8699 |
| SQZ! | $99.00 | Spreadsheet compacting | Symantec Corp.<br>10201 Torre Avenue<br>Cupertino, CA 95014<br>(800) 441-7234 |
| PKZIP | $47.00 | Compress and archive files | PKWARE, Inc.<br>9025 N. Deerwood Drive<br>Brown Deer, WI 53223<br>(414) 354-8699 |
| PK Data Compression Library | $295.00 | Compress User created Applications in most languages | PKWARE, Inc.<br>9025 N. Deerwood Drive<br>Brown Deer, WI 53223<br>(414) 354-8699 |
| SHEZ | $39.00 | Menu and mouse interface for PK utilities | California Software<br>P.O. Box 15248<br>Santa Rosa, CA 95402<br>(707) 575-9868 |

## Zero-Size Files

In addition to temporary files created when an operation is initiated, and then unexpectedly terminated, zero-size files can also show up on a disk as the result of typing mistakes.

For example, intending to type "TYPE TEXT.TXT | MORE" but mistakenly typing "TYPE TEST.TXT > MORE" creates a file by the name of MORE. If TEST.TXT does not exist, then the file size is zero. DOS informs you that the file did not exist:

```
C:\>TYPE TEST.TXT > MORE
File not found - TEST.TXT

C:\>
```

But DOS never tells you that the empty file was created. Using the FIND command, in conjunction with a DIR listing, you can discover how many files exist on the drive. Listing 8-6 shows you how.

**Listing 8-6. FIND and DIR show you how many empty files are on the drive.**

```
C:\>DIR /S | FIND " 0 "
MORE        0 11-21-92   5:52p
MERE        0 11-21-92   5:52p
MOVE        0 11-21-92   5:52p
MIRE        0 11-21-92   5:52p
MRRE        0 11-21-92   5:52p
MOREE       0 11-21-92   5:52p
   4 file(s)             0 bytes
   3 file(s)             0 bytes
   4 file(s)             0 bytes
BBDGBJDN  0 11-21-92   5:54p
BBDGBJEC  0 11-21-92   5:54p
   4 file(s)             0 bytes
   6 file(s)             0 bytes
MORE COM  0 10-18-92   12:00a
7 file(s)                0 bytes
```

```
2 file(s)            0 bytes
2 file(s)            0 bytes
7 file(s)            0 bytes

C:\>
```

The listings similar to "2 file(s)" merely indicate subdirectories that contain no entries and can be ignored. The interest lies in the listings of filenames in which the contents are blank. You may think that I've created an oversimplified example with so many variations of the MORE command, but you'll be quite surprised how many different ways an entry can be misspelled on a server used by many workers.

While we're on the subject, suppose an individual enters the filename "TEXT.TXT" correctly, but uses the wrong redirect symbol. A file will still be created, but now it does have a size, and now it's wasting even more space.

It's a good idea to run a listing on a regular basis, looking for files with the names of commands that could theoretically follow redirect commands. These commands would include MORE, FIND, SORT, DIR, and TREE. A sure clue that they're not what they should be is if they don't contain .EXE or .COM as an extension. You can use any method we've previously discussed to locate them. Here's one example:

```
C:\>FF SORT*
FF-File Find, Advanced Edition 4.50, (C) Copr 1987-88,
Peter Norton

C:\DOS
SORT.EXE  6,938 bytes  6:00 am  Mon Oct 26 92

C:\
SORT               6,938 bytes  5:00 am  Tue Apr  9 91

C:\LANG\QB45\BAS
SORT              21,689 bytes 10:06 am  Thu Sep  8 88
```

```
C:\QA\TEXT
SORT              11,488 bytes  2:25 pm  Tue Oct 20 87

4 files found

C:\>
```

One file is as it should be; the other three can, and should, be deleted.

**Listing 8-7. Here's a bonus listing showing four additional ways to use the WASTED utility.**

1. To check one file:

```
Preliminary work in progress. . .
Specify files: example *.BAT  PS.*, *.* , etc. ?
  CONFIG.SYS
Search subdirectories [n/y]: N

There are  1  files which occupy      2,048 bytes
of 33,462,272 total available in sectors of 2,048
The total occupied yet unavailable bytes =      1,914
93.46% of allocated space is vacant.
```

2. To check all SYS files in a subdirectory:

```
Preliminary work in progress. . .
Specify files: example *.BAT  PS.*, *.* , etc. ? *.SYS
Search subdirectories [n/y]: N

There are  5  files which occupy    151,552 bytes
of 33,462,272 total available in sectors of 2,048
The total occupied yet unavailable bytes =      4,242
2.80% of allocated space is vacant.
```

3. To check all SYS files on the drive:

```
Preliminary work in progress. . .
Specify files: example *.BAT  PS.*, *.* , etc. ? *.SYS
Search subdirectories [n/y]: Y

There are  26  files which occupy    421,888 bytes
of 33,462,272 total available in sectors of 2,048
The total occupied yet unavailable bytes =     27,800
6.59% of allocated space is vacant.
```

4. To check the entire drive:

```
Preliminary work in progress. . .
Specify files: example *.BAT  PS.*, *.* , etc. ? *.*
Search subdirectories [n/y]: Y

There are  995  files which occupy 29,331,456 bytes
of 33,462,272 total available in sectors of 2,048
The total occupied yet unavailable bytes = 1,104,523
3.77% of allocated space is vacant.
```

## Wrap-Up

The more streamlined a computer is—that is, the fewer steps it must take during processing and the more readily it can access needed data—the faster a user can perform operations. By optimizing the server and the workstations, you can make your network work at maximum ability and speed.

This chapter and the preceding two discussed methods of optimizing workstations and servers. Consider the following questions pertaining to all three chapters. Appendix A at the end of this book contains answers and solutions.

### Questions about optimizing servers and workstations

1. Temporary files are created as a part of the computing process; occasionally, they remain after their usefulness has passed. This chapter discussed methods of deleting these

files from the server and from the workstations. Can their removal be automated? How so, and how often?

2. The CONFIG.SYS file is crucial to optimizing workstation operations. Workstations are often so spread out that it isn't time effective or possible to physically touch them. Can you remotely check, change, and optimize the CONFIG.SYS?

3. MS-DOS 6.0 includes a command that can go into CONFIG.SYS that will change the state of the NUMLOCK key on startup. How can you do this with an operating system other than MS-DOS 6.0?

4. The WASTED utility works only with MS-DOS versions 5.0 and higher. One key reason it can't work with earlier versions is that it obtains the allocation unit size of the drive from CHKDSK, output which is different in later versions of MS-DOS than earlier ones (or in DR DOS). Another reason is that when subdirectories are included in the search, the "/S" option is used—an option that doesn't exist in other versions. Is it possible to determine allocation unit size from other versions? Is it possible to modify WASTED for use with another operating system?

5. To what extent is it possible to use file compression (PKLITE, or PKZIP, for example) and disk compression (SuperStor, DBLSPACE) on the same workstation? Are there any savings associated with doing so, or does one effectively do the job of the other? Are there drawbacks to running two types of compression at the same time? (Think in terms of decompression occurring twice.)

9 CHAPTER

# Building a Utility Toolbox

Utilities are to a supervisor what tools are to an auto mechanic. The best mechanics have, sitting around in their garages, three or four toolboxes containing contraptions far more complex than mere screwdrivers and hammers. These boxes hold specialized gear pullers, micrometers, and gauges that enable them to do a job in a fraction of the time it would otherwise take.

Supervisors use utility programs in the same way: to enable them to complete a task more quickly than they could otherwise, or to accomplish an objective that would otherwise be impossible. Some of the more commonly cited utility packages include Norton Utilities and PC Tools. This software enables users to restore deleted files, recompress fragmented sectors, and so forth. While serving very useful purposes, however, they have the disadvantage of costing money.

Of the utilities that follow, all have one very important factor in common: they're free. The first six are shareware from a bulletin board available to anyone who has a modem and can dial into a bulletin board service.

Some of these shareware utilities are just plain free, while others are offered on a trial basis; if you like and plan to use the program, then you are asked to send in a registration fee. The last four programs in this chapter are quick files aimed at automating several steps.

None of these utilities perform anything as spectacular as restoring deleted files or even defragmenting sectors, yet their functions are extremely useful.

### How to Get Free Utilities

Bulletin Board Services (BBSes) are plentiful across the United States; you can find them in almost every large city. The files they carry and the charges they assess for membership and downloading vary tremendously. One utility may be located on hundreds of bulletin boards, while another may be located on only one. Several published directories are available that list bulletin boards and membership fees; I suggest checking with your local library.

In addition to the BBSes that charge a membership fee, others operate free of charge and specialize in certain categories of computing. Many of these free BBSes are managed by publishing houses offering software as an enticement to magazine subscribers. For example, the major networking magazines offer free access to bulletin boards carrying—what else?—NetWare-specific utilities. Browsing through their periodicals, you will find advertisements for these BBSes, giving telephone numbers and dial-in protocols.

To simplify matters as much as possible, all utilities listed here can be found, along with hundreds of others, on one BBS: M&T Online.

M&T Online is a service of M&T Publishing, the organization that publishes a strong line of computer books, including this one, and the monthly magazines *Stacks: The Network Journal* and *LAN Magazine*. The BBS operates free of charge. You can communicate with this BBS using a 1200- or 2400-baud modem at 8 data bits, 1 stop bit, and no parity. You can reach it at (415) 358-8857.

All files listed contain the extension .ZIP. This extension indicates that the download consists of more than one file, all of which have been archived together to decrease modem time (saving you long-distance phone charges). To unzip the files, you'll need a copy of PKUNZIP, which you can also download from the same source.

Hundreds, if not thousands, of shareware utilities for NetWare are floating about. To list and do justice to all of them would require a volume far thicker than this book. The following list of shareware utilities is only a representative sample of those available, and reflective of my favorites.

### A bindery-related utility

ALLUSE.ZIP, from a NetWare user named Jeff Chumbley, displays a list of all users who have access to the file server, their full names, and their last login date and time. This information comes directly from the NetWare bindery.

Located in the SYS:SYSTEM directory are two or three hidden files, depending on your version of NetWare, that constitute the NetWare bindery: NET$BIND.SYS and NET$BVAL.SYS for NetWare 2.x and NET$VAL.SYS, NET$PROP.SYS, and NET$OBJ.SYS for NetWare 3.x. Together, these files build a database of users, user groups, security information, accounting charges, and file servers. ALLUSE reads from this database to gather the information it reports. This utility gathers information you can conveniently use for estimating user utilization. If user Jerry hasn't logged in for over six months, for example, maybe it's time to reallocate his workstation.

### A communication utility

NETCHAT.ZIP, from Automated Digital Offices Corporation, requires a $25 registration fee (for which you receive a memory-resident version). This program allows you to establish a link between two workstations and send messages back and forth in a split-screen format. You type messages in one screen while the responses from the other user appear in the other screen each time that user presses the <Enter> key.

Use the NetWare SEND command to signal the other person that you would like to talk. If that person then begins the program, your messages to each other enter real-time mode. Best of all, a transcript of the conversation is created under the name SYS:PUBLIC\CHAT. You can access and print this document for documentation purposes, using any ASCII-translating word-processing program.

### Monitoring utilities

METERON.ZIP, from Jim Zboncak, also requires a $25 registration fee for which you receive the complete version; the downloaded file is a restricted-usage test version. The purpose of the program is to monitor application usage. Set the number of users allowed to simultaneously access a program; if more than that number try to get into the program, an error is written in SYS:SYSTEM\NET$LOG.MSG. This error log provides a practical means of determining whether you should spend good money purchasing another network pack of a particular program to allow more simultaneous users, or if the money would be best allocated elsewhere.

LANTRAF.ZIP, whose author is uncredited, collects statistics on each workstation in the form of a TSR program to determine the station's load and efficiency. METERON determines application usage; LANTRAF does a similar job for workstations.

Specify a number of days' worth of information you wish to accumulate and, at the end of that time, you'll find the results written in SYS:LANTRAF. Also zipped with the download is a stand-alone program that enables you either to export the statistics to Lotus for intermingling or to archive the logs to conserve disk space.

### General utilities

FILESCAN.ZIP, from Tim Schwab, is a small executable utility that quickly returns a list of who is on the system and what files they presently have open. Without this program, you can obtain the user list with the NetWare USERLIST command, but the only way to see what files are open is to read them from the console. FILESCAN.ZIP runs from any workstation logged in to the server. It's a tremendous time-saver if you're experiencing application conflicts, if you have to run backups and need everyone off the server, or if you find yourself in a similar situation.

NETLIGHT.ZIP, by Andy Stevens, is a TSR program that pretends the network drive is another physical drive on the workstation. When information is sent to the server or received from it, a square block blinks in the upper-right corner of the screen as if the drive were reading and writing the same way it would were it a floppy in the A: drive. While serving as a clever novelty, this utility doubles as a convenient diagnostic tool for verifying information flow between a workstation and server.

### A convenient batch file

QUICK.BAT, shown in Listing 9-1, consists of a DOS batch file that provides numerous useful functions. While each function could be broken into a separate batch file, they're grouped together for reasons I've explained in preceding chapters, such as reducing the number of sectors occupied.

**Listing 9-1. A batch file called QUICK.BAT performs several functions.**

```
:QUICK.BAT
@ECHO OFF
IF "%1"=="" GOTO NOPARM
GOTO %1
:NOPARM
ECHO Valid options are: WHO ENV ADDP LPSTAT MESG MATH
GOTO END
:WHO
IF "%2"=="-A" GOTO WHOAM
IF "%2"=="-a" GOTO WHOAM
IF "%2"=="-Q" GOTO CNT
IF "%2"=="-q" GOTO CNT
USERLIST | FIND ":"
GOTO END
:WHOAM
WHOAMI /ALL
GOTO END
:CNT
USERLIST | FIND /C ":"
GOTO END
:ENV
IF NOT "%2"=="" GOTO SEEK
```

```
SET
MAP | FIND "Drive"
C:\NET\IPX I
C:\NET\NET3 I
GOTO END
:SEEK
ECHO %PATH% | FIND /C "%2" > TEMP.BAT
ECHO ECHO %2 is NOT in the search path > 0.BAT
ECHO ECHO %2 IS in the search path > 1.BAT
CALL TEMP.BAT
GOTO END
:ADDP
SET PATH=%PATH%;%2
IF "%3"=="" GOTO END
SHIFT
GOTO ADDP
:LPSTAT
CAPTURE SH | FIND /C "data" > TEMP.BAT
ECHO ECHO CAPTURE is NOT currently active > 0.BAT
ECHO ECHO CAPTURE IS currently active > 1.BAT
ECHO PSTAT >> 1.BAT
CALL TEMP.BAT
GOTO END
:MESG
IF "%2"=="" GOTO NOTWO
IF "%2"=="Y" CASTON
IF "%2"=="N" CASTOFF /ALL
GOTO END
:NOTWO
ECHO Usage: Quick Mesg [YN]
GOTO END
:MATH
ECHO 10 PRINT %2 %3 %4 %5 %6 %7 %8 %9 : SYSTEM >
  QCK.BAS
GWBASIC QCK.BAS
```

```
:END
FOR %%F IN (QCK.BAS TEMP.BAT 0.BAT 1.BAT) DO IF EXIST
  %%F DEL %%F
```

With this batch file, you can obtain useful environment information, modify your path statement to include additional parameters, see who or how many people are on the server, check the status of the printer, toggle message reception on and off, and perform calculations from the command line. Table 9-1 shows you parameters that you can specify.

**Table 9-1. QUICK parameters**

| PARAMETER | MEANING |
|---|---|
| QUICK WHO | Lists all users currently on the system by name and time of last login. |
| QUICK WHO -Q | Returns a count of the number of users on the system. It's more useful than the previous command if you're only interested in whether or not it's safe to do a backup; in this case you don't care who's on the network, just whether or not anyone is. Likewise, if there are 70 people on the server, you don't need to view the entire listing just to get a utilization count. |
| QUICK WHO -A | Delivers a complete list of who you are and what directory rights and security equivalences you have, as well as groups belonged to. This information is available from the command line via the NetWare WHOAMI command, but I list the parameter here to round out the WHO commands. |
| QUICK ENV | Offers a look at the environment in which the workstation is working. The information presented shows the local DOS variables, the NetWare MAP assignments, and the current versions of the local IPX and NET programs. |
| QUICK ENV C:\WP51 | Returns a yes-or-no statement telling whether the subdirectory "C:\WP51" is currently in the search path or not. If it is, executable files contained there may be run from other subdirectories; if it isn't, the executables may be run only if the full path to their address is given. |

**Table 9-1.** *(Continued)*

| PARAMETER | MEANING |
|---|---|
| QUICK ADDP C:\WP51 | Adds "C:\WP51" to the search path while retaining all that was previously there. This serves as a complement to the ENV parameter, allowing you to add a path if it wasn't found previously. |
| QUICK ADDP C:\WP51 D:\QA\KAREN D:\QA\DONNA | Adds all three directories to the search path. You may specify up to a maximum of eight at the command line, so long as they're separated by spaces. (The number of spaces between each entry is inconsequential). |
| QUICK LPSTAT | Tells the present status of the printer: If CAPTURE is currently active for the workstation, and if it is active, it tells what the current printer status is. If it isn't active, a one-line message reports that fact. |
| QUICK MESG N | Turns off message reception at the workstation. When a message is sent to the workstation, the workstation ceases processing, displays the message, and asks that you press <Ctrl>-<Enter> to clear it and restart processing. If you've ever started a long compilation just before you left for lunch, only to come back an hour later and find that someone sent you a "Don't forget softball tomorrow" message, you'll appreciate the ability to turn reception off and not interrupt any processes. |
| QUICK MESG Y | Turns message reception back on and allows the pests to descend upon you once more. The MESG parameter is using CASTON and CASTOFF, but simplifying their operation with the inclusion in the batch file. |
| QUICK MATH 7 * 1.49 | Clears the screen and returns the answer "10.43." This command makes it easy to perform immediate calculations from a command-line prompt, eliminating the need to start an application program such as Lotus or Quattro Pro just to quickly estimate utilization or perform a similar calculation. |

**Table 9-1.** *(Continued)*

| PARAMETER | MEANING | |
|---|---|---|
| QUICK MATH (7^2)–25 | Raises 7 to the second power and subtracts 25 from the result, giving an answer of 24. Just as in algebra, the brackets require the program to perform the enclosed part of the calculation first. | |
| QUICK MATH 7*1.49–3 | Gives the answer "7.43." Notice that you don't need to leave spaces between the mathematical elements: "7*1.49" will work as well as "7 * 1.49." | |
| | The mathematical symbols you may use include: | |
| | + | Addition |
| | – | Subtraction |
| | * | Multiplication |
| | / | Division |
| | \ | Division returning only the whole number - rounding |
| | () | Perform this operation first |
| | ^ | Exponential multiplication (^.5 returns the square root) |
| | MOD | Uses modulus math and returns the whole number remaining after a division (in this case, a symbol, just like the parentheses and the +). For example, QUICK MATH 22 MOD 7 gives the answer 1—the whole number left after the division of 22 by 7. |

### A few words about the batch file

QUICK.BAT was written to gather many local parameters. You may need to alter a few lines, however, and tailor them to run on your workstation, depending on your setup. The following are a few points you may need to consider concerning QUICK.BAT.

1. The math functions use the DOS BASIC program. If the DOS directory is in your search path, as it should be, all will work fine. If DOS isn't in your search path, you need to change the line "GWBASIC QCK.BAS" so that it reflects a full path: "C:\DOS\GWBASIC QCK.BAS," for example.

   If you're running DOS 5.0, GWBASIC is no longer included; it's been replaced by QBASIC. Change the line to read:

   ```
   QBASIC /RUN QCK.BAS <Enter>
   ```

2. The ENVironment subroutine acquires IPX and NET information by accessing each program; therefore, you must set the path to where the files are located on your workstation. If the files are on the D: drive in the directory NETWARE, for example, then the two lines would read:

   ```
   D:\NETWARE\IPX I
   D:\NETWARE\NETn I
   ```

   Furthermore, the name of the NET program depends on the DOS version you're running. NET3 is for DOS versions 3.x, NET5 is for DOS 5.x, and so forth. This must be set to your workstation software level to work. If you have any uncertainty, look in the AUTOEXEC.BAT or other batch file that logs the workstation in to the server and see how NETx is called.

3. At times, parameters are specified twice, in both upper- and lowercase. (For example: "IF %2==-A GOTO WHOAM" and "IF %2==-a GOTO WHOAM".) This double specification allows your command to work whether you specify "QUICK WHO -A" or "quick who -a."

### First line listing

Listing 9-2 shows the listing for the routine HEAD. Following the UNIX language utility, HEAD allows you to look at the first lines of an ASCII file, thus providing a quick reference to the contents of the file without having to TYPE the entire file to the screen.

**Listing 9-2. The routine HEAD references ASCII files.**

```
100 REM HEAD - FIRST LINE LISTING ROUTINE
DEFINT A-Z: CLS
200 IF LEN(COMMAND$) = 0 THEN PRINT "You must specify a
  file name": GOTO 1700
IF INSTR(EAD$, "*") > 0 THEN PRINT "Wildcards are not
  permitted": GOTO 1700
IF INSTR(EAD$, "?") > 0 THEN PRINT "Wildcards are not
  permitted": GOTO 1700
300 EAD$ = LTRIM$(COMMAND$) + " |"
400 IF LEFT$(EAD$, 1) <> "-" THEN GOTO 1400
500 LE = LEN(EAD$): IF LE = 4 THEN PRINT "You must
  specify a file name": GOTO 1700
IF MID$(EAD$, 2, 1) = " " THEN PRINT "You must specify
  a number": GOTO 1700
IF MID$(EAD$, 3, 1) = " " THEN DU = VAL(MID$(EAD$, 2,
  1)): EAD$ = RIGHT$(EAD$, LE - 3): GOTO 1500
IF MID$(EAD$, 4, 1) = " " THEN DU = VAL(MID$(EAD$, 2,
  2)): EAD$ = RIGHT$(EAD$, LE - 4): GOTO 1500
PRINT "Number cannot be greater than 99": GOTO 1700
1400 DU = 10: REM NO NUMBER SPECIFIED THUS USING
  DEFAULT
1500 LE = LEN(EAD$): IF LE <= 1 THEN GOTO 1700
EAD = INSTR(EAD$, " "): IF EAD < 1 THEN GOTO 1700
LED$ = LEFT$(EAD$, EAD): OPEN "I", #1, LED$: PRINT
  "*******";     LED$; "*******": FOR I = 1 TO DU
LINE INPUT #1, EA$: PRINT EA$
IF EOF(1) THEN GOTO 1600
NEXT I
```

```
1600 CLOSE #1
EAD$ = RIGHT$(EAD$, LEN(EAD$) - EAD): GOTO 1500
1700 REM THE END
```

I've including line numbering in this particular listing for purposes of explanation.

Line 200 begins a quick check for incompatibility of the parameters specified after HEAD. Since the routine prints the first lines of specified files, you must specify a filename or filenames that can't contain wildcard characters (* or ?).

Line 300 trims the parameters down and adds a space and pipe (|) symbol to the end of the request. This pipe symbol simplifies finding portions of requests.

Line 400 checks to see if a number has been requested after HEAD and before a filename (HEAD -3 JUNK.ASC). If no number has been specified, then routine 500 is skipped.

Routine 500 checks first to see if only a number was specified and no filename (HEAD -3). If that isn't the case, the number is ascertained to be one or two digits. Anything greater than the highest two-digit number (99) generates an error.

Line 1400 sets the number of lines shown to 10 if no other number has been specified.

Routine 1500 opens the first file and prints the number of specified lines from it, providing there are that many lines to the file.

Routine 1600 checks to see if more than one filename has been specified, and if so, recalls routine 1500 to do the same thing on the next file.

Routine 1700 simply exits the program.

**Listing 9-3. A sample of operations**

```
C:\>HEAD BATCH.BAT
*******BATCH.BAT *******
:BATCH.BAT
@ECHO OFF
CLS
IF "%1"=="" GOTO NOPARM
GOTO %1
:Q
CD\QA3
WF
QA
CD\

C:\>HEAD -3 BATCH.BAT

*******BATCH.BAT *******
:BATCH.BAT
@ECHO OFF
CLS

C:\>HEAD -23 BATCH.BAT

:BATCH.BAT
@ECHO OFF
CLS
IF "%1"=="" GOTO NOPARM
GOTO %1
:Q
CD\QA3
WF
QA
CD\
GOTO EXIT
:FINDER
```

```
SHIFT
CHKDSK /V | FIND "%1"
GOTO EXIT
:FINDERR
FOR %%X IN (0 1 2 ) DO IF ERRORLEVEL %%X00 SET ERR=%%X
FOR %%X IN (0 1 2 3 4 5 6 7 8 9) DO IF ERRORLEVEL
  %ERR%%%X0 SET ERR=%ERR%%%X
FOR %%X IN (0 1 2 3 4 5 6 7 8 9) DO IF ERRORLEVEL
  %ERR%%%X SET ERR=%ERR%%%X
ECHO Existing errorlevel = %ERR%
GOTO EXIT
:NOPARM
ECHO Usage BATCH {Q FINDER FINDERR}

(23 lines constitute one screen)
C:\>HEAD -5 BATCH.BAT AUTOEXEC.BAT Q.BAT

*******BATCH.BAT *******
:BATCH.BAT
@ECHO OFF
CLS
IF "%1"=="" GOTO NOPARM
GOTO %1
*******AUTOEXEC.BAT *******
@ECHO OFF
PATH C:\DOS;C:\;C:\DV
C:\MOUSE1\MOUSE
PROMPT=$P$G
:NUMLOCK
*******Q.BAT *******
@echo off
cd\qa\qa3
wf
qa
cd\

C:\>
```

### ASCII file permutation

It's often necessary to make changes to a batch file that you could make a great deal more quickly from a command line than from within a word processor—if those changes can be made from within the word processor at all.

For example, if a batch file isn't working properly due to a subdirectory path having changed, you have to load EDLIN, or WordPerfect, or whatever method you prefer for editing batch files, make the change, and then save it.

If you want to change the text of the batch file from lowercase to uppercase, there's no easy way to do it without typing the entire text over—usually on top of what already exists. No easy way, that is, unless you have access to the ASC routine.

Listing 9-4 shows the ASC routine. ASC works on ASCII files, allowing you to change the structure of a file in six different ways:

- UPPERCASE ALL LINES
- lowercase all lines
- Uppercase Every First Character
- uppercase just one WORD
- LOWERCASE JUST ONE word
- Substitute a word or phrase

**Listing 9-4. The ASC routine lets you make easy changes to batch files.**

```
ON ERROR GOTO 100
EAD$ = UCASE$(COMMAND$): IF LEN(EAD$) < 3 THEN GOTO 1
EAD$ = EAD$ + " ": F$ = LTRIM$(LEFT$(EAD$, INSTR(EAD$,
  " "))): GOTO 2
1 INPUT "Filename "; F$
IF F$ = "Q" OR F$ = "q" THEN END
IF F$ = " " THEN GOTO 1
2 SHELL "echo ZZ > TEMP.$$$"
KILL "TEMP.$$$"
NAME F$ AS "TEMP.$$$"
OPEN "TEMP.$$$" FOR INPUT AS #1
```

```
OPEN F$ FOR OUTPUT AS #2
PRINT : PRINT "1. UPPERCASE ALL LINES"
PRINT "2. lowercase all lines"
PRINT "3. Uppercase Every First Character"
PRINT "4. uppercase just one WORD"
PRINT "5. LOWERCASE JUST ONE word"
PRINT "6. Substitute a word or phrase"
PRINT "7. Quit": PRINT
INPUT "Choice (1 - 6) "; a
ON a GOTO 10, 20, 30, 40, 50, 60, 70
10 LINE INPUT #1, org$
l = LEN(org$)
FOR i = 1 TO l
z = ASC(MID$(org$, i, 1))
IF z > 96 AND z < 123 THEN org$ = LEFT$(org$, i - 1) +
CHR$(z - 32) + RIGHT$(org$, LEN(org$) - i)
NEXT i
PRINT #2, org$
IF EOF(1) THEN CLOSE : GOTO 70
GOTO 10
20 LINE INPUT #1, org$
l = LEN(org$)
FOR i = 1 TO l
z = ASC(MID$(org$, i, 1))
IF z > 64 AND z < 91 THEN org$ = LEFT$(org$, i - 1) +
CHR$(z + 32) + RIGHT$(org$, LEN(org$) - i)
NEXT i
PRINT #2, org$
IF EOF(1) THEN CLOSE : GOTO 70
GOTO 20
30 LINE INPUT #1, org$
l = LEN(org$)
FOR i = 1 TO l
z = ASC(MID$(org$, i, 1))
IF i = 1 THEN GOSUB 35
```

```
IF i > 1 THEN GOSUB 36
NEXT i
PRINT #2, org$
IF EOF(1) THEN CLOSE : GOTO 70
GOTO 30
35 IF z > 96 AND z < 123 THEN org$ = LEFT$(org$, i - 1)
  + CHR$(z - 32) + RIGHT$(org$, LEN(org$) - i)
RETURN
36 IF ASC(MID$(org$, i - 1, 1)) = 32 AND z > 96 AND z <
  123 THEN org$ = LEFT$(org$, i - 1) + CHR$(z - 32) +
  RIGHT$(org$, LEN(org$) - i)
RETURN
40 INPUT "And the word is "; old$
41 LINE INPUT #1, org$
42 IF INSTR(org$, old$) > 0 THEN GOSUB 45: GOTO 42
PRINT #2, org$
IF EOF(1) THEN CLOSE : GOTO 70
GOTO 41
45 org$ = LEFT$(org$, INSTR(org$, old$) - 1) +
  UCASE$(old$) + RIGHT$(org$, LEN(org$) - INSTR(org$,
  old$) - LEN(old$) + 1)
RETURN
50 INPUT "And the word is "; old$
51 LINE INPUT #1, org$
52 IF INSTR(org$, old$) > 0 THEN GOSUB 55: GOTO 52
PRINT #2, org$
IF EOF(1) THEN CLOSE : GOTO 70
GOTO 51
55 org$ = LEFT$(org$, INSTR(org$, old$) - 1) +
  LCASE$(old$) + RIGHT$(org$, LEN(org$) - INSTR(org$,
    old$) - LEN(old$) + 1)
RETURN
60 INPUT "And the old word/phrase is "; old$
INPUT "The new word/phrase "; new$
61 LINE INPUT #1, org$
```

```
62 IF INSTR(org$, old$) > 0 THEN GOSUB 65: GOTO 62
PRINT #2, org$
IF EOF(1) THEN CLOSE : GOTO 70
GOTO 61
65 org$ = LEFT$(org$, INSTR(org$, old$) - 1) + new$ +
  RIGHT$(org$, LEN(org$) - INSTR(org$, old$) -LEN
    (old$) + 1)
RETURN
70 IF a = 7 THEN CLOSE : KILL F$: NAME "TEMP.$$$" AS F$
IF INSTR(EAD$, "/T") > 0 THEN SHELL "TYPE " + F$
END
100 PRINT "*** INVALID FILE NAME ***": END
```

Looking at the listing, you'll see that the first line establishes a semi-error routine, while the next two lines check to see if the user specified a filename when calling ASC (ASC JUNK.ASC) or if the routine called itself (ASC). If a filename was specified, routine 1 is skipped.

Routine 1 asks for a filename and asks until it gets an entry or until you enter "Q" or "q" to quit.

Routine 2 copies the specified filename to TEMP.$$$ and empties the original file. It then asks which of the actions it should take on the file, having by now verified that it is a legitimate file. A GOTO statement sends processing to the subroutine associated with the choice made. A seventh choice is also on the menu and accepted, but not listed in the INPUT options.

Routine 10 checks the ASCII number of each character in the file to determine where it falls from "a" through "z" and if so, converts it to its uppercase equivalent by subtracting 32 from the ASCII number and then converting back to a character.

Routine 20 does the opposite, converting all "A" through "Z" characters to their lowercase equivalent by adding 32 to their ASCII value.

Routine 30 looks at the first letter of each line and at every letter following a space and uppercases it only.

Routine 40 looks for a match to a specified word and then changes it to uppercase, while routine 50 does the opposite by lowercasing just one word. If it finds a word already in that case, it overlooks that word, unlike the way the next routine works.

Routine 60 changes a specified word to another word. The word can be a whole word or a phrase contained within another word. Any match for the specified characters that are found is changed to the new value.

All of these routines are reading from TEMP.$$$ and dumping, line by line, back into the original filename. In this way, the specified file becomes the changed file, while TEMP.$$$ remains on the system as the contents of the original file. If you don't like the changes the utility has made, you may copy TEMP.$$$ back to the original file and return to where you were before processing.

Routine 70 must take into account that the contents of the original file were dumped to TEMP.$$$. If selection 7, "quit without processing," is chosen from the menu, TEMP.$$$ must be dumped back to the original file. The first line of routine 70 takes care of this task. The second line checks to see if "/T" (uppercase or lowercase) was specified as a parameter. If it was, the changed file is displayed on the screen. If it wasn't specified, the changes are not shown. The third line ends the program, while line 100, as I mentioned in the beginning, serves as the semi-error routine. Look at Listing 9-5 to see some ways to use the ASC routine.

**Listing 9-5. Some usages of the ASC routine**

```
C:\>asc
Filename ? dkjfdk
*** INVALID FILE NAME ***
C:\>asc dkdkf
*** INVALID FILE NAME ***

C:\>TYPE AUTOEXEC.BAT
echo off
path c:\dos;c:\;c:\dv
c:\mouse1\mouse
prompt=$p$g
```

```
:numlock
set temp=c:\dos
doskey
cls
cd\dv
dv

C:\>ASC AUTOEXEC.BAT

1. UPPERCASE ALL LINES
2. lowercase all lines
3. Uppercase Every First Character
4. uppercase just one WORD
5. LOWERCASE JUST ONE word
6. Substitute a word or phrase
7. Quit

Choice (1 - 6) ? 3

C:\>TYPE AUTOEXEC.BAT
Echo Off
Path C:\dos;c:\;c:\dv
C:\mouse1\mouse
Prompt=$p$g
:numlock
Set Temp=c:\dos
Doskey
Cls
Cd\dv
Dv

C:\>asc autoexec.bat /t

1. UPPERCASE ALL LINES
2. lowercase all lines
```

```
3. Uppercase Every First Character
4. uppercase just one WORD
5. LOWERCASE JUST ONE word
6. Substitute a word or phrase
7. Quit

Choice (1 - 6) ? 1
ECHO OFF
PATH C:\DOS;C:\;C:\DV
C:\MOUSE1\MOUSE
PROMPT=$P$G
:NUMLOCK
SET TEMP=C:\DOS
DOSKEY
CLS
CD\DV
DV

C:\>ASC AUTOEXEC.BAT /T

1. UPPERCASE ALL LINES
2. lowercase all lines
3. Uppercase Every First Character
4. uppercase just one WORD
5. LOWERCASE JUST ONE word
6. Substitute a word or phrase
7. Quit

Choice (1 - 6) ? 5
And the word is ? NUMLOCK
ECHO OFF
PATH C:\DOS;C:\;C:\DV
C:\MOUSE1\MOUSE
PROMPT=$P$G
:numlock
```

```
SET TEMP=C:\DOS
DOSKEY
CLS
CD\DV
DV

C:\>ASC AUTOEXEC.BAT /T

1. UPPERCASE ALL LINES
2. lowercase all lines
3. Uppercase Every First Character
4. uppercase just one WORD
5. LOWERCASE JUST ONE word
6. Substitute a word or phrase
7. Quit

Choice (1 - 6) ? 6
And the old word/phrase is ? :numl
The new word/phrase ? rem toggle numkey on and off with
numl
ECHO OFF
PATH C:\DOS;C:\;C:\DV
C:\MOUSE1\MOUSE
PROMPT=$P$G
rem toggle numkey on and off with numlock
SET TEMP=C:\DOS
DOSKEY
CLS
CD\DV
DV

C:\>
```

## File Removal

The DELETE command in DOS serves a useful function, but it's limited in that it deletes only specified files. If you want to delete all files in a directory except one, you must first delete all *.EXE, then *.COM, and then *.TXT, and so forth until the only file remaining is the one you wish to retain.

RM is a UNIX-inspired utility (as was HEAD) that allows you to delete files in a number of ways. Listing 9-6 displays the complete listing for the RM utility.

**Listing 9-6. RM (for DOS 3.3 and earlier)**

```
DEFINT A-Z
CLS
IF LEN(COMMAND$) = 0 THEN PRINT : PRINT "YOU MUST GIVE
  FURTHER SPECIFICATION": GOTO 1700
WRD$ = UCASE$(LTRIM$(COMMAND$)): WRD$ = WRD$ + " |"
IF LEFT$(WRD$, 2) = "-A" THEN GOTO 100
IF LEFT$(WRD$, 2) = "-X" THEN GOTO 200
IF LEFT$(WRD$, 2) = "-I" THEN GOTO 400
IF LEFT$(WRD$, 2) = "-R" THEN GOTO 700
IF LEFT$(WRD$, 2) = "-H" THEN GOTO 900
IF LEFT$(WRD$, 1) <> "-" THEN GOTO 1500
PRINT : PRINT "You must give further specification":
  GOTO 1700
END
100 SHELL "DEL *.*": GOTO 1700
200 LE = LEN(WRD$): IF LE = 4 THEN CLS : PRINT : PRINT
  "You must specify file parameters when using the X
    option": GOTO 1700
WRD$ = RIGHT$(WRD$, LE - 3)
210 LE = LEN(WRD$): EAD = 1: IF LE = 1 THEN GOTO 300
220 A$ = MID$(WRD$, EAD, 1): IF A$ = " " GOTO 240
230 IF EAD = LE OR EAD = 0 THEN GOTO 300
EAD = EAD + 1: GOTO 220
240 LED$ = LEFT$(WRD$, EAD): SHELL "ATTRIB +R " + LED$:
```

```
CLS : GE = LE - EAD: WRD$ = RIGHT$(WRD$, GE): GOTO 210
300 SHELL "DEL *.*"
SHELL "ATTRIB -R *.*": CLS : GOTO 1700
400 SHELL "ATTRIB +A *.*": LE = LEN(WRD$): IF LE = 4
  THEN SHELL
    "ATTRIB *.* | SORT > DOLITTLE.EAD": GOTO 500
WRD$ = RIGHT$(WRD$, LE - 3)
410 LE = LEN(WRD$): EAD = 1: IF LE = 1 THEN GOTO 500
420 A$ = MID$(WRD$, EAD, 1): IF A$ = " " GOTO 440
430 IF EAD = LE OR EAD = 0 THEN GOTO 500
EAD = EAD + 1: GOTO 420
440 LED$ = LEFT$(WRD$, EAD): SHELL "ATTRIB " + LED$ + "
>> DOLITTLE.EAD": CLS : GE = LE - EAD: WRD$ =
RIGHT$(WRD$, GE): GOTO 410
500 REM CLASS ACTION
520 OPEN "I", #1, "DOLITTLE.EAD": PRINT : PRINT
530 INPUT #1, KAREN$
KAREN$ = LTRIM$(KAREN$)
540 IF MID$(KAREN$, 6, 1) = "R" OR RIGHT$(KAREN$, 12) =
  "DOLITTLE.EAD" THEN GOTO 530
PNT = INSTR(KAREN$,":") - 1
560 DEL$ = MID$(KAREN$, PNT, (LEN(KAREN$) - (PNT - 1)))
PRINT DEL$; " ? "; : YES$ = UCASE$(INPUT$(1)): PRINT
YES$: IF YES$ = "Y" THEN KILL DEL$
IF EOF(1) THEN GOTO 570
GOTO 530
570 CLOSE #1: KILL "DOLITTLE.EAD": GOTO 1700
700 SHELL "DIR > DOLITTLE.EAD"
710 OPEN "I", #1, "DOLITTLE.EAD": PRINT : PRINT
720 INPUT #1, KAREN$
KAREN$ = LTRIM$(KAREN$)
730 IF LEFT$(KAREN$, 12) <> "Directory of" THEN GOTO
  720
CLOSE #1: SHELL "DEL *.*"
KAREN$ = RIGHT$(KAREN$, 9): EAD = 0
```

```
740 IF MID$(KAREN$, 9 - EAD, 1) = "\" THEN GOTO 750
EAD = EAD + 1: GOTO 740
750 DEL$ = RIGHT$(KAREN$, EAD): SHELL "CD ..": SHELL
  "RD " + DEL$: GOTO 1700
900 PRINT "RM WILL REMOVE ONE OR MORE FILES FROM YOUR
  DIRECTORY DEPENDING"
PRINT "UPON THE PARAMETER SPECIFICATIONS YOU PROVIDE.
  ALL DOS ENTRIES AND WILD CARDS"
PRINT "ARE ACCEPTED. PARAMETERS INCLUDE:"
PRINT "RM *.EXE *.COM     WILL DELETE ALL EXE AND COM
                          FILES FROM THE DIRECTORY"
PRINT "RM -A              WILL DELETE ALL FILES IN THE
                          DIRECTORY": PRINT
PRINT "RM -R              WILL DELETE ALL FILES AND
                          REMOVE
                          THE DIRECTORY": PRINT
PRINT "RM -I              WILL PROMPT FOR A Y BEFORE
                          DELETING THE FILE"
PRINT "                   ANYTHING BUT Y LEAVES THE
                          FILE     INTACT. IT MAY"
PRINT "                   ALSO BE USED ON A SELECTED
                          GROUP OF FILES. EXAMPLE:"
PRINT "                   RM -I *.EXE *.COM"
PRINT "                   WILL PROMPT FOR REMOVAL OF
                          ALL EXE AND COM FILES": PRINT
PRINT "RM -X              REMOVES ALL FILES BUT THOSE
                          SPECIFIED"
PRINT "                   EXAMPLE: RM -X *.EXE *.COM"
PRINT "                   WILL DELETE ALL BUT EXE AND
                          COM FILES"
PRINT
"*****************************************************
   ***********************    : GOTO 1700
1500 LE = LEN(WRD$): EAD = 1: IF LE = 1 THEN GOTO 1700
1510 A$ = MID$(WRD$, EAD, 1): IF A$ = " " GOTO 1600
```

```
1520 IF EAD = LE OR EAD = 0 THEN GOTO 1700
EAD = EAD + 1: GOTO 1510
1600 LED$ = LEFT$(WRD$, EAD): KILL LED$: GE = LE - EAD:
  WRD$ = RIGHT$(WRD$, GE): GOTO 1500
1700 REM  THIS IS THE END, MY FRIEND
```

Now here are some ways you can use RM. When you invoke the RM utility, the screen is cleared. The initial command given doesn't appear on the screen, but for purposes of clarification, I'm presenting the command and its results together in the following example, shown in Listing 9-7.

**Listing 9-7. The RM utility and its results**

```
C:\TMP>RM -H

RM WILL REMOVE ONE OR MORE FILES FROM YOUR DIRECTORY
DEPENDING UPON THE PARAMETER SPECIFICATIONS YOU
PROVIDE. ALL DOS ENTRIES AND WILD CARDS ARE ACCEPTED.
PARAMETERS INCLUDE:
RM *.EXE *.COM    WILL DELETE ALL EXE AND COM FILES FROM
                  THE DIRECTORY
RM -A             WILL DELETE ALL FILES IN THE DIRECTORY
RM -R             WILL DELETE ALL FILES AND REMOVE THE
                  DIRECTORY
RM -I             WILL PROMPT FOR A Y BEFORE DELETING
                  THE FILE ANYTHING BUT Y LEAVES THE
                  FILE INTACT. IT MAY ALSO BE USED ON A
                  SELECTED GROUP OF FILES.
                    EXAMPLE: RM -I *.EXE *.COM
                  WILL PROMPT FOR REMOVAL OF ALL EXE AND
                  COM FILES
RM -X             REMOVES ALL FILES BUT THOSE SPECIFIED
                    EXAMPLE: RM -X *.EXE *.COM
                  WILL DELETE ALL BUT EXE AND COM FILE
```

```
****************************************************

C:\TMP>DIR *.BAT

Volume in drive C is EXAMPLE
Directory of C:\TMP

Q         BAT       42 11-15-92   1:55p
FINDUR    BAT       18 11-12-92  10:33p
DIRECTOR BAT      219 08-17-91  11:36p
RUNCHA    BAT      73 04-19-89  11:55a
PATHBACK BAT       79 10-17-92  11:54p
BATCH     BAT     468 11-12-92  10:46p
FINDERR   BAT     257 10-24-92  9:00p
AUTOEXEC BAT      165 11-15-92  9:29p
8 file(s) 1321 bytes
93126656 bytes free

C:\TMP>DIR *.BAK

Volume in drive C is EXAMPLE
Directory of C:\TMP

FINDUR    BAK         14 11-12-92  10:33p
FINDER    BAK         29 08-17-91   7:24p
FRECOVER BAK      50688 05-16-92  10:46p
CONFIG    BAK        212 11-15-92   1:48p
AUTOEXEC BAK        162 11-15-92   1:44p
        5 file(s)       51105 bytes
                     93126656 bytes free

C:\TMP>RM -I *.BAT *.BAK
C:\TMP\Q.BAT ? Y
C:\TMP\FINDUR.BAT ? Y
C:\TMP\DIRECTOR.BAT ? N
```

```
C:\TMP\RUNCHA.BAT ? Y
C:\TMP\PATHBACK.BAT ? Y
C:\TMP\BATCH.BAT ? Y
C:\TMP\FINDERR.BAT ? Y
C:\TMP\AUTOEXEC.BAT ? Y
C:\TMP\FINDUR.BAK ? N
C:\TMP\FINDER.BAK ? Y
C:\TMP\FRECOVER.BAK ? Y
C:\TMP\CONFIG.BAK ? Y
C:\TMP\AUTOEXEC.BAK ? N

C:\TMP>DIR *.BA?

Volume in drive C is EXAMPLE
Directory of C:\TMP

FINDUR   BAK         14 11-12-92  10:33p
DIRECTOR BAT        219 08-17-91  11:36p
AUTOEXEC BAK        162 11-15-92   1:44p
        5 file(s)         395 bytes
                     93224960 bytes free

C:\TMP>DIR

Volume in drive C is EXAMPLE
Directory of C:\TMP

.            <DIR>        11-21-92   7:31p
..           <DIR>        11-21-92   7:31p
COMMAND  COM      53022 10-26-92   6:00a
JUNK     ASC      23824 11-03-92   7:45p
BEFSETUP MSD      13355 11-15-92   3:31a
TEST     T T         88 10-26-92  11:32p
FINDER   EAD         29 11-12-92  10:28p
MOVES    CHE        476 09-07-92   9:14p
```

```
FINDUR   BAK        14 11-12-92  10:33p
SPOOL    EAD        12 09-16-92  10:12p
AUTOEXEC CHA        57 08-03-90   7:12a
AUTOEXEC EAD       201 08-17-91   7:47p
CONFIG   CHA        86 11-10-90  11:03a
CONFIG   EAD        43 03-14-91   7:35p
HAMMER   TXT       105 07-14-92   2:11p
DIRECTOR BAT       219 08-17-91  11:36p
BANNER   EAD       788 05-03-92   6:17p
ESTIMATE EXE     31072 05-23-91  12:17a
EVENTLOG EXE     14185 08-03-90   6:46a
EXPLOSIV COM      5335 05-09-90   9:43p
NUMLOCK  BAS       192 03-14-91   8:56p
NUMLOCK  COM        11 03-14-91   8:56p
CAD      COM        17 10-26-92  11:38p
CHKLIST  MS        378 11-15-92   1:59p
QEMM386  SYS     63787 08-24-90   5:11a
REBOOT   COM        24 05-13-91   9:53p
RUNCHA   EAD       624 08-09-91  11:59p
SD       INI      2497 08-10-91  12:00a
TOM      DAT       957 03-13-88   4:00p
WINA20   386      9349 04-09-91   5:00a
IMAGE    DAT     50688 05-17-92  12:33a
WALK     BAS        26 06-24-92   4:57p
DSVXD    386      5741 10-26-92   6:00a
MOKE     COM        12 10-18-92  12:34a
CONFIG   D5        134 10-24-92  11:10p
TEST     TXT        88 10-26-92  11:32p
CONFIG   SYS       216 11-15-92   1:50p
AUTOEXEC BAK       162 11-15-92   1:44p
       38 file(s)      277814 bytes
                     93224960 bytes free

C:\TMP\RM -X *.BAS *.DAT CONFIG.SYS
```

```
All files in directory will be deleted!
Are you sure (Y/N)? Y

C:\TMP>DIR

Volume in drive C is EXAMPLE
Directory of C:\TMP

.            <DIR>        11-21-92   7:31p
..           <DIR>        11-21-92   7:31p
NUMLOCK  BAS         192  03-14-91   8:56p
TOM      DAT         957  03-13-88   4:00p
IMAGE    DAT       50688  05-17-92  12:33a
WALK     BAS          26  06-24-92   4:57p
CONFIG   SYS         216  11-15-92   1:50p
        7 file(s)       52079 bytes
                     93642752 bytes free

C:\TMP>RM -R
All files in directory will be deleted!
Are you sure (Y/N)? Y

C:\>DIR TM*

Volume in drive C is EXAMPLE
Directory of C:\

File not found

C:\>
```

## Wrap-Up

Close to 200 shareware utilities for networking are located on the M&T Online bulletin board. Describing every one of them would take more space than we have here. The few that I've presented in this chapter are my favorites, chosen for their versatility and appeal for troubleshooting.

For a complete listing of utilities available, or to find the utility you need to fulfill a specific purpose, dial in, look around, and start building your own personal toolbox.

The other routines I've presented in this chapter simplify and expound on operations necessary to all supervisors.

### Final question

The HEAD routine lists the first *n* lines of an ASCII file. This routine was inspired by a UNIX language utility that is useful in determining the contents of a file without viewing the entire file. UNIX has a LAST command that is the opposite, showing the last *n* lines of a file. How can you modify HEAD to serve this purpose?

10 CHAPTER

# NetWare Server Security

Easily the most important aspect of LAN performance is LAN security. In a time when business owners have to worry about viruses encroaching on their computer systems from corrupted floppy disks and downloaded software, about employees stealing sensitive information, and about data corruption for the sake of it, LAN security becomes a necessity.

This chapter covers security on the server. The next two chapters discuss security on workstations and combined security between server and workstation, respectively. We begin with passwords before anything else. Security is only as good as the weakest password.

After we discuss passwords, the topics will get more interesting. Read this and the next two chapters interactively—that is, sitting at your own workstation and validating. Only then will you understand the true importance of the concepts under discussion.

## Passwords

No other single item contributes as much to system security as passwords. Without access to the proper password, an intruder can't log in to a network as a valid user and cause trouble on a server or workstation. If your network uses bad or poorly chosen passwords, intruder access becomes much simpler.

Many misguided computer hackers delight in the challenge of breaking a password. Once they enter your computer system, they can do unlimited harm; some will do so, simply to let someone know they were able to do it. I can't overstress the importance of effective passwords.

Every user on your system should have a password, and it can't be the <Enter> key. It should be six to eight characters in length and contain a mix of numbers, symbols, and letters. When the password contains only numbers, the possible choices that an intruder must guess for each character are only ten (0-9). When you include the 26 letters of the alphabet, the number of guesses the intruder must make for each character is increased by 26 to 36. Including the possibility of ten symbols—**! # $ % & ' ( ) - @**—increases the number of possibilities for each character to 46. If an intruder must try 46 choices for each character and the password consists of eight characters, the number of possibilities an intruder must try is approximately 46 × 46 × 46 × 46 × 46 × 46 × 46 × 46, or 46 raised to the eighth power: 20,047,612,231,936.

Compare this to using only numbers for your eight password characters. In this case, the choices the intruder must try amount to ten raised to the eighth power, or 100,000,000. Using only three letters, it takes a maximum of 17,576 tries to crack the password. Now think how quickly a computer can spit out 17,576 entries. The BASIC routine you see in Listing 10-1 does just that—it runs through the possible 17,576 choices.

**Listing 10-1. A password-guessing routine in BASIC**

```
CLS
PRINT TIME$
FOR i = 65 TO 90
FOR j = 65 TO 90
FOR k = 65 TO 90
NEXT k
NEXT j
NEXT i
PRINT TIME$
```

The numeral 65 is the ASCII code for "A"; the numeral 90 is the ASCII code for "Z." Note that most password routines are *not* case-sensitive; if they were, it would double the number of alphabetic combinations and increase the amount of time it would take to crack a password.

How long did it take the computer to get through 17,576 combinations? Looking at the two times that were printed, we see:

```
01:29:52
01:31:18
```

One minute and 26 seconds were all that were required! And this was on a 386SX with applications running in other windows.

Clearly, the longer the password is and the more characters that are possible, the harder your password becomes to crack. Not every password must contain numbers, letters, and symbols, but the base from which choices are made must contain them to increase the number of possibilities.

NETCRACK, a shareware program found on many bulletins, is designed to show how easy it is to break into a NetWare system; in the process, it illustrates how password cracking is done. Used mostly for purposes of demonstration, NETCRACK takes a user's name provided to it, then guesses that user's password to be "A." If "A" isn't right, NETCRACK then guesses "B." After the alphabet is depleted, it guesses 0 through 9.

Not finding a match yet, NETCRACK next tries "AA" then "AB." When "A9" comes and it still hasn't been allowed in, it goes with "BA," followed by "BB," and so forth. NETCRACK uses repeated calls to the VERIFY_PASSWORD function to avoid the limitations inherent in grace logins that would otherwise cause its trial-and-error attempts to trigger an intruder alert and cause a login lockout. It can try repeatedly without being locked out because it isn't actually trying to log in, but only to verify that its attempt and the password entry are the same. When it finds a match, it tells you and you can log in, using the password it verified.

After NETCRACK tries "99" without being allowed in, it next tries "AAA," followed by "AAB," and so on. The more characters it must try the longer the search takes, but the program has nothing but time. NETCRACK keeps on trying until it finally finds the match and gets in, providing an excellent demonstration of the way password "cracking" is accomplished.

Most of the time, however, nothing this elaborate is necessary. Common sense, however, is. Many users naively pick as their password one of the following items:

- their names or maiden names
- their names spelled backwards
- the name of a loved one
- no password at all
- the <Enter> key
- the word "password"
- birth dates of themselves or their children
- social security numbers

How hard can it be for someone who works with an employee, or knows anything about him or her, to guess any of these passwords? While most supervisors don't knowingly let their users pick anything so obvious, many users change their passwords after initial password setup. Using common-sense principles has yet to injure a user, but a failure of common sense is hazardous to the security of the network.

Here are a few rules that apply to choosing a password.

- Don't use any of the choices I just listed.
- Don't use a straight English word or phrase. Many password-cracking routines begin by taking entries directly from a dictionary; this saves the time required to try combinations like "AAAA," "AAAB," and so on and allows them to gain quicker entry.
- Don't use fewer than six characters, no matter how clever the word may be.

- Don't use any names of friends, relatives, or anyone else.
- Don't use telephone or fax phone numbers.
- Don't use names of cartoon characters or pet names.
- Don't use alternate names for the computer, the work department, or even the building.
- Don't use keyboard sequences ("qwerty" is the most common).

The preceding established, how do you go about choosing a good password? Here are a few guidelines to help in that department.

- Use from six to eight characters.
- Use short words connected by numbers or symbols.
- Create "vanity license plates." (Be sure they're not actually on your car, but exist only in thought.)
- Change passwords on a regular basis, particularly if you suspect that someone may have attempted intrusion. Key passwords should always be changed when someone leaves the department. Network administrators can use NetWare to force users to change their passwords.
- Use the first letter of each word of a phrase: for example, "STGLACS" for "Salem Tastes Good Like A Cigarette Should" or WWTSP for "What Was That Stupid Password."
- Use a random password generator.

*Never* write a password down or assign it to a function key. How safe can it be if it can be located so easily? After changing a password, you might have trouble remembering it for the first few times you need it. If you must write it down, and *only* if you must, write it on a dollar bill and carry it with you. You're not likely to leave money lying carelessly about, so this is the safest way to make certain you don't leave your password lying carelessly about.

Speaking of password generators, Listing 10-2 shows you a listing for a very simple routine called CHOICES. CHOICES offers password "choices," or suggestions consisting of seven to eight characters strung together at random. The program is as follows:

**Listing 10-2. The CHOICES routine generates passwords.**

```
REM CHOICES - Random Password Generator
CLS : PRINT "Suggested choices:"
FOR Z = 1 TO 20
RANDOMIZE TIMER
A = INT(RND * 5) + 1
GOSUB 100: FIR = b
GOSUB 100: SEC = b
GOSUB 200: FIR$ = b$
RESTORE
GOSUB 200: SEC$ = b$
GOSUB 300
RESTORE: NEXT Z
END

100 b = INT(RND * 20) + 1
b = b + 33: IF b = 34 THEN b = 33
IF b > 43 THEN b = b + 4
IF b = 42 THEN b = 45
IF b = 43 THEN b = 64
RETURN

200 C = INT(RND * 433) + 1
FOR I = 1 TO C
READ b$
NEXT I
RETURN

300 IF A = 1 THEN PRINT FIR$; CHR$(FIR); CHR$(SEC);
  SEC$
IF A = 2 THEN PRINT FIR$; CHR$(SEC); SEC$
IF A = 3 THEN PRINT CHR$(FIR); FIR$; SEC$
```

```
IF A = 4 THEN PRINT CHR$(FIR); CHR$(SEC); FIR$; SEC$
IF A = 5 THEN PRINT FIR$; SEC$; CHR$(FIR)
RETURN

1000 REM Dictionary
1001 DATA ACE,ACK,ACT,ADO,AGE,AGO,AHA,AID,AIL,AIM
1002 DATA ALE,ALL,ALT,AND,ANT,ANY,ANZ,APE,APT,ARC
1003 DATA ARE,ARF,ARK,ARM,ARP,ART,ASH,ASK,ASL,ASP
1004 DATA ASS,ATE,AVE,AXE,BAD,BAG,BAK,BAM,BAN,BAR
1005 DATA BAT,BBQ,BED,BEE,BET,BIB,BID,BIG,BIN,BIT
1006 DATA BOA,BOG,BOO,BOX,BOY,BRA,BRO,BUD,BUM,BUN
1007 DATA BUS,BUT,BUY,BYE,BYT,CAB,CAD,CAM,CAN,CAP
1008 DATA CAR,CAT,CIA,COB,COD,COG,COM,CON,COP,COT
1009 DATA CUB,CUD,CUP,CUT,DAB,DAD,DAM,DAY,DEN,DEW
1010 DATA DID,DIE,DIG,DIM,DIN,DIP,DOC,DOG,DOT,DUD
1011 DATA DUM,EAR,EAT,EBB,ECO,EEK,EEL,EGA,EGG,EGO
1012 DATA ELF,ELK,ELM,EMO,EMU,EOF,EON,ERA,ERE,ETC
1013 DATA EWE,EXT,EYE,FAB,FAD,FAG,FAN,FAR,FAT,FAX
1014 DATA FBI,FDR,FEE,FEF,FIB,FIE,FIN,FIR,FIT,FIX
1015 DATA FOE,FOG,FOR,FOX,FUN,FUR,GAB,GAD,GAG,GAS
1016 DATA GAY,GEE,GEL,GEM,GET,GIG,GIN,GLO,GNU,GOB
1017 DATA GOD,GOT,GUM,GUN,GUT,HAD,HAG,HAH,HAM,HAS
1018 DATA HAT,HAY,HEE,HEM,HEN,HER,HEX,HEY,HIC,HID
1019 DATA HIM,HIP,HIS,HIT,HOB,HOE,HOG,HOP,HOT,HUB
1020 DATA HUE,HUG,HUH,HUM,HUN,HUP,HUT,IAM,IBM,ICE
1021 DATA ICK,ICY,ILK,ILL,INC,INN,INS,IRE,IRK,IVY
1022 DATA JAB,JAM,JAR,JAW,JET,JIG,JOB,JOG,JOT,JUT
1023 DATA KID,KIN,KIT,KUT,LAB,LAD,LAG,LAM,LAN,LAP
1024 DATA LAW,LAX,LAY,LED,LEG,LET,LIB,LID,LIE,LIP
1025 DATA LOB,LOG,LOT,LOW,LUG,MAG,MAN,MAP,MAR,MAT
1026 DATA MAY,MEG,MEM,MEN,MET,MID,MIN,MOB,MOD,MOM
1027 DATA MOO,MOP,MOW,MUD,MUG,MUL,MUM,NAP,NAW,NAY
1028 DATA NET,NIB,NIE,NIL,NIT,NOB,NOG,NOT,NUL,NUM
1029 DATA NUN,NUT,OAF,OAK,OAR,OAT,OBE,OBO,ODE,OFF
1030 DATA OHM,OIL,OKE,OLA,OLE,ONE,ONS,ONX,ORA,ORB
```

```
1031 DATA ORE,OUR,OUT,OWE,OWL,OXE,OYE,PAD,PAL,PAN
1032 DATA PAR,PAT,PAY,PEE,PEG,PEN,PEP,PER,PET,PLY
1033 DATA POD,POE,POP,POT,PRE,PRI,PRO,PUB,PUG,PUN
1034 DATA PUP,PUT,QUE,RAG,RAM,RAN,RAP,RAT,RAW,RBI
1035 DATA RED,REN,RIB,RID,RIG,RIM,RIP,ROB,ROM,ROT
1036 DATA RUB,RUE,RUG,RUM,RUN,RUT,SAD,SAN,SAT,SAX
1037 DATA SAY,SEE,SET,SEX,SIB,SIN,SIR,SIS,SIT,SOB
1038 DATA SOD,SOG,SON,SOS,SOW,SUB,SUM,SUN,SYS,TAB
1039 DATA TAC,TAD,TAG,TAN,TAP,TAR,TEA,TEE,TEN,TIC
1040 DATA TIE,TIN,TIP,TIT,TON,TOO,TOP,TOT,TOW,TOY
1041 DATA TUB,TYE,UCK,UGH,VAN,VAT,VIE,VOL,WAD,WAN
1042 DATA WAR,WAS,WEB,WED,WEE,WET,WIG,WIN,YAM,YAP
1043 DATA YEA,YES,YET,YOU,YUK,YUM,ZAG,ZAP,ZEN,ZIG
1044 DATA ZIP,ZIT,ZOO
```

The operation of the CHOICES routine is very straightforward; variable Z is used to generate twenty possible choices each time the routine is invoked. Variable A is a random number from one to five. This is later used in routine 300 to determine which of the five ways the password will be given:

- word_symbol_symbol_word
- word_symbol_word
- symbol_word_word
- symbol_symbol_word_word
- word_word_symbol

("Symbol" and "number" refer to the same character set in that they allow for 0 to 9 entries or punctuation.)

Routine 100 is called twice to gather two random symbols and/or numbers. If the random number is 10 or less, a symbol is generated; if it's 11 to 20, a number is generated.

Routine 200 is called twice to read the 433 three-letter words and pull out two of them. You can modify the routine by adding more words and changing the size of possible number combinations. The program does a RESTORE as each word is chosen and at the end of each password (Z) so that each word picked from the list may be before or after the one previously selected.

Since it's pulling the symbols and/or numbers and words at semi-random (true random would not include a database of words to choose from) and configuring them together, some of the choices it offers will be totally off-base (or off-color) and not suitable for use. It is for this reason that twenty choices are given in hopes that some will be suitable.

Routine 1000 begins the dictionary of words. The 433 words are very simple associations of three-letter words and computer-related phrases, as well as a few acronyms (FBI, CIA, and so on). Possible choices with this routine amount to 433 × 433 × 20 × 20, or 74,995,600 possible combinations. Other password routines are available; some are more complex than CHOICES, but all operate on the same principle.

Listing 10-3 shows some possible results. The highlighted choices are ones I deemed acceptable for use; the others are most likely too difficult to remember.

**Listing 10-3. Some passwords generated by the CHOICE routine**

```
FOGDOC%
FAB8FAX
SAD-FEE
65WETNET
6BAGRAW
BAR4AXE
IAMCOT1
MID55DAB
LOW3@PAR
TINHIP#
OWEHAT1
GOD—DID
OFUNOAK
1HOPSAN
CAPAND1
8ILLRAM
```

```
PEN77HUT
YOUMAY5
OIL!IRK
1TINCUB

C:\>
```

## Servers

Since all shared network information resides on the server, it's crucial for a network administrator to control who can and cannot get into the server and change the information that everyone else depends on. The following is a list of the NetWare commands related to security.

- ALLOW
- FLAG
- FLAGDIR
- GRANT
- LOGIN
- MAP
- PURGE
- REMOVE
- REVOKE
- RIGHTS
- SECURITY
- SETPASS
- TLIST

Chapter 1 of this book described each of these commands in detail. You should review them quickly if you're uncertain of their operation.

## The SYSCON Utility's Security Options

Think of the SYSCON menu as the key to a padlocked wealth of security parameters. In the following discussion we'll cover the basics, if for no other reason than to lay the groundwork for a secure system.

# 10 Netware Server Security

It serves no purpose to use shortcuts and utilities if a hole exists in the security at the lowest level. Only when the NetWare framework (one way you can think of SYSCON's options) is solid can you begin to be concerned with going beyond that and tightening security a bit more.

For most supervisors, this will be a reiteration of basic guidelines. If it isn't, then I strongly suggest you invest in a basic NetWare book. Only when you know the rules can you begin to broaden them.

Let's take this discussion away from the command line, into something you must attend to before any of the others come into play. I refer to the security-related options available on the SYSCON menu. Let's look at the SYSCON Available Topics menu screen, shown in Figure 10-1.

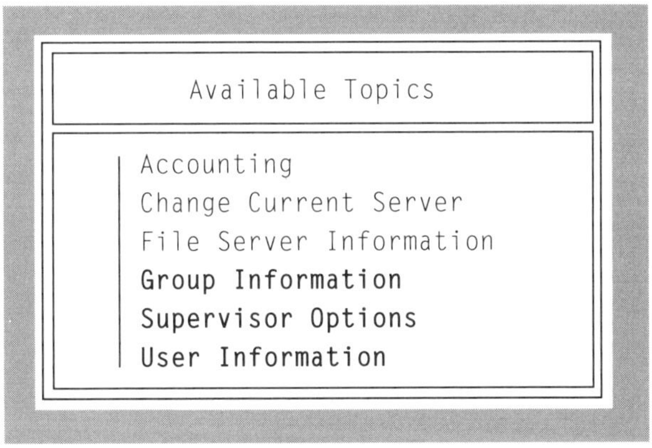


**Figure 10-1. The SYSCON menu's Available Topics menu screen**

The last three choices are of prime importance to this discussion. Group Information lists the groups that exist, gives you information about them, and lets you change the information (read that as "impose restrictions"). The Supervisor Options choice is self-explanatory. User Information lists all users on the file server, gives you information about them, and lets you change that information if you need to.

### The Group Information option

You need to know two key things about the Group Information option:

1. It's possible to assign users to groups.
2. It's possible to assign subdirectory rights to the group, thereby granting all members of the group those rights to that subdirectory.

Let's look at the group information available in SYSCON (see Figure 10-2).

```
Group Names          Trustee Directory Assignments

EVERYONE             SYS:APPL/GMK3 [RWOCDPSM]   [RWOCDPSM]
                     SYS:APPL/HELP              [RWOCDPSM]
                     SYS:APPL/PS                [RWOCDPSM]
                     SYS:APL/QA3                [RWOCDPSM]
                     SYS:APPL/QADATA            [RWOCDPSM]
                     SYS:APPL/UNIX              [RWOCDPSM]
                     SYS:APPL/WPDOC             [RWOCDPSM]
                     SYS:LOGIN                  [R O   S ]
                     SYS:MAIL                   [ W C    ]
                     SYS:PUBLIC                 [RWOC  S ]
```

**Figure 10-2. Trustee Directory Assignments in the EVERYONE group**

If Carol King belongs to the group EVERYONE, simply by virtue of belonging to that group, she has full permission to change anything, including modifying and deleting files in the subdirectories SYS:APPL/GMK3, SYS:APPL/HELP, SYS:APPL/PS, SYS:APPL/QA3, SYS:APPL/QADATA, SYS:APPL/UNIX, and in SYS:APPL/WPDOC. She has limited access to the other three subdirectories, all NetWare-specific.

Be thoughtful in choosing group assignments. Be certain that any user you assign to a group is qualified to have all rights belonging to that group. It's a common mistake to add a user to the system and think that his or her rights are limited, yet assign that user to a group that has permission to do far more than you intended to allow.

Another common practice is to assign a free-floating user, such as the GUEST name you see in the Group Members screen shown in Figure 10-3.

**Figure 10-3. The Group Members screen**

What permissions does this GUEST user have? The same as the group he or she is assigned to: in other words, the same as the other six users listed. And what is his or her password? Most of the time, a GUEST password is next-to-common knowledge. If I were attempting to break into a system, the first login I would try would be GUEST and begin working on the password, since it's undoubtedly the easiest of the lot.

How can you avoid this problem?

Don't have a GUEST user. If someone needs to use the server for a short period of time, add that person as a user, provide a password, and assign rights. Then you have established an audit trail. If KRISTIN has permission to SYS:APPL/UNIX and something goes awry there, it's much easier to point to Kristin than to the eighty people who used the default GUEST password during the last six months. Adding and deleting users on the fly isn't difficult; administrators who try to save time here have more time on their hands than they realize.

### The Supervisor Options option

Four of the items listed under Supervisor Options are significant to network security. I've highlighted those four items in Figure 10-4.

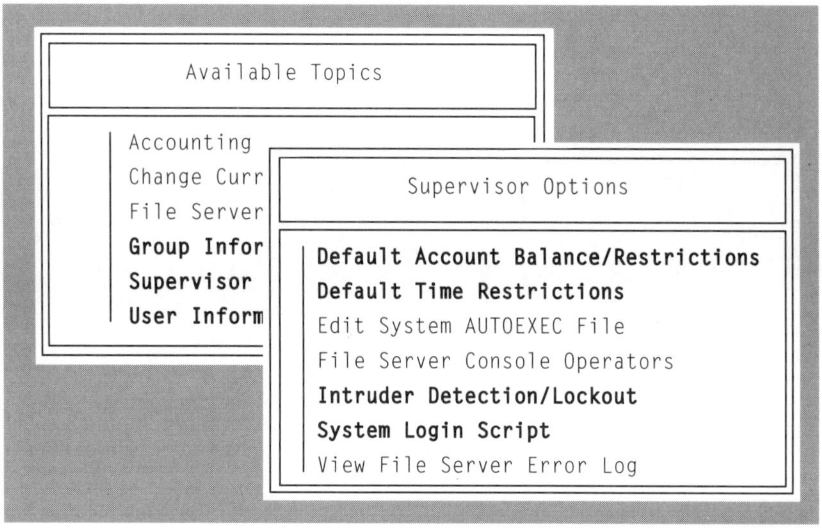


**Figure 10-4. The Supervisor Options screen**

Let's look at these four important options in detail.

**Default Account Balance/Restrictions.** The Default Account Balance/Restrictions option allows you to set the security restriction defaults that will exist for all newly created users. Figure 10-5 shows you an example of a worst-case scenario.

There's no expiration date on the account, meaning that the user may log in forever. In additional, this same user can log in on as many workstations, at the same time, as he or she can get access to. Worse yet, no passwords are required.

```
            Default Account Balance/Restrictions

Account Disabled:                         No
Account Has Expiration Date:              No
    Date Account Expires:
Limit Concurrent Connections:             No
    Maximum Connections:
Allow User to Change Password:            Yes
Require Password:                         No
    Minimum Password Length:
Force Periodic Password Changes:
    Days Between Forced Changes:
    Date Password Expires:
    Limit Grace Logins:
        Grace Logins Allowed:
        Remaining Grace Logins:
Require Unique Passwords:
```

**Figure 10-5. The Default Account Balance/Restrictions screen**

A better scenario is shown in Figure 10-6:

```
            Default Account Balance/Restrictions

Account Disabled:                         No
Account Has Expiration Date:              Yes
    Date Account Expires:                 January 1, 1994
Limit Concurrent Connections:             Yes
    Maximum Connections:                  2
Allow User to Change Password:            Yes
Require Password:                         Yes
    Minimum Password Length:              6
Force Periodic Password Changes:          Yes
    Days Between Forced Changes:          60
  Date Password Expires:                  January 22, 1993
  Limit Grace Logins:                     Yes
        Grace Logins Allowed:             3
        Remaining Grace Logins:           3
Require Unique Passwords:                 Yes
```

**Figure 10-6. A more desirable Default Account Balance Restrictions screen**

The network administrator on this NetWare network has taken several major security precautions in regard to this user.

1. The account has an expiration date and the default is January 1 of the next year. You can always change this date if you need to, but in the meantime it prevents a new user from being assigned an unlimited account.

2. The user is limited to being logged in to a maximum of two workstations at any one time. If this number turns out to be insufficient, the supervisor can raise it, but this limit provides a good starting point for most users.

3. A password is required, and the minimum length is set to six characters. In addition, the password must be changed every sixty days and the user is limited to three grace logins. Grace logins are logins using the old password after the password has expired. When users whose passwords have expired log in, NetWare informs them that the password has expired and asks if they would like to change it. Why would anyone answer "no" more than three times? More appropriately, what supervisor would allow a user to log in to the file server more than three times on an expired password?

4. The new password must be separate or unique, meaning that it can't match the password the user is changing it from. If it does match, NetWare tells the user to try again.

**Default Time Restrictions.** The second Supervisor Options screen option is Default Time Restrictions. This parameter establishes a default limit on the time that a newly added user is allowed to be logged in to the file server. These changes are not retroactive; any users already on the user list won't be affected by changes made here. This option applies only to newly created users. Figure 10-7 shows the worst-case scenario, where the user's access times have no limit whatsoever:

```
                   AM                       PM
          1                     1 1 1                   1 1
          2 1 2 3 4 5 6 7 8 9 0 1 2 1 2 3 4 5 6 7 8 9 0 1
Sunday    |************************************************|
Monday    |************************************************|
Tuesday   |************************************************|
Wednesday |************************************************|
Thursday  |************************************************|
Friday    |************************************************|
Saturday  |************************************************|
                               Sunday 12:00 am To 12:30 am
```

**Figure 10-7. Network user access with no time restrictions**

There are no limits on the times that this new user may access the file server. At three o'clock in the morning, if network security is lax enough, he or she can pop a home computer up in PC anyWHERE, dial into the file server, and download the database containing all customer information. That user can then print a message to the printer informing you that he or she won't be in this morning, and then take that little disk to the competition for a job offer. Figure 10-8 shows a better scenario:

```
                    AM                      PM
          1                     1 1 1                     1 1
          2 1 2 3 4 5 6 7 8 9 0 1 2 1 2 3 4 5 6 7 8 9 0 1
         ┌────────────────────────────────────────────────┐
Sunday   │                                                │
Monday   │              **************************        │
Tuesday  │              **************************        │
Wednesday│              **************************        │
Thursday │              **************************        │
Friday   │              **************************        │
Saturday │                                                │
         └────────────────────────────────────────────────┘
                         Saturday 11:30 pm To 12:00 am
```

**Figure 10-8. Network user access with 13-hour weekday time restrictions**

The user is allowed to connect to the file server from 7:00 a.m. to 7:00 p.m. (allowing for overtime) from Monday through Friday. No connectivity is allowed on weekends or after those hours. Outside of specified hours, a user attempting to use the file server will be logged out and not allowed to log back in.

**Intruder Detection and Lockout.** The next important choice from the Supervisor Options list is Intruder Detection and Lockout. This menu choice is self-explanatory, and straightforward enough for you to easily follow the choices. Look at the worst-case scenario, shown in Figure 10-9:

```
Intruder Detection/Lockout

Detect Intruders:                   No
Intruder Detection Threshold
Incorrect Login Attempts:
Bad Login Count Retention Time:    Days      Hours      Minutes

Lock Account After Detection:
Length of Account Lockout:          Days      Hours      Minutes
```

**Figure 10-9. Intruder Detection/Lockout with no detection or lockout settings**

Figure 10-10 shows a better scenario:

```
Intruder Detection/Lockout

Detect Intruders:                   Yes
Intruder Detection Threshold
Incorrect Login Attempts:           3
Bad Login Count Retention Time: 1 Days  0 Hours 0 Minutes

Lock Account After Detection:       Yes
Length of Account Lockout:          1 Days  0 Hours 0 Minutes
```

**Figure 10-10. Intruder Detection/Lockout with detection and lockout settings set properly**

Incorrect Login Attempts refers to a user mistyping a password. The user simply could have mistyped, or it may be an indication that someone is trying to break in. NetWare tracks the number of incorrect password attempts that occur for each user account. The number of incorrect logins on each account is automatically reset to zero as soon as the user successfully logs in or when the Bad Login Count Retention Time setting expires since the last attempt.

When the user fails to log in and exceeds the number of allowed attempts, a note is placed in the audit file and the file server errorlog (which you can see by selecting the last choice on the Supervisor Options menu—the View File Server Error Log option).

Bad Login Count Retention Time reflects the length of time that NetWare remembers a bad attempt before resetting to zero. Bear in mind that the number automatically resets to zero on a successful login.

Lock Account After Detection is the length of time the server is locked should the number of failed attempts be reached within the Count Retention Time. No one can log in to the account for the length of time specified unless the supervisor is notified. The supervisor can use SYSCON to unlock the account. If it's the supervisor's account that's locked, the command ENABLE LOGIN entered at the console will unlock it.

**System Login Script.** The final Supervisor Options choice that we'll look at is System Login Script. This routine is run for all users when they log in to the file server before their individual scripts run. The system login script is a good location to place MAP statements leading to subdirectories on every workstation that has local drives, but *never* map to a subdirectory on the file server. That mapping should be done by the individual's script after his or her login has been finalized. Figure 10-11 shows an example of MAP commands in a System Login Script:

```
System Login Script

map s6:=c:\dos
map s7:=c:\pctools
map s8:=c:\pcplus
map s9:=c:\
```

**Figure 10-11. MAP commands in a System Login Script**

### The User Information option

Now let's back out of the Supervisor Options window and return to SYSCON's Main Menu. Select the User Information option.

For each user allowed access to the file server, you may establish a variety of variables. In our discussion of server security, we're interested in six of those variables, as shown in Figure 10-12:

```
User Information

Account Balance
Account Restrictions
Change Password
Full Name
Groups Belonged To
Intruder Lockout Status
Login Script
Other Information
Security Equivalences
Station Restrictions
Time Restrictions
Trustee Directory Assignments
```

**Figure 10-12. User Information variables**

**Account Restrictions.** Account Restrictions relates to the Default Account Balance and Restrictions, but now you're dealing, not with the default, but with the real world. Figure 10-13 shows restrictions for user WILLIAM:

```
Account Restrictions For User WILLIAM

Account Disabled:                        No
Account Has Expiration Date:             No
    Date Account Expires:
Allow User To Change Password:           Yes
Require Password:                        Yes
    Minimum Password Length:             2
Force Periodic Password Changes:         Yes
    Days Between Forced Changes:         40
    Date Password Expires:               December 6, 1992
Limit Grace Logins:                      Yes
    Grace Logins Allowed:                6
    Remaining Grace Logins:              6
Require Unique Passwords:                No
Limit Server Disk Space:                 No
Maximum Server Disk Space (KB):
```

**Figure 10-13. User account restrictions for user WILLIAM**

Notice how the real world deviates from the default. The account has no expiration date; the user is allowed unlimited concurrent connections; he can have a password of only two characters (even using both letters and numbers, that's only 1,296 possible choices that need be tried to crack the password); and even though the password expires every 40 days, the user can set it back to what it was, since unique passwords are not required. Needless to say, whoever has supervisory equivalence and has made these changes has done a poor job of looking out for network security.

The Intruder Lockout Status setting shows just that. It tells you if the account is locked, how many password failures there have been, the amount of time until next reset, and the address of the possible intruder. Figure 10-14 shows normal lockout status:

```
                    Intruder Lockout Status
---------------------------------------------------------------
Account Locked:          No
Incorrect Login Count:   0
Account Reset Time:
Time Until Reset:
Last Intruder Address:   00000000:000000000000:0000
```

**Figure 10-14. Normal lockout status**

Figure 10-15 shows lockout status with an incorrect password:

```
                    Intruder Lockout Status
---------------------------------------------------------------
Account Locked:         No
Incorrect Login Count:  1
Account Reset Time:     November 23, 1992  5:15:00
Time Until Reset:       0 Days 23 Hours 58 Minutes 46 Seconds
Last Intruder Address:  00000600:00001B248440:4003
```

**Figure 10-15. Lockout status with an incorrect password**

Notice that the Intruder Address is given in terms of the physical node. A locked account is shown in Figure 10-16:

```
                    Intruder Lockout Status
---------------------------------------------------------------
Account Locked:         Yes
Incorrect Login Count:
Account Reset Time:     November 23, 1992  5:19:00
Time Until Reset:       0 Days 23 Hours 57 Minutes 14Seconds
Last Intruder Address:  00000600:00001B248440:4003
```

**Figure 10-16. A locked account**

Now I'll show you what the user saw while attempting to log in to the file server:

```
17:18|F:\>login william
Enter your password:
ANDERSON/WILLIAM: Access to server denied and you have
  been logged out.
You are attached to server ANDERSON.

17:18|F:\LOGIN>login william
Enter your password:
ANDERSON/WILLIAM: Access to server denied.
You are attached to server ANDERSON.

17:19|F:\LOGIN>login william
Enter your password:
ANDERSON/WILLIAM: Intruder detection lockout has
  disabled this account.
You are attached to server ANDERSON.

17:19|F:\LOGIN>
```

In the event that a legitimate user is attempting to log in but is genuinely unable to remember the current password, that user can come to the supervisor. The supervisor can type "N" at this screen to change the display as shown in Figure 10-17:

```
                  Intruder Lockout Status

Account Locked:         No
Incorrect Login Count: 0
Account Reset Time:
Time Until Reset:
Last Intruder Address: 00000600:00001B248440:4003
```

**Figure 10-17. An unlocked account**

The System Error Log entry looks like this:

```
NOVEMBER 22, 1992      5:19:06 pm
Intruder lock-out on account WILLIAM
[00000600:00001B248440]
248440]
```

Security Equivalences, also included as an option in the User Information window, merely shows the group(s) the user belongs to.

The Station Restrictions option allow you to prevent a user from using any of the workstations not included in a list you configure. To configure the list, you must know the eight-digit hex number physical node of the workstation. The easiest way to get this information is to use the USERLIST /A option.

In the example I just showed you, to confine WILLIAM to logging in only from the workstation he kept failing on, you'd use the address 1B248440.

Time Restrictions is the real-world equivalent of the default established earlier. Trustee Directory Assignments shows the directories in which the user is a trustee.

Every supervisor should be aware of these security measures available in the SYSCON utility. With SYSCON, you can prevent the kinds of security problems I discussed at the beginning of this chapter.

## Command-Line Functions

In returning to a discussion of command-line institutions, I'd like to bring up a few facts about two commands that I didn't cover in Chapter 1. I discuss them here because they relate to security issues and are items that operate independently, or invisibly, to the command.

The first command-line function I want to discuss here is the LOGIN command. LOGIN returns an errorlevel value based on whether or not it was successful. If the login was successful, meaning that the user provided a proper username and corresponding password, the errorlevel returned is zero.

If the user provides a wrong username, or a good username and not a corresponding password, then the errorlevel returned is zero. You can use this errorlevel in a batch file, as I'm about to show you, to alert the user to his or her failed attempts, thus preventing someone from mistyping the password and hours later being unable to obtain file server information.

If you mistype your password, you don't get on the network, but your AUTOEXEC.BAT may continue operation whether or not the network connection was properly connected. As a result, you could run WordPerfect on your local drive with no problem, but be unable to access a network database. If this scenario happens to a user on your network, more than likely he or she will call to complain that the network has "crashed" once more.

Listing 10-4 shows you the LOGIN routine when a user mistypes a password.

**Listing 10-4. The LOGIN routine for a mistyped password**

```
:LOG.BAT
@ECHO OFF
:LOGIN
F:LOGIN
IF ERRORLEVEL 1 GOTO RETRY
GOTO EXIT
:RETRY
CLS
ECHO Your login attempt was unsuccessful
ECHO Please try again
GOTO LOGIN
:EXIT
```

If the login is successful, nothing appears on the screen. If it isn't successful, the message is displayed and the user attempts to log in again. This pattern will repeat itself until the user enters the password incorrectly enough times that the Intruder Lockout, if properly set, prevents any further login attempts.

It's also possible to specify a username on the command line with LOGIN and the executable file will attempt to log in the user as that person: for example, LOGIN WILLIAM. Instead of prompting for a username, the executable drops to asking for a password.

Worse yet, LOGIN will accept the output of a DOS file as input for its operations. Suppose, for example, that William places a file in his root drive called GETMEIN, and its contents are but one line:

`TURKEY` <Enter>

With "TURKEY" as his password, William can place the following command in a batch file:

`LOGIN WILLIAM < C:\GETMEIN` <Enter>

and anyone running that batch file will be logged in as user William. At this time, I know of no good method of circumventing this little workaround. If a user performs such an operation, it could take you a while to find out about it. Chapter 2 gives you a batch file, called FINDPASS.BAT, that searches for a password in a file, but you must know the password before being able to search for it. A good recommendation would be to use that batch file and search for the word LOGIN in all batch files.

The second command-line function I want to discuss in this context is SETPASS. You can use the SETPASS command to change a password from the command line. (The supervisor or user can also change it in SYSCON.) SETPASS also returns an errorlevel value based on whether or not it was able to successfully change a password. If it succeeds, the errorlevel returned is zero. If it fails, either because the user didn't enter the proper password or didn't enter the new password the same way twice, then the errorlevel returned is 254.

You can use the batch file shown in Listing 10-5 to alert the user that he or she hasn't successfully completed the operation.

**Listing 10-5. A batch file to inform users of password creation failure**

```
:PWD.BAT
@ECHO OFF
SETPASS
IF ERRORLEVEL 254 GOTO FAIL
GOTO EXIT
:FAIL
ECHO Entries did not match
ECHO and password was not changed
ECHO.
ECHO Please try again.
:EXIT
```

NetWare 2.2 and NetWare 3.11 provide such error messages, but earlier versions don't.

## Sniffers

Sniffers are devices and/or software packages used to analyze and diagnose problems on LANS. These devices are designed to run quietly, without interfering with normal network operations, and report on what they see.

The problem is that they see everything. They see users logging in, and they see them logging out. They see them entering passwords, and they see the passwords being verified. Therefore, anyone who attaches a sniffer to your network can watch all transactions taking place, including logging in.

NetWare 3.x uses password encryption rather than reading the password exactly as typed in. This new approach alleviates the problem to some extent. The sniffer sees the encrypted password, and the intruder must go to the extra trouble of decrypting it. Versions of NetWare before NetWare 2.15c sent the password exactly as it was typed in.

## Wrap-Up

This chapter has covered network security as it pertains to the server. The next chapter discusses workstations, and the following chapter will discuss security relating to the server and the workstation together. Following that chapter, there will be questions pertaining to all three chapters.

Read on.

11 CHAPTER

# NetWare Workstation Security

The two main components of a network are a server and a workstation. The previous chapter discussed security on the server; this chapter covers security measures for the second major network component, the workstation. The next chapter, completing the trilogy, will discuss across-the-board security techniques not restricted to server or workstation alone.

## The DR DOS PASSWORD Command

DR DOS contains a convenient command, PASSWORD, that you can use to assign a password up to eight characters long to files and directory paths. Unfortunately, you can use it only on local drives, not on the file server. Three different security levels within this command, established by optional parameters, may be applied to a file and/or directory.

**Table 11-1. PASSWORD parameter-defined security levels**

| PARAMETER | SECURITY LEVEL |
|---|---|
| /D | Any user can read and modify the file, but the user must give the password in order to delete a file. |

**Table 11-1.** *(Continued)*

| PARAMETER | SECURITY LEVEL |
|---|---|
| /W | Any user can read and copy the file, but the user must give a password in order to modify, rename, or delete a file. |
| /R | A password is required for a user to read, write, copy, delete, or rename a file. |

Issuing the PASSWORD shows you the current attributes assigned to all files, as shown in Listing 11-1.

**Listing 11-1. File attributes displayed by the PASSWORD command**

```
C:\>PASSWORD
---   c:io.sys
---   c:msdos.sys
---   c:ibmbio.com
---   c:config.sys
---   c:ibmdos.com
---   c:command.com
---   c:sstordrv.sys
---   c:devswap.com
---   c:diskmap.dat
---   c:autoexec.wms
---   c:temp.net
---   c:@dlwatch.dat
---   c:autoexec.bak
---   c:autoexec.bat
---   c:finderr.bat
---   c:who.txt
---   c:finderr.bak
---   c:check.bak
---   c:test.bat
---   c:check.bat
---   c:config.bak
---   c:ead

C:\>
```

The following text shows how to add the second level of protection to the AUTOEXEC.BAT and CONFIG.SYS files and establish a password of TURKEY.

```
C:\>PASSWORD AUTOEXEC.BAT /W:TURKEY
-wd  c:autoexec.bat

C:\>PASSWORD CONFIG.SYS /W TURKEY
c:config.sys ...protection level not changed: file has
no password
TURKEY ...file not found

C:\>PASSWORD CONFIG.SYS /W:TURKEY
-wd  c:config.sys

C:\>
```

Notice first of all that assigning W adds the D, the next level down. If you were to assign R, it would add the attributes R, W, and D.

Notice also what took place in the second attempt. The colon (:) was left out and this caused the command to fail, but in that failure, it interpreted the password TURKEY as being the name of a file, meaning that you can specify more than one file on the same command line. Look at the following text:

```
C:\>PASSWORD TEST.BAT /W:TURKEY CHECK.BAT
-wd  c:test.bat
-wd  c:check.bat

C:\>
```

What happens when a user attempts to manipulate CHECK.BAT around? Let's look at the possibilities shown in Listing 11-2.

**Listing 11-2. Viewing a file after password assignment**

```
C:\>TYPE CHECK.BAT
:check.bat
@echo off
cls
echo Do you want
echo
echo 1.
echo 2.
echo 3.
echo
switch ba, bb, bc
echo Goodbye
exit
:ba
echo one
return
:bb
echo two
return
:bc
echo three
return

C:\>COPY CHECK.BAT CHECK2.BAT
       1 File(s) copied

C:\>DEL CHECK.BAT
File not erased: CHECK.BAT - Invalid Password

C:\>
```

And what of CHECK2.BAT, which was created by this user?

```
C:\>DEL CHECK2.BAT

C:\>
```

Since this user has permission to create CHECK2 from CHECK, he or she has permission to delete and modify CHECK2 as desired. To illustrate:

```
C:\>COPY CHECK.BAT CHECK2.BAT
        1 File(s) copied

C:\>PASSWORD CHEC*.*
---   c:check.bak
-wd   c:check.bat
---   c:check2.bat

C:\>
```

The password structure isn't carried over from a password-protected file if the user doing the copying has permission to do so. (Without permission to do so, the user wouldn't be able to copy it over.)

How do you go about performing an operation on a file that requires password clearance? Issue the command and follow it with a semicolon and the password, like this:

```
C:\>DEL CHECK.BAT;TURKEY

C:\>
```

The password is *not* case-sensitive; therefore, "TURKEY," "Turkey," and "turkey" all pass the test.

To assign password protection to a subdirectory instead of a file, use the /P parameter. The /P parameter is the only way to protect a subdirectory; when you use it, you impose protection levels R, W, and D. Listing 11-3 shows you an example of using the /P parameter to password-protect one of the subdirectories on the root of C:.

**Listing 11-3. Password-protecting a subdirectory**

```
C:\>DIR *.

Volume in drive C is EXAMPLE
Directory of  C:\

OLDDOS          <DIR>    9-10-92  9:44a
QEMM            <DIR>    9-10-92  9:57a
NET             <DIR>    9-10-92 10:03a
TMP             <DIR>   11-08-92  9:19p
DV              <DIR>    9-10-92 10:16a
CHA             <DIR>    9-10-92 11:00a
PCPLUS          <DIR>    9-14-92  7:36a
REFLECT         <DIR>    9-14-92 12:51p
DOS             <DIR>    9-29-92  1:05p
TEMP            <DIR>    9-29-92  1:05p
ANYIII          <DIR>   10-18-92  1:20p
EAD                  1135      11-08-92  9:46p
           12 File(s)    52641792 bytes free

C:\>PASSWORD TEMP /P:TURKEY
rwd  c:TEMP

C:\>DIR *.

Volume in drive C is EXAMPLE
Directory of  C:\

OLDDOS          <DIR>  9-10-92  9:44a
QEMM            <DIR>  9-10-92  9:57a
NET             <DIR>  9-10-92 10:03a
TMP             <DIR>  8-08-92  9:19p
DV              <DIR>  9-10-92 10:16a
CHA             <DIR>  9-10-92 11:00a
PCPLUS          <DIR>  9-14-92  7:36a
```

```
REFLECT         <DIR>  9-14-92 12:51p
DOS             <DIR>  9-29-92  1:05p
TEMP            <DIR>  9-29-92  1:05p
ANYIII          <DIR>  2-18-92  1:20p
EAD                 1135     1-08-92  9:46p
          12 File(s) 52641792 bytes free

C:\>
```

Note that the directory is still visible.

```
C:\>CD TEMP
Invalid Password

C:\>CD TEMP;TURKEY


C:\TEMP>DIR

Volume in drive C is EXAMPLE
Directory of  C:\TEMP

.         <DIR>   9-29-92  1:05p
..        <DIR>   9-29-92  1:05p
EAD           450     11-08-92  9:21p
          3 File(s)  52641792 bytes free

C:\TEMP>PASSWORD
---  c:ead

C:\TEMP>
```

A user must give a password to enter the subdirectory, since it's protected. Once the user has gained access, however, the contents of the subdirectory are not protected. DOS assumes that if you're able to get this far, you have the proper rights. However, there's an old joke about what happens when one assumes, so it's a good idea to go an extra step and assign passwords to files inside password-protected subdirectories, like this:

```
C:\TEMP>PASSWORD EAD /W:HAM
-wd  c:ead

C:\TEMP>
```

Use the /S parameter to perform an operation throughout subdirectories. "PASSWORD *.BAT /W:TURKEY /S," if initiated from the root directory, will password all batch files throughout the drive. You can also use this method in conjunction with the FIND command to search for all protected files and subdirectories, as follows:

```
C:\>PASSWORD /S | FIND /V "---"
c:\temp ...path password?
-wd  c:\config.sys
--d  c:\autoexec.bak
-wd  c:\autoexec.bat
******
-wd  c:\temp\ead

C:\>
```

The /N parameter removes password protection from a file, and /NP removes password protection from a subdirectory. The only remaining parameter is the most important one of all: /G. This parameter allows you to feed DR DOS a global password variable that it will store and attempt to use each time you perform an operation that requires a password. This approach reduces the number of prompts that come up, but still provides password protection on the workstation. Let's look at this series of steps and then discuss what happens.

```
C:\>REN AUTOEXEC.BAT AUTOEXEC.BCK
Invalid Password

C:\>PASSWORD /G:TURKEY

C:\>REN AUTOEXEC.BAT AUTOEXEC.BCK

C:\>DEL C:\TEMP\EAD
File not erased: C:\TEMP\EAD - Invalid Password

C:\>DEL C:\TEMP\EAD;HAM

C:\>REN AUTOEXEC.BCK AUTOEXEC.BAT

C:\>
```

First, the password wasn't specified, so the REN couldn't be carried out. (REN, unlike COPY, does transfer over the password protection to the newly created file.) Next, a global password was entered to allow the operation to be carried out without a password prompt.

Third, C:\TEMP\EAD couldn't be deleted, since the password for it isn't the same as the global password. (You could delete it, however, by specifying the proper password.) Finally, the REN can still take place, since /G stays in effect until the system is rebooted or another /G is given.

## Screen Blanking

When users walk away from running workstations, they're walking away from files stored on their local drives. They're also walking away from access to the file server—access they gained by issuing a user name and password at the beginning of the day.

If someone malicious wants to change things on the file server that only the supervisor can change, why should that person go to all the trouble of trying to break the password when he or she can sit down at the supervisor's workstation during the lunch hour?

Screen-blanking utilities clear what's on the screen and keep wandering eyes from seeing what was previously displayed there. Good screen-blanking utilities also include password protection that requires the user to give a password before being able to exit the screen blanker and access other programs. Listing 11-4 shows a quick utility that provides such protection.

**Listing 11-4. A screen-blanking utility**

```
REM Blank routine
LINE INPUT "WORD? "; pass$
10 CLS
LINE INPUT " ", test$
IF UCASE$(test$) <> UCASE$(pass$) THEN SOUND 700, 36:
  GOTO 10
CLS
END
```

The routine is very simple and straightforward. Every time you invoke it, it asks you for a password that it will then require to exit the program. This approach is much more effective than using a static password that's the same every time you use it. With this routine, you can enter the same thing every time, or enter whatever you feel like entering on that day.

When you run the screen-blanking utility, the screen blanks and sits there awaiting input. There's no prompt. Never should a password prompt be something to the effect of "Please enter password:". This prompt tells snooping eyes that the machine is awaiting a password. It's far better for the screen to be blank and await the entry, or, if it's absolutely necessary that a prompt be displayed, the prompt should be something cryptic that an intruder could mistake for a system message. "Abort, Retry, Fail?" is a favorite.

If you enter the password correctly (notice that it isn't case-sensitive, but you can change this feature if you want to by removing the UCASE$ command), the blanking stops and the prompt returns. If you enter the password improperly, the machine beeps one steady beep for approximately two seconds.

BLANK works very well, given its limited language. Unfortunately, there is a way of escaping it without entering the password: by pressing <Ctrl>-<Break> or <Ctrl>-<C>. What the user sees is:

```
Break
Hit any key to return to system

C:\>
```

This problem is inherent in many programs because DOS always checks at a prompt to see if this key combination has been pressed. If so, it stops processing.

To compensate, you need to do three things. First, modify BLANK by adding the two lines highlighted in Listing 11-5.

**Listing 11-5. A modification of the BLANK utility**

```
REM Blank routine
LINE INPUT "WORD? "; pass$
SHELL "ECHO HEY > C:\BLANK.BLK"
10 CLS
LINE INPUT " ", test$
IF UCASE$(test$) <> UCASE$(pass$) THEN SOUND 700, 36:
  GOTO 10
CLS
KILL "C:\BLANK.BLK"
END
```

Listing 11-5 creates a dummy file upon beginning, and removes the dummy file upon successful execution. If the file was already there, it's overwritten (>).

The second thing to do is create a program called SCREECH. Listing 11-6 shows you how.

**Listing 11-6. The SCREECH utility**

```
REM Screech
FOR I = 700 TO 2000
SOUND I, 1080
NEXT I
END
```

And the third thing to do is write a batch file to invoke BLANK and invoke SCREECH only if BLANK is interrupted and doesn't successfully complete its assignment. Listing 11-7 shows this procedure.

**Listing 11-7. Invoking SCREECH if BLANK is interrupted**

```
:BLANKER.BAT
@ECHO OFF
BLANK
IF EXIST C:\BLANK.BLK GOTO SCREECH
GOTO EXIT
:SCREECH
SCREECH
:EXIT
```

Now invoke BLANKER. BLANKER calls BLANK, which creates the dummy file, accepts a password for later comparison, and clears the screen until that password is entered. If someone enters the proper password, the dummy file is erased, BLANK is exited, and BLANKER.BAT is exited.

If BLANK is exited by someone pressing <Ctrl>-<Break> or <Ctrl>-<C>, the dummy file remains and SCREECH is called. SCREECH sounds one annoying tone on the computer for one full minute, then changes the tone slightly and releases another one-minute note, incrementing from 700 to 2000—approximately 1300 minutes, or 21 hours. Since SCREECH doesn't pause or accept any input, there's no way of breaking out of it with a <Ctrl> combination. The only way out is to reboot the computer, causing the server to have a user name and password reentered in the process.

## Substitute and Assign

Suppose someone has to use your workstation to access a word processor on the file server, and this person must change files located in C:\TEMP while you're out to lunch. You can't turn the computer off, and you can't invoke the blanker utility if someone else is going to use your workstation. One way of handling this is to limit the workstation to seeing only the C:\TEMP subdirectory. You can impose this limitation by combining two DOS commands: SUBST (substitute) and ASSIGN.

SUBST allows you to use a different drive specification to refer to a path; ASSIGN tells DOS to redirect requests for one drive to another drive. This process requires only three steps, as follows:

1. Step one is simple. Since the data you want to protect is on C:, pick another drive at random. D: will work nicely. Either at the command line or in a batch file, invoke the command:

   `SUBST D: C:\TEMP` <Enter>

2. Step two involves assigning the root drive to the new drive. This assignment will reduce the root drive to the new drive *only*. As a consequence, all external DOS commands, batch files, and the like will be lost. At the command line or in your batch file, type:

   `ASSIGN C=D` <Enter>

3. Step three involves changing the PATH statement to reflect the new dimensions. Listing 11-5 shows the process as you'd see it on your screen.

**Listing 11-5. Using ASSIGN to screen your data from view**

```
C:\>dir *.

Volume in drive C does is EXAMPLE
Directory of  C:\

OLDDOS          <DIR>    9-10-92   9:44a
QEMM            <DIR>    9-10-92   9:57a
NET             <DIR>    9-10-92  10:03a
TMP             <DIR>   11-08-92   9:19p
DV              <DIR>    9-10-92  10:16a
CHA             <DIR>    9-10-92  11:00a
PCPLUS          <DIR>    9-14-92   7:36a
REFLECT         <DIR>    9-14-92  12:51p
DOS             <DIR>    9-29-92   1:05p
TEMP            <DIR>    9-29-92   1:05p
ANYIII          <DIR>   10-18-92   1:20p
EAD                 1135      11-08-92   9:46p
         12 File(s)  51904512 bytes free

C:\>cd TEMP


C:\TEMP>dir

Volume in drive C is EXAMPLE
Directory of  C:\TEMP

.          <DIR>         7-29-92  1:05p
..         <DIR>         9-29-92  1:05p
ERROR    BAT      5157   7-24-92  8:34a
DCANCEL  EXE      2064   5-03-90  3:11a
DCHKSUM  EXE      8512   5-03-90  3:11a
DINSTALL EXE     35175   5-03-90  3:11a
DLOGOFF  EXE      9671   5-03-90  3:11a
```

```
DLOGVIEW EXE     39191   5-03-90   3:11a
DNY      CNF     46592   5-31-91   9:08a
DNY      EXE    130887   5-03-90   3:11a
DNY      LOG      2995  11-22-92  10:21p
DNY      MNU        56   5-03-90   3:11a
DNY      TRM       642   5-03-90   3:11a
DPLAY    EXE     33911   5-03-90   3:11a
DREMOTE  CNF      1159   5-03-90   3:11a
DREMOTE  SCR      7616   5-03-90   3:11a
DSEND    EXE     41575   5-03-90   3:11a
DT-PIF   DVP       416   5-03-90   3:11a
DTERM    CNF       640   3-19-92   3:56p
DTERM    EXE     87127   5-03-90   3:11a
DTERM    LOG       340   1-11-91  11:29a
DTERMLAP EXE     87767   5-03-90   3:11a
DW-PIF   DVP       416   5-03-90   3:11a
DWMODEM  CNF     26112   5-03-90   3:11a
DIALDIR  PRM      2054   3-19-92   3:56p
PCPLUS   DIR     15050   8-20-91   7:03a
PCPLUS   KEY       500   8-20-91   7:02a
PCPLUS   PRM      1190   8-20-91   7:02a
PCPLUS   XLT       256   8-20-91   7:02a
READ     ME       5289   5-03-90   3:11a
REMOVEAW EXE      1368   5-03-90   3:11a
EAD                  8  11-10-92   8:06a
EMMETT   ZIP     10067  11-12-92  11:51a
        33 File(s)  51904512 bytes free

C:\TEMP>SUBST D: C:\TEMP

C:\TEMP>subst
D: => C:\TEMP

C:\TEMP>ASSIGN C=D
```

```
C:\>DIR

Volume in drive C is EXAMPLE
Directory of  C:\

.           <DIR>        9-29-92  1:05p
..          <DIR>        9-29-92  1:05p
ERROR    BAT       515   7-24-92  8:34a
DCANCEL  EXE      2064   5-03-90  3:11a
DCHKSUM  EXE      8512   5-03-90  3:11a
DINSTALL EXE     35175   5-03-90  3:11a
DLOGOFF  EXE      9671   5-03-90  3:11a
DLOGVIEW EXE     39191   5-03-90  3:11a
DNY      CNF     46592   5-31-91  9:08a
DNY      EXE    130887   5-03-90  3:11a
DNY      LOG      2995  11-22-92 10:21p
DNY      MNU        56   5-03-90  3:11a
DNY      TRM       642   5-03-90  3:11a
DPLAY    EXE     33911   5-03-90  3:11a
DREMOTE  CNF      1159   5-03-90  3:11a
DREMOTE  SCR      7616   5-03-90  3:11a
DSEND    EXE     41575   5-03-90  3:11a
DT-PIF   DVP       416   5-03-90  3:11a
DTERM    CNF       640   3-19-92  3:56p
DTERM    EXE     87127   5-03-90  3:11a
DTERM    LOG       340   1-11-91 11:29a
DTERMLAP EXE     87767   5-03-90  3:11a
DW-PIF   DVP       416   5-03-90  3:11a
DWMODEM  CNF     26112   5-03-90  3:11a
DIALDIR  PRM      2054   3-19-92  3:56p
PCPLUS   DIR     15050   8-20-91  7:03a
PCPLUS   KEY       500   8-20-91  7:02a
PCPLUS   PRM      1190   8-20-91  7:02a
PCPLUS   XLT       256   8-20-91  7:02a
READ     ME       5289   5-03-90  3:11a
```

```
REMOVEAW EXE      1368  5-03-90  3:11a
EAD                  8 11-10-92  8:06a
EMMETT   ZIP     10067 11-12-92 11:51a
          33 File(s)  51904512 bytes free

C:\>D:

D:\>DIR

Volume in drive D is EXAMPLE
Directory of  D:\
.           <DIR>        9-29-92  1:05p
..          <DIR>        9-29-92  1:05p
ERROR    BAT       515  7-24-92  8:34a
DCANCEL  EXE      2064  5-03-90  3:11a
DCHKSUM  EXE      8512  5-03-90  3:11a
DINSTALL EXE     35175  5-03-90  3:11a
DLOGOFF  EXE      9671  5-03-90  3:11a
DLOGVIEW EXE     39191  5-03-90  3:11a
DNY      CNF     46592  5-31-91  9:08a
DNY      EXE    130887  5-03-90  3:11a
DNY      LOG      2995 11-22-92 10:21p
DNY      MNU        56  5-03-90  3:11a
DNY      TRM       642  5-03-90  3:11a
DPLAY    EXE     33911  5-03-90  3:11a
DREMOTE  CNF      1159  5-03-90  3:11a
DREMOTE  SCR      7616  5-03-90  3:11a
DSEND    EXE     41575  5-03-90  3:11a
DT-PIF   DVP       416  5-03-90  3:11a
DTERM    CNF       640  3-19-92  3:56p
DTERM    EXE     87127  5-03-90  3:11a
DTERM    LOG       340  1-11-91 11:29a
DTERMLAP EXE     87767  5-03-90  3:11a
DW-PIF   DVP       416  5-03-90  3:11a
DWMODEM  CNF     26112  5-03-90  3:11a
```

```
DIALDIR  PRM      2054  3-19-92  3:56p
PCPLUS   DIR     15050  8-20-91  7:03a
PCPLUS   KEY       500  8-20-91  7:02a
PCPLUS   PRM      1190  8-20-91  7:02a
PCPLUS   XLT       256  8-20-91  7:02a
READ     ME       5289  5-03-90  3:11a
REMOVEAW EXE      1368  5-03-90  3:11a
EAD                  8 11-10-92  8:06a
EMMETT   ZIP     10067 11-12-92 11:51a
         33 File(s)  51904512 bytes free

D:\>C:

C:\>PATH=C:\
```

Now, for all practical purposes, there's only one drive, and one directory on the hard drive, and the contents of it are what was in C:\TEMP.

To return to normal operations, insert a DOS floppy disk containing a copy of ASSIGN.COM. Then type "ASSIGN" to return things to their original state.

Carrying this thought one step further, you can use ASSIGN.COM as a "software disable" of the floppy drives. Issuing the command ASSIGN A=C

<Enter> reassigns all requests to the A: drive to the C: drive. Use SUBST in conjunction and you can drop A: into a dummy TEMP directory containing nothing.

### Hide and Protect Files

Rather than worrying about protecting a workstation, sometimes the only things you need to protect are key files that you don't want others to see. One of the simplest ways to reduce the likelihood of others looking into your files is to avoid giving your files attention-catching names. Anything named "RESUME" or "PRIVATE" is bound to catch attention, as well as items ending with extensions such as "PVT," "PER," and so forth.

Another way to conceal files is to place them in a directory not addressed in the PATH statement and then give them extensions of .COM and .EXE. They'll appear to be executable files rather than data files.

Another old rule of protecting files is to include an invisible character in the file name. If ANSI.SYS has been installed as a driver in the CONFIG.SYS file, then you can type an invisible space by holding down the <Alt> key and entering "255" on the numeric keypad. This produces a character that exists, but isn't visible in DIR listings. To view the file, you must give its entire name, including the unseen, invisible character.

Listing 11-6 shows how you can use the invisible character to hide files.

**Listing 11-6. Hiding files with an invisible character**

```
C:\>DIR *.BAT

Volume in drive C is EXAMPLE
Directory of C:\

Q        BAT       42 11-15-92   1:55p
FINDUR   BAT       18 11-12-92  10:33p
DIRECTOR BAT      219 08-17-91  11:36p
RUNCHA   BAT       73 04-19-89  11:55a
BATCH    BAT      468 11-12-92  10:46p
FINDERR  BAT      257 10-24-92   9:00p
AUTOEXEC BAT      165 11-15-92   9:29p
BLANKER  BAT      106 11-22-92  10:04p
        8 file(s)       1348 bytes
                    93339648 bytes free
```

```
C:\>TYPE BLANKER.BAT
:BLANKER.BAT
@ECHO OFF
BLANK
IF EXIST C:\BLANK.BLK GOTO SCREECH
GOTO EXIT
:SCREECH
SCREECH
:EXIT
```

`C:\>REN BLANKER.BAT BLANKER .BAT` (The space is where the <Alt>-255 is.)

```
C:\>DIR *.BAT

 Volume in drive C is EXAMPLE
 Directory of C:\

Q        BAT        42 11-15-92   1:55p
FINDUR   BAT        18 11-12-92  10:33p
DIRECTOR BAT       219 08-17-91  11:36p
RUNCHA   BAT        73 04-19-89  11:55a
BATCH    BAT       468 11-12-92  10:46p
FINDERR  BAT       257 10-24-92   9:00p
AUTOEXEC BAT       165 11-15-92   9:29p
BLANKER  BAT       106 11-22-92  10:04p
        8 file(s)        1348 bytes
                     93339648 bytes free

C:\>TYPE BLANKER.BAT
File not found - BLANKER.BAT

C:\>TYPE BLANKER?.BAT
Invalid filename or file not found
```

Simply leaving a space (the ASCII value of 32) doesn't solvethe problem:

```
C:\>TYPE BLANKER .BAT
Too many parameters - .BAT
```

The only way to view or change the file is to specify the <Alt>-255 character when addressing it. Listing 11-7 shows you how to use the character to make your computer screech at an intruder.

**Listing 11-7. Viewing a file by using an invisible character**

```
C:\>TYPE BLANKER .BAT
:BLANKER.BAT
@ECHO OFF
BLANK
IF EXIST C:\BLANK.BLK GOTO SCREECH
GOTO EXIT
:SCREECH
SCREECH
:EXIT

C:\>
```

The <Alt>-255 character provides a useful method of preventing the average user from viewing files. Unfortunately, this method has been around for a while. A new twist on this old trick, however, is to create an entire subdirectory named <Alt>-255 and hide files in it. Listing 11-8 shows you how to do it.

**Listing 11-8. Creating an invisible subdirectory**

```
C:\>MD <Alt>255

C:\>DIR *.

Volume in drive C is EXAMPLE
```

```
Directory of C:\

DOS           <DIR>      11-15-92   3:58a
QA            <DIR>      11-15-92   4:02a
              <DIR>      11-22-92  11:30p
LANG          <DIR>      11-15-92   4:09a
BATCH         <DIR>      11-15-92   4:13a
QEMM          <DIR>      11-15-92   4:13a
COMM          <DIR>      11-15-92   4:14a
DV            <DIR>      11-15-92   4:15a
GMK3          <DIR>      11-15-92   4:18a
MOUSE1        <DIR>      11-15-92   4:24a
NEWPS         <DIR>      11-15-92   4:24a
PBRUSH        <DIR>      11-15-92   4:26a
UTILITY       <DIR>      11-15-92   4:27a
TEMP          <DIR>      11-22-92  10:53p
       14 file(s)          2010 bytes
                       93306880 bytes free

C:\>
```

You've created the subdirectory, and it's able to hold information. However, it's still a bit too obvious to anyone looking closely. Listing 11-9 shows a way to hide it even better.

**Listing 11-9. Hiding a subdirectory from DIR listings**

```
C:\>ATTRIB +H

C:\>DIR *.

Volume in drive C is EXAMPLE
Directory of C:\

DOS           <DIR>      11-15-92   3:58a
QA            <DIR>      11-15-92   4:02a
```

```
LANG          <DIR>      11-15-92   4:09a
BATCH         <DIR>      11-15-92   4:13a
QEMM          <DIR>      11-15-92   4:13a
COMM          <DIR>      11-15-92   4:14a
DV            <DIR>      11-15-92   4:15a
GMK3          <DIR>      11-15-92   4:18a
MOUSE1        <DIR>      11-15-92   4:24a
NEWPS         <DIR>      11-15-92   4:24a
PBRUSH        <DIR>      11-15-92   4:26a
UTILITY       <DIR>      11-15-92   4:27a
TEMP          <DIR>      11-22-92  10:53p
       13 file(s)          2010 bytes
                       93306880 bytes free

C:\>
```

The subdirectory now doesn't even show up in DIR listings and is ready to hold files that will take a great deal of snooping to unearth.

Another file-renaming strategy involves using a File Allocation Table editor, such as Norton's NU utility, to locate the name of the file in question. Using such a utility, you can change a character in the name of the file from an uppercase character to a lowercase character. All commands given to DOS convert the command to uppercase. Even though the file still exists and is in plain sight, there's no method of accessing, viewing, modifying, deleting, or doing anything else to the file until the affected character is reverted to its original state.

Listing 11-10 shows an example of this approach to hiding files. (You would encounter the same menu choices I've shown in Figures 11-1 through 11-9, but I've altered the actual look to replace the color screens with black-and-white printing.)

**Listing 11-10. Using the FAT to hide a file**

```
C:\TEMP>DIR
Volume in drive C is EXAMPLE
Directory of  C:\TEMP
```

```
.              <DIR>      10-24-91   3:42p
..             <DIR>      10-24-91   3:42p
TMP            <DIR>       5-05-92   3:18p
CHOWN     EXE     11792    5-31-91   3:56a
FRIENDS   TXT       145   11-23-92  12:09p
        5 File(s)   2281472 bytes free

C:\TEMP>TYPE FRIENDS.TXT
kristi    1026
jim       1007
jess      1022
tom       1023
tony      1017
doug      1077
shannon   2006
jan       2007
bill      2010

C:\TEMP>NU C:\
```

```
                Main Menu

  Explore disk
  UnErase
  Disk Information
  Quit the Norton Utilities
```

**Figure 11-1. Norton Utilities main menu screen**

```
Explore disk

Choose item
Information on item
Edit/display item
Search item/disk for data
Write item to disk
Return to main menu
```

**Figure 11-2. The Explore disk screen**

```
Search item/disk for data

Where to search
Text to search for
(start search)
(display found text)
(continue search)
Leave search
```

**Figure 11-3. The Search item/disk for data screen**

```
Where to search

All of DOS disk
Data area
Erased file space
Selected item: Root dir
```

**Figure 11-4. The Where to search screen**

```
Search item/disk for data

Where to search
Text to search for
(start search)
(display found text)
(continue search)
Leave search
```

**Figure 11-5. The Search item/disk for data screen**

```
Text to search for

Search data, in character format
FRIENDS
```

**Figure 11-6. The Text to search for screen**

```
Search item/disk for data

Where to search
Text to search for
Start search
(display found text)
(continue search)
Leave search
```

**Figure 11-7. The Search item/disk for data screen**

```
Searching cluster 74
       Found!

Press any key to continue . . .
```

**Figure 11-8. The Searching screen**

The screen will appear garbled as it displays the file allocation table in hex and ASCII format. Hex will be on the left, constituting two thirds of the screen, and the ASCII will be on the right. Pay attention only to the ASCII and make the change.

```
20202010 00000000 00000000 00005C7D .          ..........\}
2E2E2020 20202020 20202010 00000000 XJ.......        ....
58170000 00000000 544D5020 20202020 ......\}X......TMP
00000000 00004E7A A5184B00 00000000    ..........NzÑ
                                                    K.....
45584520 00000000 00000000 00001A1F CHOWN   EXE .........
46524945 4E445320 54585420 00000000 ¬Ö...FRIENDS TXT ....
-æ...........
00000000 00000000 00000000 00000000 .....................
00000000 00000000 00000000 00000000 .....................
```

(make the change and press <Esc>)

```
20202010 00000000 00000000 00005C7D .          ..........\}
2E2E2020 20202020 20202010 00000000 XJ.......        ....
58170000 00000000 544D5020 20202020 ......\}X......TMP
00000000 00004E7A A5184B00 00000000    ..........NzÑ
                                                    K.....
45584520 00000000 00000000 00001A1F CHOWN   EXE .........
46526945 4E445320 54585420 00000000 ¬Ö...FRiENDS TXT ....
-æ...........
00000000 00000000 00000000 00000000 .....................
00000000 00000000 00000000 00000000 .....................
```

```
Save or discard changes made to data

You have made changes to the cluster in memory
(Changes are made and shown highlighted when
data is displayed in the hexadecimal format)

Write the changed data
Review the changed data
Discard the changes
```

**Figure 11-9. The Save or discard changes screen**

```
12:31|C:\TEMP>DIR

Volume in drive C is EXAMPLE
Directory of  C:\TEMP

.            <DIR>      10-24-91   3:42p
..           <DIR>      10-24-91   3:42p
TMP          <DIR>       5-05-92   3:18p
CHOWN    EXE     11792   5-31-91   3:56a
FRiENDS  TXT       145  11-23-92  12:09p
        5 File(s)   2281472 bytes free

12:31|C:\TEMP>TYPE FRiENDS.TXT
File not found

12:31|C:\TEMP>type friends.txt
File not found

12:31|C:\TEMP>
```

## Renaming Delete and Erase Commands

MS-DOS 5.0 contains the DOSKEY utility, which serves many functions, one of which is creating macros. In an earlier chapter, I mentioned that DOS takes a command and looks in the internal commands for a match. If it doesn't find a match, it then looks in the current working directory for a .COM file by that name. Not finding it, it looks for an .EXE file by that name, and then a .BAT file. If it can't find any matches, it goes to the first directory in the PATH statement and checks three times there, in the order I've just specified.

Macros fall into the equation above the search in the internal commands, thereby taking precedence over everything. This arrangement makes it possible to reassign internal commands to macro operations. Here's how. But first, create a quick batch file, as shown in Listing 11-11.

**Listing 11-11. A batch file to begin reassigning internal commands**

```
:PERM.BAT
@ECHO OFF
CLS
ECHO Permission denied
```

Second, if DOSKEY isn't installed as a TSR, install it by simply typing DOSKEY <Enter> at the command-line prompt.

Third, type the following statements at the command-line prompt:

```
DOSKEY DEL=PERM <Enter>
DOSKEY ERASE=PERM <Enter>
```

Now when a user attempts to delete a file by entering either command, the screen will clear and the user will receive the message "Permission denied."

Although DOSKEY is handy, not everyone has a copy, and it must be reloaded as a TSR each time the workstation is booted up. Additionally, the command to revert to DEL being equal to the delete function is the same as if you were unsetting an environment variable:

```
DOSKEY DEL=
```

A far better approach is to rename the internal commands altogether. You can rename commands with SID on DR DOS, DEBUG on MS-DOS, or, easiest of all, with NU from Norton Utilities. Here's how to use NU to rename the internal commands:

1. Start NU addressing the COMMAND.COM file:

   `C:\>NU C:\COMMAND.COM` <Enter>

2. Use the Search item/disk for data menu selection and enter ERASE as the text to search for. The display will look something like the following (not all characters are shown):

   ```
   45012612 0352454E 01261205 45524153   REN....ERAS
   45BD1104 44454C45 019E1203 52454D02   E...DEL..TY
   ```

   Change the first "E" in ERASE to "Z" and change the "D" in DEL to "Z" as well:

   ```
   45012612 0352454E 01261205 5A524153   REN....ZRAS
   45BD1104 5A454C45 019E1203 52454D02   E...ZEL..TY
   ```

3. Save the changes and exit. Reboot the workstation to reread the new COMMAND.COM file.

Now that you've renamed ERASE and DEL, the choices for what their replacements can do is limitless. Three possibilities appear in the following scenarios.

In all three scenarios, you create and make executable two files—DEL.EXE and ERASE.EXE—to prevent a user from viewing files. You must place these two files in the DOS subdirectory to be found when either of these two commands is summoned.

In the first scenario, the file deletion occurs without the user knowing that anything different has taken place, but an entry is made in a dummy DOS file called SLICE.EXE. Listing 11-12 shows the two new files.

**Listing 11-12. Creating two files that track file deletions**

```
REM DEL.EXE to maintain a transaction of file deletions
OPEN "C:\DOS\SLICE.EXE" FOR APPEND AS #1
PRINT #1, DATE$; " "; TIME$; " "; COMMAND$
CLOSE #1
KILL COMMAND$
END

REM ERASE.EXE to maintain a transaction of file
  deletions
OPEN "C:\DOS\SLICE.EXE" FOR APPEND AS #1
PRINT #1, DATE$; " "; TIME$; " "; COMMAND$
CLOSE #1
KILL COMMAND$
END
```

Listing 11-13 shows you what transpires when you use these new executables.

**Listing 11-13. Using DEL.EXE and ERASE.EXE**

```
C:\TEMP>DIR

Volume in drive C is EXAMPLE
Directory of C:\TEMP

.             <DIR>      11-22-92  10:53p
..            <DIR>      11-22-92  10:53p
COMMAND  COM       53022 10-26-92   6:00a
        3 file(s)       53022 bytes
                     93241344 bytes free
```

```
C:\TEMP>DEL COMMAND.COM

C:\TEMP>DIR

Volume in drive C is EXAMPLE
Directory of C:\TEMP

.            <DIR>      11-22-92  10:53p
..           <DIR>      11-22-92  10:53p
        2 file(s)            0 bytes
                      93339648 bytes free

C:\TEMP>CD\DOS

C:\DOS>DIR SL*

Volume in drive C is EXAMPLE
Directory of C:\DOS

SLICE    EXE         33 11-23-92   6:22p
        1 file(s)           33 bytes
                      93339648 bytes free

C:\DOS>TYPE SLICE.EXE
11-23-1992 18:22:41 COMMAND.COM

C:\DOS>
```

In the second scenario, depicted in Listing 11-14, the same transactions take place, except that the files are moved to a TRASHCAN directory within the hidden subdirectory created with the <Alt>-255 combination earlier in this chapter.

Naturally, if this option is the one you choose, the files need to be named DEL.EXE and ERASE.EXE and not DEL2 and ERASE2, as depicted here for purposes of differentiating examples.

```
Listing 11-14. Moving files to a TRASHCAN directory
REM DEL2.EXE to maintain transaction of deletions and
  copy over
OPEN "C:\DOS\SLICE.EXE" FOR APPEND AS #1
PRINT #1, DATE$; " "; TIME$; " "; COMMAND$
CLOSE #1
NAME COMMAND$ AS "C:\<Alt>255\TRASHCAN\" + COMMAND$
END

REM ERASE2.EXE to maintain transaction of deletions
  and copy over
OPEN "C:\DOS\SLICE.EXE" FOR APPEND AS #1
PRINT #1, DATE$; " "; TIME$; " "; COMMAND$
CLOSE #1
NAME COMMAND$ AS "C:\<Alt>255\TRASHCAN\" + COMMAND$
END
```

What transpires:

```
C:\TEMP>DIR

Volume in drive C is EXAMPLE
Directory of C:\TEMP

.            <DIR>     11-22-92  10:53p
..           <DIR>     11-22-92  10:53p
AUTOEXEC BAT       165 11-15-92   9:29p
        3 file(s)        165 bytes
                    93290496 bytes free

C:\TEMP>DEL AUTOEXEC.BAT
```

```
C:\TEMP>DIR

Volume in drive C is EXAMPLE
Directory of C:\TEMP

.            <DIR>      11-22-92  10:53p
..           <DIR>      11-22-92  10:53p
        2 file(s)            0 bytes
                      93290496 bytes free

C:\TEMP>CD\DOS

C:\DOS>TYPE SLICE.EXE
11-23-1992 18:22:41 COMMAND.COM
11-23-1992 18:32:27 AUTOEXEC.BAT

C:\DOS>CD\ \TRASHCAN

C:\ \TRASHCAN>DIR

Volume in drive C is EXAMPLE
Directory of C:\ \TRASHCAN

.            <DIR>      11-23-92   6:31p
..           <DIR>      11-23-92   6:31p
AUTOEXEC BAT        165 11-15-92   9:29p
        3 file(s)          165 bytes
                      93290496 bytes free

C:\ \TRASHCAN>
```

The third option, illustrated in Listing 11-15, doesn't keep a log or copy the files over to a TRASHCAN subdirectory, but instead prompts for a password before carrying out the action. If the password, a static one, isn't satisfied, then no action is carried out. If the password is properly satisfied (remember the discussion of how a password prompt should never say, "Please enter the password:", but should be far more cryptic?), then the action is performed.

**Listing 11-15. Using a password to block deletions**

```
REM DEL3.EXE to prompt for a password on deletions
PRINT : INPUT "Current drive is no longer valid>";
  PASS$
IF UCASE$(PASS$) <> "PLEASE" THEN GOTO 100
KILL COMMAND$
100 END

REM ERASE3.EXE to prompt for a password on deletions
PRINT : INPUT "Current drive is no longer valid>";
  PASS$
IF UCASE$(PASS$) <> "PLEASE" THEN GOTO 100
KILL COMMAND$
100 END
```

What transpires:

```
C:\TEMP>DIR

Volume in drive C is EXAMPLE
Directory of C:\TEMP

.            <DIR>      11-22-92  10:53p
..           <DIR>      11-22-92  10:53p
CONFIG   SYS        216 11-15-92   1:50p
        3 file(s)         216 bytes
                    93224960 bytes free

C:\TEMP>DEL CONFIG.SYS

Current drive is no longer valid>? c:
```

```
C:\TEMP>DIR

Volume in drive C is EXAMPLE
Directory of C:\TEMP

.             <DIR>      11-22-92  10:53p
..            <DIR>      11-22-92  10:53p
CONFIG   SYS        216 11-15-92   1:50p
        3 file(s)         216 bytes
                     93224960 bytes free

C:\TEMP>DEL CONFIG.SYS

Current drive is no longer valid>? Please

C:\TEMP>DIR

Volume in drive C is EXAMPLE
Directory of C:\TEMP

.             <DIR>      11-22-92  10:53p
..            <DIR>      11-22-92  10:53p
        2 file(s)           0 bytes
                     93224960 bytes free

C:\TEMP>
```

Since the password is compared on a non-case-sensitive basis, "PLEASE," "Please," "please," and all case variations thereof pass for the correct entry. To be more specific, remove the UCASE$ and enable case sensitivity.

In all three examples, as the individual who made the changes, you are aware that the original DEL and ERASE still exist and can still be performed, bypassing all three of the previous modifications, but only by someone who knows that they now operate as ZRASE and ZEL.

## Wrap-Up

The previous chapter dealt with security on the server, while this one discussed methods of making the workstation more secure. But we're not through yet. There's one more chapter in this trilogy; it will discuss security methods that work on both the server and the workstations.

Questions and discussion follow the next chapter.

12 CHAPTER

# NetWare Server and Workstation Security

Chapter 10 covered security techniques on file servers, and Chapter 11 discussed practices applicable to workstations. This chapter covers security techniques that apply equally to file servers and workstations.

## Read-Only

All .EXE, .COM, and bug-proofed .BAT files (meaning you've used them enough times to know that they work the way you intend them to) should have their attributes set to read-only. Since they are compiled programs (with the exception of .BAT), no user should be able to view or alter the contents. The only ones usually trying to write to .EXE and .COM files are viruses looking for a good place to attach themselves.

This situation is especially true of the COMMAND.COM file, which contains the internal DOS commands. Considering the material we covered in the previous chapter, how hard would it be to change the definition of COPY to DEL? If the change can be made this easily, think what a virus or worm could do, given the opportunity. In short, the more protection you can place on your files, the better off you are. For example, one way to use the Read-Only attribute to protect your COMMAND.COM file is to type, at the command line:

```
ATTRIB +R *.COM <Enter>
```

This command will read-protect your .COM files. You can do the same with .EXE and .BAT files, although I caution against doing so to SLICE.EXE if you're using it as a dummy file to write a deletion record as outlined at the end of Chapter 11.

Not only is read protection a good idea, but hiding files is as well. Setting the attribute bit of a file to Hide doesn't prevent DOS from finding it; it only prevents the file from appearing in directory listings. Listing 12-1 shows you what happens when you use the Hidden attribute on DEMO.BAT.

**Listing 12-1. Using the Hidden attribute to hide a file**

```
C:\>ECHO @ECHO OFF > DEMO.BAT

C:\>ECHO ECHO I CAN STILL BE PROCESSED >> DEMO.BAT

C:\>ECHO ECHO EVEN WHEN HIDDEN >> DEMO.BAT

C:\>ECHO ECHO       - DEMO.BAT >> DEMO.BAT

C:\>DIR *.BAT

Volume in drive C is EXAMPLE
Directory of C:\

Q        BAT       42 11-15-92   1:55p
FINDUR   BAT       18 11-12-92  10:33p
DIRECTOR BAT      219 08-17-91  11:36p
RUNCHA   BAT       73 04-19-89  11:55a
BATCH    BAT      468 11-12-92  10:46p
FINDERR  BAT      257 10-24-92   9:00p
AUTOEXEC BAT      165 11-15-92   9:29p
BLANKER  BAT      106 11-22-92  10:04p
DEMO     BAT       92 11-23-92   7:45p
```

```
        9 file(s)      1440 bytes
                    93224960 bytes free

C:\>ATTRIB +H DEMO.BAT

C:\>DIR *.BAT

Volume in drive C is EXAMPLE
Directory of C:\

Q        BAT        42 11-15-92   1:55p
FINDUR   BAT        18 11-12-92  10:33p
DIRECTOR BAT       219 08-17-91  11:36p
RUNCHA   BAT        73 04-19-89  11:55a
BATCH    BAT       468 11-12-92  10:46p
FINDERR  BAT       257 10-24-92   9:00p
AUTOEXEC BAT       165 11-15-92   9:29p
BLANKER  BAT       106 11-22-92  10:04p
        8 file(s)      1348 bytes
                    93224960 bytes free

C:\>DEMO
I CAN STILL BE PROCESSED
EVEN WHEN HIDDEN
      - DEMO.BAT
C:\>
```

Notice that the number of bytes in use diminishes when DEMO.BAT is hidden. The only clue that it's still there is that the number of bytes free didn't change. At the bare minimum, you should set three files to read-only *and* hidden: COMMAND.COM, AUTOEXEC.BAT, and CONFIG.SYS. These three files determine how the system operates; having them readily available for anyone to see is ludicrous.

## Passwords in Files

Programs that require passwords must store the password somewhere so they will know what to compare a user's entry with. Good utility programs store this information in an encrypted or compiled form; poor utility programs store it in plain old ASCII files begging to be viewed.

The short batch file, FINDPASS.BAT, examines ASCII files in a subdirectory and looks for a given word—a password in this case, or the word LOGIN as I explained in Chapter 10. Listing 12-2 shows you this simple batch file.

**Listing 12-2. Using FINDPASS.BAT to locate a password**

```
:FINDPASS.BAT
@ECHO OFF
FOR %%I IN (*.*) DO FIND "%1" %%I
```

"FINDPASS CU0SOON" goes through all files in the current directory and looks for a match to "CU0SOON." The batch file can't search files that are not in ASCII format; it skips over them, checking only the filenames. For ASCII files, it examines their entire contents and prints any matches it finds to the screen. (It prints to the screen the name of each file as the search progresses, as well.)

## Communications Programs

Remote communications and operations programs are a must in most networking environments today. They allow users to dial in to a workstation from the road or from home and perform operations exactly as if they were sitting at the workstation in the office.

From a security standpoint, this ability presents an interesting concept. Is the person who actually dials in at night and accesses a workstation the same person who should be dialing in? Or is it someone else who stumbled across the telephone number of an answering modem and decided to look around?

Password requirements should be turned on for *all* remote communications software. In addition to the file server password, the remote user now also needs a dial-up password to access the workstation via the modem.

Another safeguard against remote intruders is to turn on transaction logging, or at the bare minimum, logging of who dialed in and when. Listing 12-3 shows a sample activity record from PC anyWHERE by Symantec.

**Listing 12-3. A log of dial-in activity**

```
Activity Report for ANYWHERE.LOG

          Time   Time   Time
Date      On     Off    Online  Description     Project
--------  -----  -----  ------  --------------  -------
09-05-92  16:30  16:35  0:05    Emmett Working  Late
09-07-92  07:56  08:05  0:09    Emmett Working  Late
09-07-92  08:15  09:06  0:51    Emmett Working  Late
09-07-92  20:24  20:36  0:12    Emmett Working  Late
10-26-92  20:56  21:05  0:09    Emmett Working  Late
10-27-92  19:40  20:12  0:32    Emmett Working  Late
10-27-92  20:27  21:07  0:40    Emmett Working  Late
10-27-92  22:17  22:56  0:39    Emmett Working  Late
10-28-92  22:39  23:02  0:23    Emmett Working  Late
11-22-92  13:45  16:31  2:46    Emmett Working  Late
11-22-92  16:49  17:42  0:53    Emmett Working  Late
11-22-92  22:31  22:42  0:11    Emmett Working  Late
```

## Non-Standard Filenames

Everyone knows that "A" through "Z" and "0" through "9" are valid entries for filenames. DOS also accepts symbols and characters; think, for example, of temporary files with extensions of $$$.

When discussing passwords in Chapter 10, I mentioned several symbols as being valid choices. Eight of those same symbols are acceptable for use in filenames. In ASCII order, they are as follows:

**! # $ % & ' ( )**

These eight symbols begin with ASCII 33 and progress to 41, whereas "A" does not begin until 65. What benefit does this provide? If you use a symbol as the first character of a filename, and the subdirectory is sorted, the files with the symbols will sort alphabetically ahead of those numbers and letters. This provides a quick way of creating files that are easily located and not as prone to being examined by snooping eyes as more revealing filenames may be.

## Application Passwords

Many applications, whether word processors, databases, or something else, allow the user to assign a password to the application files. This password capability is often more than adequate. Since the application developers designed how the file would be laid out, they should know best how to prevent its being viewed.

To use the continuing example of Q&A by Symantec, this database program allows you to assign passwords to databases. Note the plural. More than one user can be assigned to a database, and each user is required to log in to the database just as any user must log in to the file server. A user name and password are required; the user name is common knowledge, while the password can be encrypted.

Different users can have different rights as to what they can see, delete, alter, and print. Only those assigned administrative access can assign users and change their permissions.

Lotus and Quattro Pro allow passwords to be assigned to spreadsheets. WordPerfect allows password encryption. Even PKLite allows you to encrypt executable files so they can't be returned to their original form without the proper password being given. In short, check the software you're using and see if it offers file-protection benefits.

## Locking a File

Sometimes you don't care whether or not a user accesses a file, but you don't want him or her to be accessing it at this moment. If such is the case, then you can lock the file and prevent it from being used, *providing* (very important point) the DOS command SHARE is running on the workstation. In most networking environments, SHARE is always running.

LOCKEDUP is a utility routine you can use to open a file whose name you give on the command line. It then locks that file and prevents anyone else from accessing it until you enter an uppercase "Z." It also provides a "shell" that allows you to make other requests while it's essentially locking the file in the background. It provides a clue that it's running by printing the prompt on one line and accepting input on the second line, as opposed to the usual one line for both.

While LOCKEDUP is fine in theory and practice, it doesn't look as nice as running directly from the DOS prompt does. Consequently, if you're running Windows or DesqView, I strongly suggest opening LOCKEDUP in one session and using another session in which to continue your business. When you're ready to release the file, revert to the original session and use the uppercase Z to unlock the file. Listing 12-4 shows you how to make this setup work.

> **NOTE:** TRUENAME is a command associated with MS-DOS 5.0 and higher. On other operating systems, substitute the CD command and it will perform a similar function.

**Listing 12-4. The LOCKUP utility**

```
REM LOCKEDUP
OPEN COMMAND$ FOR RANDOM AS #1
LOCK #1
10 SHELL "TRUENAME"
```

```
LINE INPUT ""; c$
IF c$ = "Z" THEN UNLOCK #1: END
IF c$ <> "" THEN SHELL c$
GOTO 10
```

What transpires:

```
C:\>DIR AUTO*

Volume in drive C is EXAMPLE
Directory of C:\

AUTOEXEC CHA        57 08-03-90   7:12a
AUTOEXEC EAD       201 08-17-91   7:47p
AUTOEXEC BAK       162 11-15-92   1:44p
AUTOEXEC BAT       165 11-15-92   9:29p
        4 file(s)        585 bytes
                    93192192 bytes free

C:\>TYPE AUTOEXEC.BAK
@ECHO OFF
PATH C:\DOS;C:\;C:\DV;C:\UTILITY\NORTON
C:\MOUSE1\MOUSE
PROMPT=$P$G
:NUMLOCK
SET TEMP=C:\DOS
DOSKEY
CLS
CD\DV
DV

C:\>LOCKEDUP AUTOEXEC.BAK
C:\
DIR AUTO*
```

```
Volume in drive C is EXAMPLE
Directory of C:\

AUTOEXEC CHA        57 08-03-90   7:12a
AUTOEXEC EAD       201 08-17-91   7:47p
AUTOEXEC BAK       162 11-15-92   1:44p
AUTOEXEC BAT       165 11-15-92   9:29p
        4 file(s)        585 bytes
                    93192192 bytes free
```

(Notice that the prompt and input are now on separate lines. Remember, this separation of prompt and input is the clue that LOCKEDUP is active.)

```
C:\
TYPE AUTOEXEC.BAK

Lock violation reading drive C
Abort, Retry, Fail?A

C:\
Z

C:\>TYPE AUTOEXEC.BAK
@ECHO OFF
PATH C:\DOS;C:\;C:\DV;C:\UTILITY\NORTON
C:\MOUSE1\MOUSE
PROMPT=$P$G
:NUMLOCK
SET TEMP=C:\DOS
DOSKEY
CLS
CD\DV
DV

C:\>
```

The prompt and the input are once again on the same line, indicating that LOCKEDUP is no longer active. If you have trouble invoking the utility, you'll probably receive an error message like the following one to indicate that the DOS SHARE utility isn't active:

```
C:\>LOCKEDUP AUTOEXEC.BAK

Permission denied in module LOCKEDUP at address
21DD:005A

Hit any key to return to system

C:\>
```

## Wrap-Up

This chapter and the preceding two chapters have covered network security. Computers revolve around data; the safer you can keep that data, the more productive the work environment will be.

Cliff Stoll wrote a book entitled *The Cuckoo's Egg* (see Suggested Reading in Appendix B) about a hacker who was able to gain access to the Berkeley Lab. Countless articles have been written about Robert Morris, the Cornell University student who created the Internet Worm that "temporarily" disabled approximately 3,000 computers.

Computer hackers and virus creators gain public attention, and that attention gives rise to others who thrive on that notoriety. You must therefore make it as difficult as possible for such individuals to thwart your system. Let them look for a system with easier access and easier passwords.

In addition to these exogenous threats, you must also deal with employees who have passwords and trustee rights, and who want to look at data that they shouldn't see. While allowing them access to the system, you must limit that access.

It's dangerous and costly to be careless with your network's security.

## A Few Good Questions

1. The Server Login Restrictions option in SYSCON pertains to failed attempts and limits on access time. What about users who have left the employ of the company? How do you prevent them from accessing the system? How do you make certain all information pertaining to them is deleted?

2. We renamed ERASE and DEL, both internal commands. Should the same be done with external commands? If so, which ones, and how would it best be performed?

Consider these questions, and then find the answers in Appendix A.

# 13 CHAPTER

# NetWare Troubleshooting with Utilities

Optimization is a wonderful concept, and security is a comforter that keeps you cozy and guarded from the outside world. But even under the best conditions, things do go wrong. And as sad as it may be, nothing lasts forever—with the exception of milk jugs and plastic diapers, as the ecology crowd would quickly point out.

With computers, and particularly with networks, you try to keep things running as smoothly as possible for as long as possible. Then when something does go wrong, you attempt to isolate the problem, seal it off from the rest of the network, and evaluate the extent of the damage. You minimalize that damage as much as possible.

Once you know the source of the difficulty, you correct the problem and try to restore everything to proper working order. The first secret is in knowing what the problem is. Was it noise on line, and if so, where did the noise come from? Did the file server take a surge? And what could be wrong with that blasted laser printer?

## Avoiding Trouble

Many troublesome networking complications occur as the result of one small problem: lack of power. If a server loses power while files are opened, the subsequent network crash can damage the files so severely that you have to restore them from a backup tape.

Databases often open indexes and pointers to the data inside. If a disruption in power occurs while the file is opened, the indexes and pointers become unreliable. They can point to the wrong data, or they can point to data that doesn't exist at all.

There's an old saying that absolute power corrupts absolutely. This may be true in terms of world leaders and underground figures, but with networks, it's the unexpected absence of power that corrupts absolutely.

As for supplying electrical input to the server and workstations, it's the supervisor's responsibility to see that he or she has the proper power supplies and power surge protectors. Bear in mind that you can sink a great deal of money into protecting the electrical current flowing into a server, but that server is only as secure as the electrical protection on the workstation that it's connected to via an Ethernet cable. If a surge comes into the workstation and goes out the Ethernet cable, will the server be affected? Probably.

Never skimp on power protection.

That said, never skimp on file protection, either. When you turn the server off, be absolutely certain that no open files are floating about. It goes without saying that you should always use the DOWN command to shut the server down properly. If DOWN returns the message, "*** WARNING *** ACTIVE FILES OPEN. HALT NETWORK?" what should you do?

The answer is that you should never turn off the server when this message is on the console screen, regardless of how certain you are that no users were logged on 15 minutes ago when you went for coffee and a Danish. Use the NetWare FCONSOLE utility to confirm that no one is connected. Let's look at the FCONSOLE Available Options screen shown in Figure 13-1.

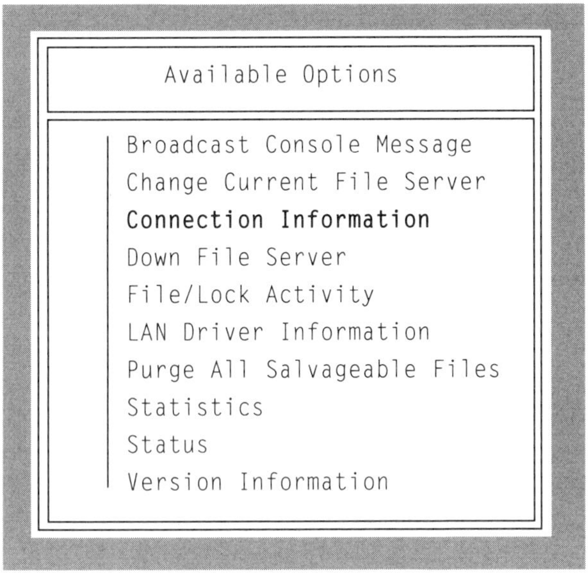


**Figure 13-1. The Available options screen**

Next, look at the Connection Information option, shown in Figure 13-2.

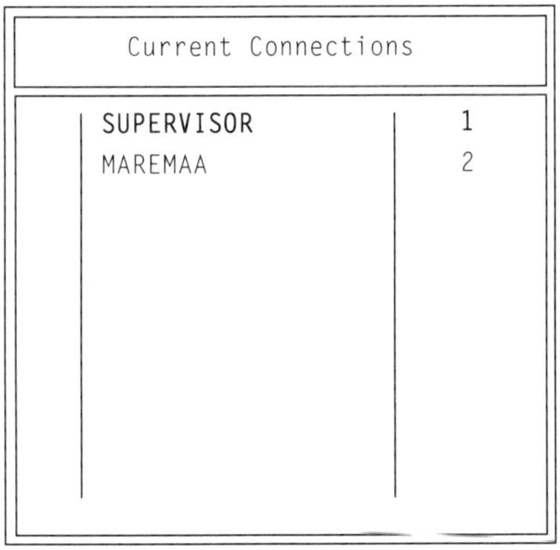


**Figure 13-2. The Connection Information option**

In this case, it appears that MAREMAA has logged on and now there are open files. FCONSOLE can show you what those files are. It can also be useful if you're having problems accessing a particular file by checking to see if anyone else is presently accessing the same file. For example, try using FCONSOLE to follow up on MAREMAA's open files.

First select the user from the current connections screen, and then choose Open Fles from the next menu that appears, as shown in Figure 13-3.

```
Current Connections

SUPERVISOR        1
MAREMAA           2
```

```
Connection Information

Broadcast Console Message
Clear Connection
Logical Record Locks
Open Files/Physical Records
Other Information
Semaphores
Task Information
Usage Statistics
```

**Figure 13-3. Choosing the Open Files/Physical Records option in the Connection Information screen**

```
Files In Use By MAREMAA[2]                      Task

SYS:APPL/QA3/QA.DIS                              9
SYS:APPL/QA3/QA1.EXE                             9
```

**Figure 13-4. A list of files in use by MAREMAA**

One of the best features of FCONSOLE, however, is its unmatched capability to give you a quick look at file server statistics and determine what's really happening from the standpoint of the file server.

Let's consider a representation of a small network with only three workstations running. Look at the Available Options menu shown in Figure 13-5:

**Figure 13-5. The Available options menu**

Select the Statistics option:

```
File Server Statistics

Cache Statistics
Channel Statistics
Disk Mapping Information
Disk Statistics
File System Statistics
LAN I/O Statistics
Summary
Volume Information
```

**Figure 13-6. The File Server Statistics menu—select Summary**

The Statistics option offers you a Summary option that gives you helpful information, such as the summary of server statistics shown in Listing 13-1.

**Listing 13-1. Server Statistics Summary**

```
File Server Up Time:  1 Day   0 Hours 20 Minutes 55 Seconds

Number Of File Service Processes: 5 Current Server Utiliza-
  tion:0%

Disk Requests Serviced From Cache: 96%  Packets Routed: 0

Total Packets Received:  58,858  File Service Packets: 0

Total Number Of Cache Buffers: 265  Dirty Cache Buffers: 0

Total Server Memory:  2,097,152  Unused Server Memory:4,096
```

```
                    Maximum      Peak Used Currently In Use
Routing Buffers:        40               1              0
Open Files:            504             108             14
Indexed Files:          10               0              0
Transactions:          N/A             N/A            N/A
Bindery Objects:       500              10             10
Connections:           100               3              3
Dynamic Memory 1:   17,914           1,764            814
Dynamic Memory 2:   52,812           4,576          4,328
Dynamic Memory 3:   47,104             712            120
```

The number of open files is configured for a maximum of 504, yet only 108 have ever been used, and only 14 are currently open. Bindery objects are set for a maximum of 500 (this roughly translates to 500 users); a glance here shows there are only 10. The statistics offered by this summary can come in handy in many troubleshooting situations.

## Course of Action

Several courses of action constantly reappear when attempting to correct network server problems. The following list of procedures is a step-by-step summary of the way to approach a suspected dilemma. When you use this short outline for troubleshooting your network, expect the first two steps to correct your problem, but be willing to perform the other two if you must.

1. Run diagnostic software, such as SYSCON and PCONSOLE, to identify problems. If you're using NetWare 2.2 or NetWare 3.11, note that many FCONSOLE functions have been taken over by the MONITOR utility. As a network administrator, you're either quite familiar with these utilities or you have access to the documentation.

2. Reboot the server. (The reboot process itself is simple, but making sure everyone is logged out at the time is sometimes difficult.)

3. Run BINDFIX. If simpler solutions don't work, the problem could be with the bindery.

4. Run VREPAIR. This step is a serious, last-desperate-measure attempt to resolve network problems. It can disable the hard drive, so try everything else first.

## Troubleshooting the Database

The routine presented in Listing 13-2, called TROUBLE, is a database of some of the more common NetWare problems. By working through a menu system, it can provide advice on paths to follow to arrive at a solution.

Not *every* NetWare problem is listed; I don't believe there to be a large enough database to hold all things that happenstance can create. Besides, you have access to NetWare's on-line help, and you should have the NetWare Technical Reference disk. Nevertheless, the TROUBLE routine is quite useful, and it serves a needed function in demonstrating its operation. Again, I use NetWare 2.15 as the lowest common denominator to generate solutions that will work with virtually every NetWare version presently in use.

**Listing 13-2. Using the TROUBLE routine to troubleshoot the network**

```
REM TROUBLE
1000 A$ = "TROUBLESHOOTING DATABASE - VERSION ONE"
B$ = "PRINTING WORKSTATION SERVER QUIT"
GOSUB 7000

1200 REM MAIN MENU SELECTION
INPUT A
IF A > 5 OR A < 1 THEN GOTO 1200
ON A GOTO 2000, 3000, 4000, 5000
```

```
RETURN

1300 INPUT B
IF B > LIM OR B < 1 THEN GOTO 1300
IF B = LIM THEN GOTO 1000
GOTO 8000

2000 REM PRINTING PROBLEM
A$ = "PRINTING PROBLEM"
B$ = "ILLEGAL BANNER ILLEGAL Q. NAMENO DEFAULT QUE NO
  RESPONSE NOT AUTHORIZED "
B$ = B$ + "NOT ENOUGH MEM Q. NOT EXIST   QUEUE IS FULL
  QUEUE HALTED   SCRAMBLED JOBS "
B$ = B$ + "SERVER ERROR   SPOOLER ERROR  UNKOWN QUEUE
  RETURN TO MAIN "
GOSUB 7000: LIM = 14
GOTO 1300

3000 REM WORKSTATION PROBLEM
A$ = "WORKSTATION PROBLEM"
B$ = "ACCESS DENIED  COM INTERPRETERCONN. NO
  LONGERENVIRON SPACE INVALID DRIVE   "
B$ = B$ + "IPX NOT LOADED NETWORK FAIL LDNOT FILES OPEN
  OUT OF MEMORY  PARITY ERROR   RETURN TO MAIN "
GOSUB 7000: LIM = 11
GOTO 1300
4000 REM SERVER PROBLEM
A$ = "SERVER PROBLEM"
B$ = "ACCESS DENIED  ADDR. COLLISIONBAD BLOCK
  CANNOT ADD USERFATAL DIR ERRORFILE HANDLES   "
B$ = B$ + "I/O READ ERROR NO FREE CONNECTNOT OPEN
  BINDEROUT OF BOUNDS  PARITY ERROR   "
B$ = B$ + "PRT. DRIVE FAILSTACK OVERFLOW RETURN TO MAIN"
GOSUB 7000: LIM = 14
```

```
GOTO 1300

5000 END

6000 DATA The banner flag was used without specifying a
  banner
DATA RETYPE THE ENTRY - WATCHING SYNTAX
DATA Mistyped or misspecified queue name
DATA USE PCONSOLE TO VERIFY VALID QUEUE NAMES
DATA Print queues are lost or disabled
DATA SUPERVISOR NEEDS TO CREATE OR REENABLE QUEUES
DATA The printer is off-line or out of paper
DATA CHECK AND CORRECT THE PROBLEM ON THE PRINTER
DATA The printer server cannot access the queue
DATA USE PCONSOLE AND ADD THE PRINT SERVER
DATA On a workstation there is not enough memory to
  hold escape sequences
DATA ADD MORE MEMORY TO THE WORKSTATION
DATA The queue name was improperly typed in or called
  from a BAT file
DATA CHECK PCONSOLE FOR VALID QUEUES
DATA The station running as Pserver does not have
  enough memory
DATA ADD ADDITIONAL MEMORY TO THE PSERVER
DATA The queue operator has disabled additional entries
  DATA USE PCONSOLE TO REENABLE
DATA The CAPTURE statement is timing out before the
  entire job is sent
DATA INCREASE THE LENGTH OF THE ti VARIABLE
DATA The NetWare Bindery files are corrupted
DATA USE BINDFIX TO REBUILD THE HIDDEN SYSTEM FILES
DATA Print job was deleted while it was spooling
DATA CHECK SYS FOR UNNEEDED TEMP FILES AND FREE UP
  SPACE
DATA There was a problem with the cabling connection
```

```
DATA SEND THE REQUEST AGAIN
DATA THIS SPACE INTENTIONALLY LEFT BLANK
DATA THIS SPACE INTENTIONALLY LEFT BLANK
DATA THIS SPACE INTENTIONALLY LEFT BLANK
DATA THIS SPACE INTENTIONALLY LEFT BLANK
DATA User attempting to login after too many failed
  attempts
DATA WAIT UNTIL RESTRICTION TIME EXPIRES OR SUPERVISOR
CAN REENABLE LOGIN
DATA The COMMAND.COM file has been deleted or rendered
  unsuitable
DATA REBOOT FROM A DISKETTE AND COPY OVER A NEW
  COMMAND.COM
DATA Connection no longer valid - the server has been
  downed or time restriction
DATA CHECK THE SERVER THEN CHECK THE USER TIME
  RESTRICTIONS
DATA The space allotted for environmental variables
  has been depleted
DATA SET UNNEED VARIABLES = {nothing} AND\OR USE
  COMMAND.COM TO ALLOT MORE SPACE
DATA If root drive then system files have been rendered
  useless
DATA REINSTALL THE TWO HIDDEN DOS FILES FROM A FLOPPY
DATA An attempt has been made to run NET.n without
  loading IPX
DATA LOAD IPX FIRST THEN NET.n
DATA The board address and memory do not match
DATA RUN IPX I FOR INFO THEN RECONFIGURE THE BOARD
DATA The number or open files exceeds the number
  allowed
DATA INCREASE FILES= IN CONFIG.SYS
DATA The workstation is using all recognizable memory
DATA ADD MORE MEMORY
DATA RAM memory is not reading properly
```

```
DATA REBOOT THE WORKSTATION
DATA THIS SPACE INTENTIONALLY LEFT BLANK
DATA THIS SPACE INTENTIONALLY LEFT BLANK
DATA THIS SPACE INTENTIONALLY LEFT BLANK
DATA THIS SPACE INTENTIONALLY LEFT BLANK
DATA THIS SPACE INTENTIONALLY LEFT BLANK
DATA THIS SPACE INTENTIONALLY LEFT BLANK
DATA THIS SPACE INTENTIONALLY LEFT BLANK
DATA THIS SPACE INTENTIONALLY LEFT BLANK
DATA THIS SPACE INTENTIONALLY LEFT BLANK
DATA THIS SPACE INTENTIONALLY LEFT BLANK
DATA Passwords have been corrupted/scrambled
DATA RUN BINDFIX TO REBUILD THE HIDDEN SYSTEM FILES
DATA Two networks are using the same address
DATA CHANGE THE NETWORK ADDRESS OF ONE LAN
DATA Interrupts passed an undefined message
DATA REBOOT THE SERVER
DATA The NetWare hidden system files are corrupted
DATA RUN BINDFIX TO RECOVER
DATA Server power was lost without the server being
  properly downed
DATA THE VREPAIR UTILITY MUST BE RUN
DATA An application is requiring more file handles than
  are configured
DATA CHECK FCONSOLE STATISTICS FOR MAX. OPEN FILES AND
  CURRENT - ADD MORE
DATA Server processing other requests
DATA CHECK FCONSOLE FOR OTHER USERS USING THE FILE
DATA The users workstation number has been exceeded
DATA EXIT THE USER FROM WORKSTATIONS THEY ARE NOT USING
DATA Corruption in NetWare hidden system files
DATA REBUILD THE BINDERY WITH BINDFIX
DATA The server was turned off without properly downing
DATA USE THE VREPAIR UTILITY
DATA Problem with RAM
```

```
DATA REBOOT THE SERVER
DATA Mirroring has switched to the second disk
DATA REPLACE THE PRIMARY DISK AND REINITIALIZE
  MIRRORING
DATA A memory failure in RAM exists
DATA REBOOT THE SERVER

7000 REM MENU DISPLAYS
CLS
PRINT A$: PRINT : PRINT "What category does the problem
  match:": PRINT
FOR C = 1 TO LEN(B$) STEP 15
PRINT INT(C / 15) + 1; "  "; MID$(B$, C, 15)
NEXT C
RETURN

8000 REM PROBLEM\SOLUTION DISPLAYS
CLS
F = 14
PRINT MID$(B$, (B * 15) - F, 15); ":"
D = (((A * 15) - 15) + B)
PRINT : PRINT
FOR E = 1 TO D
READ E$, F$
NEXT E
PRINT "CAUSE: "; E$
PRINT "SOLUTION: "; F$
RESTORE
PRINT : PRINT "Press X to exit, or any other key to go
  back": PRINT
INPUT " "; C$
IF UCASE$(C$) = "X" THEN END
G = A
ON G GOTO 2000, 3000, 4000
```

## Comments on the TROUBLE Routine

The three available categories of problems are defined in routine 1000 as printing, workstations, and servers. You can create additional menu choices by adding them to variable B$ in increments of 15 characters.

Routines 2000, 3000, and 4000 are the submenus beneath the main menu, each offering its allocation of problems. You can create additional submenu choices in any of these categories, again by expanding B$ in increments of 15 characters.

As presently defined, the submenu choices are limited to 15 selections and 15 characters. This limitation creates a variable B$ of 225 characters, for purposes of having a workable length. You can modify this setup, however, if you need to allow for more and longer entries.

Routine 6000 gives the DATA statements containing each problem in two sections: the problem and the solution. The problem is listed first in lowercase, while the solution follows in uppercase text. Because each submenu is defined for 15 entries, those that have less have "THIS SPACE INTENTIONALLY LEFT BLANK" added as their data statements. When a submenu choice is added as new problems occur, all you need to do is to change two of the BLANK lines into a problem-and-solution listing.

Routine 7000 displays the submenus, and 8000 the solutions. The operation is illustrated in Listing 13-3, with the exception of the CLS procedures.

**Listing 13-3. Results from running the TROUBLE routine**

```
Which of the following categories does the problem
match?

  1 PRINTING
  2 WORKSTATION
  3 SERVER
  4 QUIT
? 2
```

```
WORKSTATION PROBLEM

Which category does the problem match?

 1 ACCESS DENIED
 2 COM INTERPRETER
 3 CONN. NO LONGER
 4 ENVIRON SPACE
 5 INVALID DRIVE
 6 IPX NOT LOADED
 7 NETWORK FAIL LD
 8 NOT FILES OPEN
 9 OUT OF MEMORY
10 PARITY ERROR
11 RETURN TO MAIN
? 6

IPX NOT LOADED :

CAUSE: An attempt has been made to run NET.n without
loading IPX
SOLUTION: LOAD IPX FIRST THEN NET.n

Press X to exit, or any other key to go back

 ?
WORKSTATION PROBLEM

What category does the problem match?

 1 ACCESS DENIED
 2 COM INTERPRETER
 3 CONN. NO LONGER
 4 ENVIRON SPACE
 5 INVALID DRIVE
```

```
 6  IPX NOT LOADED
 7  NETWORK FAIL LD
 8  NOT FILES OPEN
 9  OUT OF MEMORY
10  PARITY ERROR
11  RETURN TO MAIN
? 11

TROUBLESHOOTING DATABASE - VERSION ONE

What category does the problem match?

 1  PRINTING
 2  WORKSTATION
 3  SERVER
 4  QUIT
? 3

SERVER PROBLEM

What category does the problem match?

 1  ACCESS DENIED
 2  ADDR. COLLISION
 3  BAD BLOCK
 4  CANNOT ADD USER
 5  FATAL DIR ERROR
 6  FILE HANDLES
 7  I/O READ ERROR
 8  NO FREE CONNECT
 9  NOT OPEN BINDER
10  OUT OF BOUNDS
11  PARITY ERROR
12  PRI. DRIVE FAIL
13  STACK OVERFLOW
```

```
14  RETURN TO MAIN
? 2

ADDR. COLLISION:

CAUSE: Two networks are using the same address
SOLUTION: CHANGE THE NETWORK ADDRESS OF ONE LAN

Press X to exit, or any other key to go back

 ?

SERVER PROBLEM

What category does the problem match?

 1  ACCESS DENIED
 2  ADDR. COLLISION
 3  BAD BLOCK
 4  CANNOT ADD USER
 5  FATAL DIR ERROR
 6  FILE HANDLES
 7  I/O READ ERROR
 8  NO FREE CONNECT
 9  NOT OPEN BINDER
10  OUT OF BOUNDS
11  PARITY ERROR
12  PRI. DRIVE FAIL
13  STACK OVERFLOW
14  RETURN TO MAIN
? 4

CANNOT ADD USER:

CAUSE: The NetWare hidden system files are corrupted
```

```
SOLUTION: RUN BINDFIX TO RECOVER

Press X to exit, or any other key to go back

 ? x
```

## Wrap-Up

Troubleshooting involves recognizing that a problem exists, and then proceeding to correct that problem in the most expedient and effective manner. The more you know, the more quickly and effectively you can act.

The routine TROUBLE should benefit you in diagnosing common problems, and you can add to it as situations arise to create a quick database reference of problems and solutions.

While this concluding chapter has dealt exclusively with troubleshooting, it has been the intent of this entire book to present shortcuts and solutions that enable NetWare administrators to have an easier time performing their obligations.

And obligations they are, for it's the responsibility of an administrator to make certain that the network operates as efficiently and productively as possible. I hope that the utilities presented throughout this book and included on the disk will enable you to fulfill your obligations more easily.

APPENDIX

# A

# Answers to Chapter Questions

Several chapters in this book concluded with pertinent questions about network administration. Answers to those questions are given in this appendix.

## Chapter 5

At the conclusion of Chapter 5, we left the discussion of MAIL.BAT on the note that

```
mail send c:\qa\qadoc\letter.dat karen <Enter>
```

won't work, while

```
MAIL SEND C:\QA\QADOC\LETTER.DAT KAREN <Enter>
```

will work. The reason is that the MAIL.BAT file looks for the existence of a second parameter and branches processing to the second parameter if it finds one. In this instance, a second parameter is found (send) and it attempts to branch processing, but can't since it's case-sensitive and no match is found (SEND is uppercase).

With the BASIC language, you can convert the given string to uppercase before processing by using the UCASE$ command. Unfortunately, there is no comparable way to perform this function in simple batch language. The simplest solution to this problem is to specify two pointers to the same location, one uppercase and one lowercase, as follows:

```
:MAIL.BAT
@ECHO OFF
IF NOT "%1"=="" GOTO %1
SET ALLAN=\MAIL\B0025
SET DONNA=\MAIL\11004D
SET ERNESTINE=\MAIL\E003B
SET JENNIFER=\MAIL\A001D
SET JERRY=\MAIL\D0033
SET KAREN=\MAIL\290067
SET LORRAINE=\MAIL\20007
CALL YOU.BAT
F:
CD %ME2%
IF EXIST *.DAT ECHO You have new mail - use %0 READ to
  view
PAUSE
GOTO END
:READ
:read
IF NOT "%2"=="" GOTO VIEW
CLS
ECHO New messages are:
C:
DIR F:%ME2%\*.DAT | FIND /V "Volume" | FIND /V "
  Directory" | FIND /V "(s"
ECHO Saved messages are:
DIR F:%ME2%\*.-AT | FIND /V "Volume" | FIND /V "
  Directory" | FIND /V "File not" | FIND /V "(s"
ECHO Use %0 %1 FILENAME.EXT TO VIEW
GOTO END
```

```
:VIEW
:view
F:
CD %ME2%
IF NOT EXIST %2 ECHO Invalid File Name and/or Extension
IF NOT EXIST %2 GOTO END
MORE < %2
REN %2 *.-AT
ECHO Message has been saved.  Use MAIL PURGE FILENAME
  to permanently remove.
:PURGE
:purge
IF "%2"=="" ECHO You must specify a File Name
IF "%2"=="" GOTO END
IF NOT EXIST %2.-AT ECHO Invalid File Name.  Leave off
  the Extension.
IF NOT EXIST %2.-AT GOTO END
F:
CD %ME2%
DEL %2.-AT
GOTO END
:SEND
:send
IF "%3"=="" ECHO Correct syntax is MAIL SEND Path
 Person
IF "%3"=="" ECHO Such as MAIL SEND C:\WP\LETTER %ME%
IF "%3"=="" GOTO END
SET ABC=%3
CALL YOU B40
F:
CD %ME2%
COPY %2
SEND "You have received mail" %3
ECHO MAIL HAS BEEN SENT
SET ABC=%ME%
```

```
CALL YOU TOO
GOTO END
:COMPOSE
:compose
IF "%2"=="" ECHO Correct syntax is MAIL COMPOSE Person
  Document.DAT
IF "%2"=="" ECHO Such as MAIL COMPOSE %ME% LETTER.DAT
IF "%2"=="" GOTO END
SET ABC=%2
CALL YOU B40
F:
CD %ME2%
CLS
ECHO Begin writing. . . use {CTRL-Z} on a blank line
  when finished
COPY CON %3
SEND "You have received mail" %2
ECHO MAIL HAS BEEN SENT
SET ABC=%ME%
CALL YOU TOO
GOTO END
:HELP
:help
:INFO
:info
:INFORMATION
:information
:?
CLS
TYPE MAIL.HLP
ECHO.
PAUSE
CLS
:END
C:
CD\
```

This takes care of the MAIL.BAT program. A problem, however, still exists in the execution of YOU.BAT. In the example given, the receiver of the document is also given in lowercase. MAIL.BAT doesn't care how the entry is given; it's only concerned with the existence of a third parameter and passes execution to YOU.BAT. YOU.BAT *does* care about the case sensitivity when it performs its IF statement check. It's looking for %ABC% to be equal to a variable, and it replaces %ABC% with the variable, so that the statement at time of programming looks like this:

```
IF karen==KAREN SET ME2=\MAIL\290067
```

The two parameters are not the same and %ABC% doesn't match with anything in the IF statement lists. The result is that ME2 stays what it originally was, not giving the proper directory, and the file is not copied.

It's possible to write a BASIC program to accept the variables and convert them to uppercase, and then send them back to the batch file. But the easiest solution in this scenario of limited users is to follow the same pattern as MAIL.BAT and simply state each user twice, like this:

```
:YOU.BAT
@ECHO OFF
CLS
IF NOT "%1"=="" GOTO ASCERTAIN
C:
WHOAMI | FIND "You are" > TEMP.BAT
TEMP.BAT
:ASCERTAIN
IF NOT "%1"=="are" GOTO NEXT
SET ME=%3
DEL TEMP.BAT
SET ABC=%ME%
:NEXT
IF %ABC%==ALLAN SET ME2=\MAIL\B0025
```

```
IF %ABC%==allan SET ME2=\MAIL\B0025
IF %ABC%==DONNA SET ME2=\MAIL\11004D
IF %ABC%==donna SET ME2=\MAIL\11004D
IF %ABC%==ERNESTINE SET ME2=\MAIL\E003B
IF %ABC%==ernestine SET ME2=\MAIL\E003B
IF %ABC%==JENNIFER SET ME2=\MAIL\A001D
IF %ABC%==jennifer SET ME2=\MAIL\A001D
IF %ABC%==JERRY SET ME2=\MAIL\D0033
IF %ABC%==jerry SET ME2=\MAIL\D0033
IF %ABC%==KAREN SET ME2=\MAIL\290067
IF %ABC%==karen SET ME2=\MAIL\290067
IF %ABC%==LORRAINE SET ME2=\MAIL\20007
IF %ABC%==lorraine SET ME2=\MAIL\20007
```

If the user issues a command that doesn't exist, such as

`MAIL LOOK` <Enter>

he or she will receive the message "Label not found" since there's no LOOK to branch to. Unfortunately, the batch file won't return an errorlevel, and it isn't possible to predict all the possible entries a user might type in. The only possibility here would be, instead of sending processing immediately to the second parameter, to verify that it's a valid parameter in the following way:

```
:MAIL.BAT
@ECHO OFF
IF "%1"=="" GOTO SET
IF "%1"=="READ" GOTO READ
IF "%1"=="read" GOTO READ
IF "%1"=="VIEW" GOTO VIEW
IF "%1"=="view" GOTO VIEW
IF "%1"=="PURGE" GOTO PURGE
IF "%1"=="purge" GOTO PURGE
IF "%1"=="SEND" GOTO SEND
```

```
IF "%1"=="send" GOTO SEND
IF "%1"=="COMPOSE" GOTO COMPOSE
IF "%1"=="compose" GOTO COMPOSE
GOTO HELP
:SET
SET ALLAN=\MAIL\B0025
SET DONNA=\MAIL\11004D
SET ERNESTINE=\MAIL\E003B
SET JENNIFER=\MAIL\A001D
SET JERRY=\MAIL\D0033
SET KAREN=\MAIL\290067
SET LORRAINE=\MAIL\20007
CALL YOU.BAT
F:
CD %ME2%
IF EXIST *.DAT ECHO You have new mail - use %0 READ to
  view
PAUSE
GOTO END
:READ
IF NOT "%2"=="" GOTO VIEW
CLS
ECHO New messages are:
C:
DIR F:%ME2%\*.DAT | FIND /V "Volume" | FIND /V "
  Directory" | FIND /V "(s"
ECHO Saved messages are:
DIR F:%ME2%\*.-AT | FIND /V "Volume" | FIND /V "
  Directory" | FIND /V "File not" | FIND /V "(s"
ECHO Use %0 %1 FILENAME.EXT TO VIEW
GOTO END
:VIEW
F:
CD %ME2%
IF NOT EXIST %2 ECHO Invalid File Name and/or Extension
```

```
IF NOT EXIST %2 GOTO END
MORE < %2
REN %2 *.-AT
ECHO Message has been saved.  Use MAIL PURGE FILENAME
  to permanently remove.
:PURGE
IF "%2"=="" ECHO You must specify a File Name
IF "%2"=="" GOTO END
IF NOT EXIST %2.-AT ECHO Invalid File Name.  Leave off
  the Extension.
IF NOT EXIST %2.-AT GOTO END
F:
CD %ME2%
DEL %2.-AT
GOTO END
:SEND
IF "%3"=="" ECHO Correct syntax is MAIL SEND Path
  Person
IF "%3"=="" ECHO Such as MAIL SEND C:\WP\LETTER %ME%
IF "%3"=="" GOTO END
SET ABC=%3
CALL YOU B40
F:
CD %ME2%
COPY %2
SEND "You have received mail" %3
ECHO MAIL HAS BEEN SENT
SET ABC=%ME%
CALL YOU TOO
GOTO END
:COMPOSE
IF "%2"=="" ECHO Correct syntax is MAIL COMPOSE Person
  Document.DAT
IF "%2"=="" ECHO Such as MAIL COMPOSE %ME% LETTER.DAT
IF "%2"=="" GOTO END
```

```
SET ABC=%2
CALL YOU B40
F:
CD %ME2%
CLS
ECHO Begin writing. . . use {CTRL-Z} on a blank line
  when finished
COPY CON %3
SEND "You have received mail" %2
ECHO MAIL HAS BEEN SENT
SET ABC=%ME%
CALL YOU TOO
GOTO END
:HELP
CLS
TYPE MAIL.HLP
ECHO.
PAUSE
CLS
:END
C:
CD\
```

A batch file programmer should pay particular attention to two aspects of this routine. First, by checking for valid %1 entries at the beginning of the routine, branching is done if the parameter is one specified and the HELP routine is performed if any other parameter is given. Second, the case sensitivity is examined at the beginning, as well. This double-checking eliminates the need to have two labels for each routine (:SEND and :send) by moving such checking to the beginning.

## Chapter 8

### *Can you remotely change the CONFIG.SYS file?*

You can update CONFIG.SYS any time the workstation is up and running, since it is read once, and only once, during each session—at start-up. To change the CONFIG.SYS on a remote workstation, create a batch file in the PUBLIC directory on the server and change the LOGIN script as described in Chapter 3 to run the batch file.

This batch file can replace the CONFIG.SYS with a new version. Either type

```
COPY CONFIG.SYS C:\CONFIG.SYS <Enter>
```

at the command-line prompt, or add lines to the existing version in the following manner:

```
ECHO DEVICE=PASS.SYS >> C:\CONFIG.SYS <Enter>
```

### *Can you turn NUMLOCK off without MS-DOS 6.0?*

MS-DOS 6.0 contains the NUMLOCK command that doesn't come with other versions of DOS. To automatically turn the NUMLOCK key off via a COM file, enter the following as a DEBUG or SID file, or copy directly from the accompanying disk. I offer it here as a DEBUG script.

```
E 0100 B8 40 00 8E D8 80 26 17 00 DF C3 FF 07 07 08 07
  FF
N NUM.COM
RCX
0011
W
Q
```

***How do you determine allocation unit size without MS-DOS 5.0 or greater?***

You can determine allocation unit size with versions of DOS that don't offer such information at CHKDSK by performing the following steps:

1. Perform a DIR listing and note the "bytes free."

2. At the command-line prompt, type ECHO HELLO > JUNK.TXT <Enter>.

3. Perform a DIR listing and notice the difference in "bytes free" from the first time.

While you can perform this process manually, you can also do it with a quick BASIC file, or modify WASTED to do so.

***Is it possible to use file compressors and disk compressors together?***

PKLITE and DBLSPACE can and should be used together in that they don't interfere with each other's operations. Both will optimize the disk, one by reducing the size of the file and the other by essentially increasing the amount of free space. There are no known problems with using both, though the processing time slightly increases as the file is expanded twice. This increase in processing time is barely noticeable and the benefits far outweigh this slight inconvenience.

## Chapter 9

***Can you modify HEAD to show the last lines of a file?***

A few modifications to the HEAD routine allow it to show the last lines of a file, from one to ninety-nine, with a default of ten:

```
100 REM TAIL - LAST LINE LISTING ROUTINE
DEFINT A-Z: CLS
```

```
200 IF LEN(COMMAND$) = 0 THEN PRINT "You must specify a
  file name": GOTO 1600
IF INSTR(EAD$, "*") > 0 THEN PRINT "Wildcards are not
  permitted": GOTO 1600
IF INSTR(EAD$, "?") > 0 THEN PRINT "Wildcards are not
  permitted": GOTO 1600
300 EAD$ = LTRIM$(COMMAND$)
400 IF LEFT$(EAD$, 1) <> "-" THEN GOTO 1400
500 LE = LEN(EAD$): IF LE = 4 THEN PRINT "You must
  specify a file name": GOTO 1600
IF MID$(EAD$, 2, 1) = " " THEN PRINT "You must specify
  a number": GOTO 1600
IF MID$(EAD$, 3, 1) = " " THEN DU = VAL(MID$(EAD$, 2,
  1)): EAD$ = RIGHT$(EAD$, LE - 3): GOTO 1500
IF MID$(EAD$, 4, 1) = " " THEN DU = VAL(MID$(EAD$, 2,
  2)): EAD$ = RIGHT$(EAD$, LE - 4): GOTO 1500
PRINT "Number cannot be greater than 99": GOTO 1600
1400 DU = 10: REM NO NUMBER SPECIFIED THUS USING
  DEFAULT
1500 REM COUNT LINES IN FILE
LINES = 0
OPEN "I", #1, EAD$
1510 LINE INPUT #1, EA$: LINES = LINES + 1
IF EOF(1) THEN CLOSE  ELSE GOTO 1510
1520 LA = LINES - DU
OPEN "I", #1, EAD$
IF LA < 1 THEN GOTO 1540
1530 FOR NE = 1 TO LA
LINE INPUT #1, EA$
NEXT NE
1540 LINE INPUT #1, EA$
PRINT EA$
IF EOF(1) THEN CLOSE : GOTO 1600
GOTO 1540
1600 REM THE END
```

First, the number of lines in the file are counted within the utility by opening the file and incrementing the LINES variable. After all have been read, the file is closed. Next, the number of lines specified to be shown are subtracted from this, if no number has been specified; then the default of ten is used.

The file is opened once again, and all of the lines up to the starting point are read and ignored. The utility program reads the remaining lines and prints them to the screen.

## Chapter 12

### *How do you delete users who have left the company?*

The best method of deleting all information pertaining to employees who have left the company and preventing them from gaining further access is to remove the user from the USERLIST, and then run BINDFIX to rebuild the bindery, making certain that their mail directories and other related information are not built into the new bindery files.

### *Should external DOS commands be renamed?*

ERASE and DEL are both internal commands that I showed you how to alter to make it more difficult for untrustworthy users to endanger processing. You can apply the same concept to external commands by renaming them to something less obvious and creating new files with those names. I suggest you follow this procedure for your DEBUG.EXE, FORMAT.COM, and XCOPY.EXE commands.

B APPENDIX

# Suggested Reading


Bishop, Matt. "Foiling Password Crackers." *UnixWorld*, March, 1992.

Day, Michael, and Ken Neff. *Troubleshooting NetWare for the 386*. Redwood City, CA: M&T Books, 1991. $27.95. Tips for maintaining a NetWare 3.11 LAN.

Hayes, Frank. "Is Your System Safe?" *UnixWorld*, June, 1990.

Liebing, Edward. *NetWare User's Guide v2.2*. Redwood City, CA: M&T Books, 1991. $24.95. Excellent discussion of getting the most from NetWare 2.2, particularly the command-line and menu utilities.

McCann, John, with Adam Ruef, and Steven Guengerich. *NetWare Supervisor's Guide*. Redwood City, CA: M&T Books, 1990. $29.95. Undocumented reference of commands and utilities.

Milligan, Christine. *NetWare 386 User's Guide*. Redwood City, CA: M&T Books, 1990. $29.95. Common-sense technical reference.

Rash, Wayne Jr., and Peter Stephenson. *The Novell Connection.* New York: Brady Books, 1990. $24.95. Covers LAN system set-up and command reference.

Stoll, Cliff. *The Cuckoo's Egg*. New York: Pocket Books, 1990. $5.99. A true tale of a hacker who was able to break into U.S. computer systems and steal secrets.

C APPENDIX

# ASCII Table

| Number | Character | Number | Character | Number | Character |
|---|---|---|---|---|---|
| 0 | NUL | 23 | ↨ | 46 | . |
| 1 | ☺ | 24 | ↑ | 47 | / |
| 2 | ☻ | 25 | ↓ | 48 | 0 |
| 3 | ♥ | 26 | SUB | 49 | 1 |
| 4 | ♦ | 27 | ESC | 50 | 2 |
| 5 | ♣ | 28 | FS | 51 | 3 |
| 6 | ♠ | 29 | GS | 52 | 4 |
| 7 | BELL | 30 | RS | 53 | 5 |
| 8 | BS | 31 | US | 54 | 6 |
| 9 | HT | 32 | SPACE | 55 | 7 |
| 10 | LF | 33 | ! | 56 | 8 |
| 11 | ♂ | 34 | " | 57 | 9 |
| 12 | FF | 35 | # | 58 | : |
| 13 | CR | 36 | $ | 59 | ; |
| 14 | ♪ | 37 | % | 60 | < |
| 15 | ☼ | 38 | & | 61 | = |
| 16 | ► | 39 | ' | 62 | > |
| 17 | ◄ | 40 | ( | 63 | ? |
| 18 | ↕ | 41 | ) | 64 | @ |
| 19 | ! | 42 | * | 65 | A |
| 20 | ¶ | 43 | + | 66 | B |
| 21 | § | 44 | , | 67 | C |
| 22 | ▬ | 45 | - | 68 | D |

| Number | Character | Number | Character | Number | Character |
|---|---|---|---|---|---|
| 69 | E | 108 | l | 147 | ô |
| 70 | F | 109 | m | 148 | ö |
| 71 | G | 110 | n | 149 | ò |
| 72 | H | 111 | o | 150 | û |
| 73 | I | 112 | p | 151 | ù |
| 74 | J | 113 | q | 152 | ÿ |
| 75 | K | 114 | r | 153 | Ö |
| 76 | L | 115 | s | 154 | Ü |
| 77 | M | 116 | t | 155 | ¢ |
| 78 | N | 117 | u | 156 | £ |
| 79 | O | 118 | v | 157 | ¥ |
| 80 | P | 119 | w | 158 | ₧ |
| 81 | Q | 120 | x | 159 | ƒ |
| 82 | R | 121 | y | 160 | á |
| 83 | S | 122 | z | 161 | í |
| 84 | T | 123 | { | 162 | ó |
| 85 | U | 124 | \| | 163 | ú |
| 86 | V | 125 | } | 164 | ñ |
| 87 | W | 126 | ~ | 165 | Ñ |
| 88 | X | 127 | • | 166 | ª |
| 89 | Y | 128 | Ç | 167 | º |
| 90 | Z | 129 | ü | 168 | ¿ |
| 91 | [ | 130 | é | 169 | ⌐ |
| 92 | \ | 131 | â | 170 | ¬ |
| 93 | ] | 132 | ä | 171 | ½ |
| 94 | ^ | 133 | à | 172 | ¼ |
| 95 | _ | 134 | å | 173 | ¡ |
| 96 | ` | 135 | ç | 174 | « |
| 97 | a | 136 | ê | 175 | » |
| 98 | b | 137 | ë | 176 | ░ |
| 99 | c | 138 | è | 177 | ▒ |
| 100 | d | 139 | ï | 178 | ▓ |
| 101 | e | 140 | î | 179 | │ |
| 102 | f | 141 | ì | 180 | ┤ |
| 103 | g | 142 | Ä | 181 | ╡ |
| 104 | h | 143 | Å | 182 | ╢ |
| 105 | i | 144 | É | 183 | ╖ |
| 106 | j | 145 | æ | 184 | ╕ |
| 107 | k | 146 | Æ | 185 | ╣ |

# C

## ASCII Table

| Number | Character | Number | Character |
|---|---|---|---|
| 186 | | 221 | |
| 187 | | 222 | |
| 189 | | 223 | |
| 190 | | 224 | α |
| 191 | | 225 | β |
| 192 | | 226 | Γ |
| 193 | | 227 | π |
| 194 | | 228 | Σ |
| 195 | | 229 | σ |
| 196 | | 230 | μ |
| 197 | | 231 | τ |
| 198 | | 232 | Φ |
| 199 | | 233 | Θ |
| 200 | | 234 | Ω |
| 201 | | 235 | δ |
| 202 | | 236 | ∞ |
| 203 | | 237 | ∅ |
| 204 | | 238 | ∈ |
| 205 | | 239 | ∩ |
| 206 | | 240 | ≡ |
| 207 | | 241 | ± |
| 208 | | 242 | ≥ |
| 209 | | 243 | ≤ |
| 210 | | 244 | ⌠ |
| 211 | | 245 | ⌡ |
| 212 | | 246 | ÷ |
| 213 | | 247 | ≈ |
| 214 | | 248 | ° |
| 215 | | 249 | ∘ |
| 216 | | 250 | · |
| 217 | | 251 | √ |
| 218 | | 252 | $^n$ |
| 219 | | 253 | $^2$ |
| 220 | | 254 | ■ |

D APPENDIX

# About the Source Disk

The disk that accompanies this book contains copies of every program and program listing presented in the text. The listings are arranged according to the chapters in which I discussed them. Consequently, if I give a different AUTOEXEC.BAT file in two different chapters, you can locate the correct file in the subdirectory for the chapter in question.

All .BAS, .BAT, and .TXT files are in ASCII format and viewable with the TYPE command. I've run PKLITE on all .EXE and .COM files to reduce their sizes to minimums. The compiled programs are not viewable, but every compiled program has a corresponding ASCII listing.

APPENDIX

# E

# Internal DOS Commands

The following commands are contained within the DOS interpreter, COMMAND.COM. DOS therefore understands them at startup regardless of the PATH or current directory.

| | |
|---|---|
| BREAK | |
| CALL | |
| CD | |
| CHCP | |
| CHDIR | |
| CLS | |
| COPY | |
| CTTY | |
| DATE | |
| DEL | |
| DELQ | (DR DOS only) |
| DIR | |
| ECHO | |
| ERASE | |
| ERAQ | (DR DOS only) |
| EXIST | |
| EXIT | |

```
FOR
GOTO
HILOAD
IF
IN DO
MD
MKDIR
NOT ERRORLEVEL
PATH
PAUSE
PROMPT
RD
REM
REN
RENAME
RMDIR
SET
SHIFT
TIME
TYPE
VER
VERIFY
VOL
```

(DR DOS only) — applies to HILOAD

F APPENDIX

# External DOS Commands and Files

The following commands are contained within the DOS directory. They must be locatable within a PATH statement, or processing must be in the current directory; otherwise, these commands won't work. I've also listed selected .SYS files and others commonly located in the DOS directory.

| | |
|---|---|
| 1050.CPI | |
| 4201.CPI | |
| 4208.CPI | |
| 5202.CPI | |
| ANSI.SYS | |
| APPEND.EXE | |
| ASSIGN.COM | |
| ATTRIB.EXE | |
| BACKUP.COM | |
| CHKDSK.COM | |
| COMP.COM | |
| COUNTRY.SYS | |
| CURSOR.EXE | (DR DOS only) |
| DEBUG | (MS DOS only) |
| DELPURGE.EXE | (DR DOS only) |

| | |
|---|---|
| DELWATCH.EXE | (DR DOS only) |
| DISKCOMP.COM | |
| DISKCOPY.COM | |
| DISKMAP.EXE | (DR DOS only) |
| DISKOPT.EXE | (DR DOS only) |
| DISPLAY.SYS | |
| DOSBOOK.EXE | (DR DOS only) |
| DOSKEY.COM | (MS DOS only) |
| DRDOS.INI | (DR DOS only) |
| DRIVER.SYS | |
| EDIT.COM | (MS DOS only) |
| EDIT.HLP | (MS DOS only) |
| EDITOR.EXE | (DR DOS only) |
| EGA.CPI | |
| EMM386.SYS | |
| EXE2BIN.EXE | |
| FASTOPEN.EXE | |
| FC.EXE | |
| FDISK.COM | |
| FILELINK.EXE | (DR DOS only) |
| FIND.EXE | |
| FORMAT.COM | |
| GRAFTABL.COM | |
| GRAPHICS.COM | |
| JOIN.EXE | |
| KEYB.COM | |
| LABEL.COM | |
| LOCK.EXE | (DR DOS only) |
| MEM.EXE | |
| MEMMAX.EXE | (DR DOS only) |
| MODE.COM | |
| MOVE.EXE | (DR DOS only) |
| NLSFUNC.EXE | |
| PASSWORD.EXE | (DR DOS only) |
| PCKWIK.SYS | (DR DOS only) |

| | |
|---|---|
| PCKWIN.SYS | (DR DOS only) |
| PRINT.COM | |
| PRINTER.SYS | |
| README | |
| RECOVER.COM | |
| RENDIR.EXE | |
| REPLACE.EXE | |
| RESTORE.COM | |
| SCRIPT.EXE | (DR DOS only) |
| SETUP.EXE | |
| SHARE.EXE | |
| SID.EXE | (DR DOS only) |
| SORT.EXE | |
| SSTOR.EXE | (DR DOS only) |
| SUBST.EXE | |
| SUPERPCK.EXE | (DR DOS only) |
| SYS.COM | |
| TASKMAX.EXE | (DR DOS only) |
| TASKMAX.INI | (DR DOS only) |
| TOUCH.EXE | (DR DOS only) |
| TREE.COM | |
| UNDELETE.EXE | |
| UNFORMAT.COM | |
| UNINSTAL.EXE | |
| VDISK.SYS | |
| VIEWMAX | (DR DOS only) |
| VIEWMAX.EXE | (DR DOS only) |
| XCOPY.EXE | |
| XDEL.EXE | (DR DOS only) |
| XDIR.EXE | (DR DOS only) |

# Index

## O



## P



## Q



## R



## S

# A Library of Technical References from M&T Books

## Building Local Area Networks with Novell's NetWare Versions 2.2 and 3.X
### by Patrick H. Corrigan and Aisling Guy

From the basic components to complete network installation, here is the practical guide that PC system integrators will need to build and implement PC LANs in this rapidly growing market. The specifics of building and maintaining PC LANs, including hardware configurations, software development, cabling, selection criteria, installation, and on-going management are described in a clear "how-to" manner with numerous illustrations and sample LAN management forms. Covers Novell's NetWare, version 2.2, and 3.11 for the 386. Additional topics covered include the OS/2 LAN Manager, Tops, Banyan VINES, internetworking, host computer gateways, and multisystem networks that link PCs, Apples, and mainframes. 704 pp.

Book/Disk (MS-DOS) $39.95 #239X

Level: Beginning - Advanced

## Building Local Area Networks with Novell's NetWare
### by Patrick H. Corrigan and Aisling Guy

The best-selling guide to selecting and installing LANs. Covers Novell's NetWare version 2.1 and NetWare for Macintosh. Useful tips and software utilities are provided on MS/PC-DOS disk. 635 pp.

Book/Disk $39.95 #0257

Level: Beginning - Advanced

**1-800-688-3987**

**M&T BOOKS**

# A Library of Technical References from M&T Books

## NetWare User's Guide
## by Edward Liebing

The best-selling guide to using Novell's NetWare, versions 2.1 through 2.15. It introduces new users to NetWare services and provides a reference for the experienced NetWare user as well. "...a superior presentation style...intelligent organization..." says *LAN Times*. A solid reference book for NetWare users!

Book $24.95 #0710

Level: Beginning - Intermediate

## NetWare for Macintosh User's Guide
## by Kelley J.P. Lindberg

NetWare for Macintosh! Here's the complete guide on how to increase productivity, protect files and share printers, applications, and files with other network users. Simple instructions for accessing the network, printing, and working with security. Plus descriptions of NetWare 286 and 386 security, hints on sharing files with MS-DOS and OS/2 users, and practical tips on troubleshooting workstation problems. Covers versions 1.0, 1.1, and 2.0. 280 pp.

Book $29.95 #1261

Level: Beginning-Advanced

**1-800-688-3987**

# ORDER FORM

**To Order:**

Return this form with your payment to M&T Books, 411 Borel Avenue, Suite 100, San Mateo, CA 94402 or **call toll-free 1-800-533-4372 (in California, call 1-800-356-2002).**

| ITEM # | DESCRIPTION | DISK | PRICE |
|---|---|---|---|
| | | | |
| | | | |
| | | | |
| | | | |
| | | | |
| | | | |
| | | | |
| | | | |
| | | | |
| | | Subtotal | |
| | | CA residents add sales tax ___% | |
| | | Add $4.50 per item for shipping and handling | |
| | | TOTAL | |

**Charge my:**

- ❑ **Visa**
- ❑ **MasterCard**
- ❑ **AmExpress**

❑ **Check enclosed, payable to M&T Books.**

CARD NO. ______________________________

SIGNATURE ______________________ EXP. DATE ______________

NAME ______________________________

ADDRESS ______________________________

CITY ______________________________

STATE ______________________ ZIP ______________

**M&T GUARANTEE:** If your are not satisfied with your order for any reason, return it to us within 25 days of receipt for a full refund. Note: Refunds on disks apply only when returned with book within guarantee period. Disks damaged in transit or defective will be promptly replaced, but cannot be exchanged for a disk from a different title.

3108

# ***Tell us what you think and we'll send you a free M&T Books catalog***

It is our goal at M&T Books to produce the best technical books available. But you can help us make our books even better by letting us know what you think about this particular title.Please take a moment to fill out this card and mail it to us. Your opinion is appreciated.

***Tell us about yourself***

Name ______________________

Company ______________________

Address ______________________

City ______________________

State/Zip ______________________

***Title of this book?***

______________________

***Where did you purchase this book?***

☐ Bookstore
☐ Catalog
☐ Direct Mail
☐ Magazine Ad
☐ Postcard Pack
☐ Other

***Why did you choose this book?***

☐ Recommended
☐ Read book review
☐ Read ad/catalog copy
☐ Responded to a special offer
☐ M&T Books' reputation
☐ Price
☐ Nice Cover

***How would you rate the overall content of this book?***

☐ Excellent
☐ Good
☐ Fair
☐ Poor

***Why?***

______________________

______________________

***What chapters did you find valuable?***

______________________

______________________

______________________

***What did you find least useful?***

______________________

______________________

______________________

***What topic(s) would you add to future editions of this book?***

______________________

______________________

______________________

***What other titles would you like to see M&T Books publish?***

______________________

______________________

______________________

***Which format do you prefer for the optional disk?***

☐ 5.25" ☐ 3.5"

***Any other comments?***

______________________

______________________

______________________

☐ Check here for M&T Books Catalog

M&T BOOKS

3108

NO POSTAGE
NECESSARY
IF MAILED
IN THE
UNITED STATES

**BUSINESS REPLY MAIL**

FIRST CLASS MAIL PERMIT 2660 SAN MATEO, CA

POSTAGE WILL BE PAID BY ADDRESSEE


**M&T BOOKS**
411 Borel Avenue, Suite 100
San Mateo, CA 94402-9885


PLEASE FOLD ALONG LINE AND STAPLE OR TAPE CLOSED